Immigration Law and Human Rights: The Unequal, Disorganized, and Consequential Movement of People

Marko Nikolić

SOCIETY Publishing

www.societypublishing.com

Immigration Law and Human Rights: The Unequal, Disorganized, and Consequential Movement of People

Marko Nikolić

Society Publishing
224 Shoreacres Road
Burlington, ON L7L 2H2
Canada
www.societypublishing.com
Email: orders@arclereducation.com

ISBN: 978-1-77469-062-8 (Hardcover)

ABOUT THE AUTHOR

Marko obtained his Master's degree from University of Belgrade - Faculty of Law in 2014. He specialized in Criminal Law, Family Law and Environmental Law. He spent his Master year studying about international child abduction in modern world. He was employed in Ministry of Defense's Legal Department and was also working as a legal secretary in numerous educational institutions. His freelance engagements are including more than 40 long-term clients and he also established a consulting agency in 2021. In addition to professional literature editing, he published a novel on the subject of history and mythology.

TABLE OF CONTENTS

LIST OF FIGURES

LIST OF ABBREVIATIONS

CMW	Committee on Migrant Workers
ILO	International Labor Organization
TCI	Third Culture Individuals
TCK	Third Culture Kids
UAE	United Arab Emirates
UDHR	Universal Declaration of Human Rights
WTO	World Trade Organization

PREFACE

Immigration is a fact of life, and for centuries, people have moved from place to place. Similarly, there have always been efforts to control immigration. The difference is that modern technology has provided various ways in which these controls can be exercised; a luxury that was not available to early immigration officers. Of course, the penalties have slackened somewhat. For example, during the Elizabethan era traveling without the express sanction of the monarch and their council of ministers could be construed to be treason; a crime that could very easily led to losing one's head. Today, the penalties include long periods of detention or even incarceration if convicted of a specific immigration crime.

The discourse surrounding immigration has become even more bigoted. There have been national and international leaders that have used immigrants as scapegoats for the failings of their administrations. Meanwhile, the general populace has been fed and believed a number of "truths" that cannot withstand any form of scrutiny, no matter how obsequious. A case in point is the notion that immigrations are taking away job from the indigenous population. Any casual review of the employment statistics quickly disabuses the reader of this dangerous assumption. In reality, immigrants tend to do essential jobs that nobody else who is a citizen of the country would want to do.

Then there is that gripe about immigrants who diminish the local economy by sending remittances back to their home countries. What these anti-immigrant voices miss or deliberately ignore, is the fact that immigrants pay taxes and do actual jobs that are necessary for a healthy economy. If the COVID-19 virus has taught developed nations anything, it is the fact that immigrants working in the health services are a very valuable segment of their communities. Those that are willing to accept these potential benefits of immigration, then turn to another arm of criticism. That arm is the toxic debate surrounding illegal immigrants. These are accused of all sorts of heinous abuses (some of which are true in certain cases).

The reality is that the restriction on immigrants from poor countries has made applications even more desperate. If there is no accessible route to immigration, the potential applications may turn to alternative means. That means that economic migrants turn to the asylum system, which they abuse in order to gain residence. Those that come on visits or short work stays, end up not going home because they know that it will be very difficult for them to return. In fact, the current global immigration system is designed to favor white people from industrialized nations and disfavor black immigrants from poorer nations. A lot of platitudes may be adopted to mask this reality, but that does not change its factual basis.

This book attempts to untangle the complex issues of immigration from a perspective of human rights. It considers how the law and practice can be amalgamated in order to better understand our responses to immigration. In doing so, the book implicitly makes a case for a rational immigration framework that takes into account the needs of the indigenous people, but does not treat immigrants in an inhumane way. After all, the biggest "nation of immigrants" in the USA and it remains the most advanced nation on earth despite the presence of a multitude of immigrants.

CHAPTER 1

UNDERSTANDING THE CONTEXT OF INTERNATIONAL MIGRATION

CONTENTS

The opening chapter of this book will layout the context of international migration; if only to lay the foundation of understand why and how people move from place to place. The first section of this chapter focuses on the thorny issue of sovereignty and how it has impacted on the policy formulation with regards to international immigration. In the second section, we attempt to understand the categories of immigrants that are looking to work and earn a living; as opposed to the stereotype of immigrants that are looking for an "easy cushion" of state benefits without responsibility. The third section places the immigration policy within the context of economic development in order to understand how the world order has determined the patterns of international migration. The fourth section of this chapter shows some of the impacts of emigration on the sending countries in the form of positive aspects (such as remittances) and the negative aspects (such as the notorious "brain drain" within the developing world). The chapter will close with a section on the links between migration patterns and global crises, arguing that the latter is a cause rather than a symptom of international migration. Let us begin this chapter by looking at how national sovereignty has and can be protected in the age of global travel.

1.1. BALANCING NATIONAL SOVEREIGNTY WITH IMMIGRATION POLICY

One of the cardinal privileges of national sovereignty is the ability to control who and how people move in and out of the country (Kasimis, 2012; Kelson and DeLaet, 1999; King, 2009; Lopez, 2005; Lorentzen, 2014; Mehan, 1997; Melis, 2001). During the Tudor era, it was even more controlled with a mercantilist view of immigration which considered the unauthorized exit of people to be an act of treason (Miller, 2015, 2016; Molnar and Gill, 2018; Money, 1998; Morris, 2002, 2016; Motomura, 1999). Today, there are millions of people on the move, and there have been efforts to ease movement for certain categories of people (Nethery and Holman, 2016; Newman, Proctor, and Dudley, 2013; Oberman, 2016; Orfanos, 2019; Ozdowski, 1985). The reality is that if you are white, and at least middle class; you can travel freely and easily to most places on earth (Taylor, 2000; Thym, 2008; Webber, 2012; Welch, 2002; Wexler, 2007; Wilcox, 2009; Zúñiga and Hernández-León, 2005; Zwi and Mares, 2015). By the same token, if you are non-white and poor; it is virtually impossible to travel outside your home country (Sassen, 1996, 1997; Shohamy and McNamara, 2009; Smith, 2014; Soysal, 2012; Spijkerboer and Van Walsum, 2007).

The efforts to control immigration have been couched in patriotic terms, including the need to "protect our way of life" (Saadi et al., 2020; Samers, 2004; Sampson, Mitchell, and Bowring, 2011; Sanggaran, Haire, and Zion, 2016). These are code words to signify the desire to maintain a fairly homogenous mix of people in any given locality (Paz, 2016, Peberdy, 2001; Ramji-Nogales, 2007; Rubio-Marín, 2014; Ruhs, 2010; Ryan and Mitsilegas, 2010). Some of the key categorizations that are considered in such a policy include race, class, and even political views (Nethery and Holman, 2016; Newman, Proctor, and Dudley, 2013; Oberman, 2016; Orfanos, 2019; Ozdowski, 1985). In an effort to control the entrance of unwanted migrants, the more prosperous countries (see Figure 1.1 for the example of Canada) have developed increasingly sophisticated ways of tracking the so-called "unwanted immigrants" (Miller, 2015, 2016; Molnar and Gill, 2018; Money, 1998; Morris, 2002, 2016; Motomura, 1999). Enforcement action, including imprisonment and deportation, can then be undertaken in a fairly predictable way (Kasimis, 2012; Kelson and DeLaet, 1999; King, 2009; Lopez, 2005; Lorentzen, 2014; Mehan, 1997; Melis, 2001).

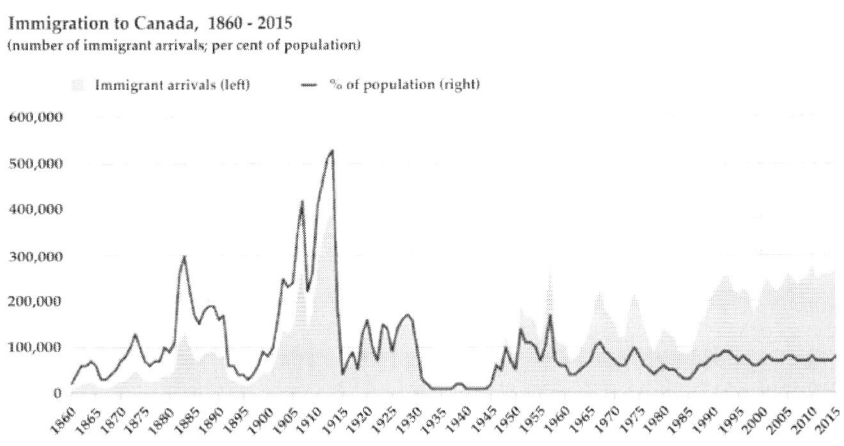

Figure 1.1: Unwanted immigration in Canada 1860 to 2015.

Source: CGAI CA.

The sovereignty argument is something of a tool. Hence, when a country wants to limit the number of Muslims in its borders; it will invoke a number of anti-terror acts that equate being a Muslim to being a terrorist (Hollifield, Martin, and Orrenius, 2014; Jacobson, 1996; Johnson, 1996; Joppke, 1998, 1999, 2010). Because many of the international terrorists that are selectively publicized by the media are actually Muslim or from Muslim-majority countries; the xenophobic Donald Trump administration in the USA feels free to place a blanket ban on people from Muslim-majority of countries, regardless of their personal circumstances. Similarly, because there are certain Mexican immigrants that are criminal in their conduct; the same US regime can justify building a wall on the Mexican border and separating migrant children from their parents. Such actions open up discourses in which immigration becomes a nationalist battle cry for purposes of protecting parochial interests and rejecting the notion of a global community in which most people are able to travel freely (Guild and Niessen, 1996; Hailbronner, 2000; Hayter, 2000; Heisler, 2000; Hernandez-Truyol and Johns, 1997).

There are practical implications and explanations that cannot be ignored (Acer and Goodman, 2009; Ackerman and Furman, 2014; Adelman, 2002; Aynsley-Green et al., 2012; Bacon, 1996). For example, the reality is that no country can afford to take in all immigrants from the world (Baldwin-Edwards, 2006; Bangarth, 2003; Barak-Erez, 2008; Becerra, 2016; Brané and Lundholm, 2007). Furthermore, there are immigrants who behave in ways that are harmful to the host country. However, acknowledging those facts may not necessarily be a justified cause for an insensitive and ultimately cruel immigration policy (Brochmann and Hammar, 2020; Chavez, 2001; Chin, 1999; Cook, 2003; Cornelisse, 2004, 2010).

At the same time, governments have to pay heed to the needs, perceptions, and aspirations of their constituencies (Costello, 2012; Dauvergne, 2012; Den Heijer, 2010; Dudley et al., 2012; Dunn, 2001, 2010; Exdell, 2009). That constituency are the citizenry who may have been conditioned by media narratives to dislike immigrants and be suspicious of them (Fiske, 2016; Flynn, 2013; Frederking, 2012; Gilman, 2013; Guia, Koulish, and Mitsilegas, 2016; Guild, 2001). No government that goes against the express wishes of its people is going to last for long (Guild and Niessen, 1996; Hailbronner, 2000; Hayter, 2000; Heisler, 2000; Hernandez-Truyol and Johns, 1997). Therefore, a context that is marred by anti-migrant sentiment is fertile ground for reactionary policies by the state (Hollifield, Martin, and Orrenius, 2014; Jacobson, 1996; Johnson, 1996; Joppke, 1998, 1999, 2010).

The challenge for politicians is in balancing the needs of the proper administration of immigration law and quietening public anxieties about the visible, invisible, actual, or imagined immigrants (Fiske, 2016; Flynn, 2013; Frederking, 2012; Gilman, 2013; Guia, Koulish, and Mitsilegas, 2016; Guild, 2001). International law demands some standardization with regards to human rights, and that means that even the most rightwing governments have certain red lines that they will not cross when implementing immigration policy (Costello, 2012; Dauvergne, 2012; Den Heijer, 2010; Dudley et al., 2012; Dunn, 2001, 2010; Exdell, 2009). A case in point is the studious avoidance of any mention of racist intentions in the policy, despite the fact that the outcomes of immigration policies are by definition discriminatory (Brochmann and Hammar, 2020; Chavez, 2001; Chin, 1999; Cook, 2003; Cornelisse, 2004, 2010).

One of the key considerations are the potential and actual benefits of immigration, which are often ignored by the popular press in its anti-immigrant animus (Baldwin-Edwards, 2006; Bangarth, 2003; Barak-Erez, 2008; Becerra, 2016; Brané and Lundholm, 2007). For example, the health and hospitality industries in the developed world could not function without the contribution of migrant workers (Acer and Goodman, 2009; Ackerman and Furman, 2014; Adelman, 2002; Aynsley-Green et al., 2012; Bacon, 1996). Given their general vulnerability, these are the types of workers that are prone to exploitation and will generally be subject to working conditions that are below the minimum standards that are expected for "home" applicants (Paz, 2016; Peberdy, 2001; Ramji-Nogales, 2007; Rubio-Marín, 2014; Ruhs, 2010; Ryan and Mitsilegas, 2010). Whereas many laws are enacted to protect workers, few of them address the specific needs of migrant workers despite their demonstrable relative vulnerability to exploitation (Saadi et al., 2020; Samers, 2004; Sampson, Mitchell, and Bowring, 2011; Sanggaran, Haire, and Zion, 2016).

Because immigrants are generally treated as either second-class citizens or non-persons; the same patterns are experienced in the implementation of immigration policy (Sassen, 1996, 1997; Shohamy and McNamara, 2009; Smith, 2014; Soysal, 2012; Spijkerboer and Van Walsum, 2007). This is true in as far as the human rights of immigrants are not always considered as being of the essence (Taylor, 2000; Thym, 2008; Webber, 2012; Welch, 2002; Wexler, 2007; Wilcox, 2009; Zúñiga and Hernández-León, 2005; Zwi and Mares, 2015). Indeed, some of the enforcement agents are in effect violating the human rights of immigrants (Acer and Goodman, 2009; Ackerman and Furman, 2014; Adelman, 2002; Aynsley-Green et al., 2012; Bacon, 1996). The governments tend to ignore these incidents or otherwise justify them on the basis that they are a necessary aspect of immigration enforcement (Ackerman and Furman, 2014; Adelman, 2002; Aynsley-Green et al., 2012; Bacon, 1996; Baldwin-Edwards, 2006). Some even callously question why immigrants continue preferring to settle in industrialized nations where they are treated badly (Adelman, 2002; Aynsley-Green et al., 2012; Bacon,

1996; Baldwin-Edwards, 2006; Bangarth, 2003; Barak-Erez, 2008). The implication is that "if they do not like it here, they can go right back home." However, such an assertion fails to recognize the diverse motivations for immigration (Bacon, 1996; Baldwin-Edwards, 2006; Bangarth, 2003; Barak-Erez, 2008; Becerra, 2016; Brané and Lundholm, 2007). Some of these motivations may include saving lives in cases of violence against certain communities. Another motivation involves "looking for a better life" where the migrant intends to expand their job prospects by moving abroad (Baldwin-Edwards, 2006; Bangarth, 2003; Barak-Erez, 2008; Becerra, 2016; Brané and Lundholm, 2007; Brochmann and Hammar, 2020).

When the three arms of government are considered (executive, judiciary, and legislature); it is the executive that is at the forefront of implementing immigration policy (Bangarth, 2003; Barak-Erez, 2008; Becerra, 2016; Brané and Lundholm, 2007; Brochmann and Hammar, 2020; Chavez, 2001). Moreover, the legislature may be under pressure to legislate in such a way as to discourage immigrants while at the same time maintain existing immigrants in perpetual servitude (Barak-Erez, 2008; Becerra, 2016; Brané and Lundholm, 2007; Brochmann and Hammar, 2020; Chavez, 2001; Chin, 1999). A case in point are the undocumented migrants in the USA who are caught up in limbo since the legislature never quite passes immigration reform legislation, despite saying the right things all the time (Becerra, 2016; Brané and Lundholm, 2007; Brochmann and Hammar, 2020; Chavez, 2001; Chin, 1999; Cook, 2003).

Some have argued that there is bipartisan hypocrisy when it comes to making laws concerning immigration (Brané and Lundholm, 2007; Brochmann and Hammar, 2020; Chavez, 2001; Chin, 1999; Cook, 2003; Cornelisse, 2004). Indeed, some researchers have found that leftwing governments are as harsh as rightwing governments when it comes to legislating against immigrants (Brochmann and Hammar, 2020; Chavez, 2001; Chin, 1999; Cook, 2003; Cornelisse, 2004, 2010; Costello, 2012). Part of this is driven by concern about the plight of working-class indigenous people who may be disadvantaged by the presence of a productive labor force of immigrants (Chavez, 2001; Chin, 1999; Cook, 2003; Cornelisse, 2004, 2010; Costello, 2012; Dauvergne, 2012; Den Heijer, 2010).

Whereas many governments have focused on keeping undesirable immigrants out, there are some that are considered the possibility of tackling this problem from its source (Chin, 1999; Cook, 2003; Cornelisse, 2004, 2010; Costello, 2012; Dauvergne, 2012; Den Heijer, 2010; Dudley et al.,

2012). Given the impetus to tackle the issue of joblessness, there have been discussions about improving the lives of people in developing countries so as to reduce the push factors that drive them to become immigrants (Cook, 2003; Cornelisse, 2004, 2010; Costello, 2012; Dauvergne, 2012; Den Heijer, 2010; Dudley et al., 2012). For example, ethical purchasing patterns and practices are designed to ensure that producers in the developing world get a fair price for their efforts and that their incomes do not fall even as things become cheaper in the consumerist export destinations of Europe and North America. It is the migrants that wish to work and earn a living that will be the next consideration in the following section of this chapter.

1.2. MIGRANTS WHO WANT TO WORK AND EARN A LIVING

Perhaps the most important group of immigrants are those that work and earn a living (Cornelisse, 2004, 2010; Costello, 2012; Dauvergne, 2012; Den Heijer, 2010; Dudley et al., 2012; Dunn, 2001). This is because this category forms the largest portion of immigrants (Cornelisse, 2010; Costello, 2012; Dauvergne, 2012; Den Heijer, 2010; Dudley et al., 2012; Dunn, 2001, 2010). Secondly, it has the possibility of great economic impact in terms of creating and taking up domestic jobs (Costello, 2012; Dauvergne, 2012; Den Heijer, 2010; Dudley et al., 2012; Dunn, 2001, 2010; Exdell, 2009; Fiske, 2016). Thirdly, this group of migrants can increase demand and consumption within the local economy (Wexler, 2007; Wilcox, 2009; Zúñiga and Hernández-León, 2005; Zwi and Mares, 2015). Fourth, working, and productive migrants tend to send remittances at home which reflect a form of capital drain on the host nation (Welch, 2002; Wexler, 2007; Wilcox, 2009; Zúñiga and Hernández-León, 2005; Zwi and Mares, 2015). In fact, this is a category of migrants that is not protected by asylum laws and can therefore be deported at the whims of the administration in power (Webber, 2012; Welch, 2002; Wexler, 2007; Wilcox, 2009; Zúñiga and Hernández-León, 2005; Zwi and Mares, 2015). There are many geographical distribution patterns that elicit certain considerations such as gender (see Figure 1.2 for an example of geographical spread of female migrant domestic workers).

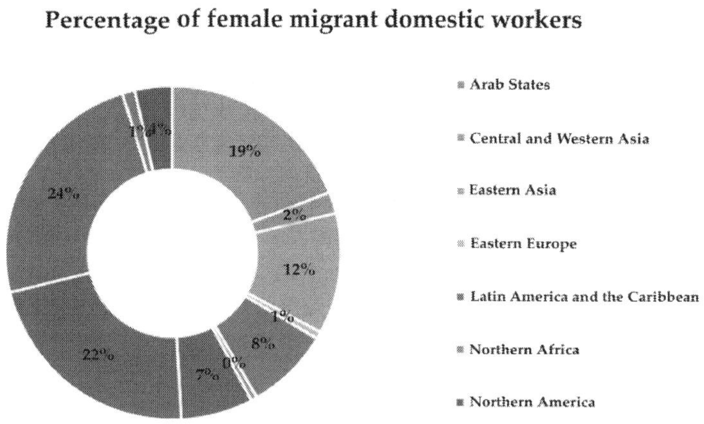

Figure 1.2: Geographical distribution of migrant female domestic workers 2013.

Source: Derived from Migration Data Portal via ILO.

Whereas economic migrants generally contribute to the development of the host nation, they are often characterized in the popular press as agents of globalization who take away jobs and opportunities that would ideally belong to the indigenous population (Thym, 2008; Webber, 2012; Welch, 2002; Wexler, 2007; Wilcox, 2009; Zúñiga and Hernández-León, 2005; Zwi and Mares, 2015). This opens up a narrative of discrimination that focuses on the potential for harm, whilst paying only scant attention to the positive side of economic migrants (Taylor, 2000; Thym, 2008; Webber, 2012; Welch, 2002; Wexler, 2007; Wilcox, 2009; Zúñiga and Hernández-León, 2005).

The International Labor Organization (ILO) goes further than many domestic governments by advocating for a rights-based approach in dealing with the needs of economic migrants (Spijkerboer and Van Walsum, 2007; Taylor, 2000; Thym, 2008; Webber, 2012; Welch, 2002; Wexler, 2007; Wilcox, 2009). This is a significant part of the workforce and therefore deserving of policy attention. For example, it is estimated that there were over 100 million people who were economically active outside the country of their birth. This represents about 50% of people that live outside their home countries. Clearly migrants will continue being an important facet of labor planning and demography generally (Soysal, 2012; Spijkerboer and Van Walsum, 2007; Taylor, 2000; Thym, 2008; Webber, 2012; Welch, 2002; Wexler, 2007). When we speak of economically productive immigrants, we cast a very wide net because that definition can include those that are self-employed, those that are employed by others, and those who are doing business (Smith, 2014; Soysal, 2012; Spijkerboer and Van Walsum, 2007; Taylor, 2000; Thym, 2008; Webber, 2012; Welch, 2002). In fact, even including refugees in the mix shows that the vast majority of immigrants are economically active (Shohamy and McNamara, 2009; Smith, 2014; Soysal, 2012; Spijkerboer and Van Walsum, 2007; Taylor, 2000; Thym, 2008).

This belies the oft-repeated myth that immigrants are only interested in securing welfare benefits from the host country (Sassen, 1997; Shohamy and McNamara, 2009; Smith, 2014; Soysal, 2012; Spijkerboer and Van Walsum, 2007). Indeed, many countries condition their welfare benefits on being out of work and not engaging in work on the sidelines (Sassen, 1996, 1997; Shohamy and McNamara, 2009; Smith, 2014; Soysal, 2012; Spijkerboer and Van Walsum, 2007). That means that for immigrants, it does not make sense for them to rely on meager state benefits whilst failing to work (Sanggaran, Haire, and Zion, 2016; Sassen, 1996, 1997; Shohamy and McNamara, 2009; Smith, 2014).

One of the motivations to work hard and quickly is the fact that migrants spend a lot of money organizing their migration to the more popular and exclusive spots such as North America and Western Europe (Sampson, Mitchell, and Bowring, 2011; Sanggaran, Haire, and Zion, 2016; Sassen, 1996, 1997; Shohamy and McNamara, 2009). The receipt of state welfare benefits (which are in any case forbidden for economic migrants) would not be sufficiently lucrative to take them away from the world of work (Samers, 2004; Sampson, Mitchell, and Bowring, 2011; Sanggaran, Haire, and Zion, 2016; Sassen, 1996, 1997). The process of migrating is not an easy one, even for those that have a legal status (Guia, Koulish, and Mitsilegas, 2016; Guild, 2001; Guild and Niessen, 1996; Hailbronner, 2000; Hayter, 2000; Heisler, 2000). First of all, there is the financial undertaking that is required in order to make the journey and resettle in a new place. Secondly, there is an emotional toll involved in leaving loved ones and familiar settings behind to look for greener pastures elsewhere (Gilman, 2013; Guia, Koulish, and Mitsilegas, 2016; Guild, 2001; Guild and Niessen, 1996; Hailbronner, 2000; Hayter, 2000).

It is generally accepted, even in the most virulent press coverage, that economic migrants outnumber other categories (such as asylum seekers and refugees) (Saadi et al., 2020; Samers, 2004; Sampson, Mitchell, and Bowring, 2011; Sanggaran, Haire, and Zion, 2016; Sassen, 1996). However, that acceptance of the factual statistics does little to dispel the myth that migrants travel for the sole purpose of securing state benefits from their host country; regardless of how ridiculous such a proposition is (Ryan and Mitsilegas, 2010; Saadi et al., 2020; Samers, 2004; Sampson, Mitchell, and Bowring, 2011; Sanggaran, Haire, and Zion, 2016). In the absence of another motivator, it is difficult to explain how someone might liquidate their entire asset base and go into debt for thousands of dollars in order to receive the meager pickings of state benefits (Ruhs, 2010; Ryan and Mitsilegas, 2010; Saadi et al., 2020; Samers, 2004; Sampson, Mitchell, and Bowring, 2011). Perhaps a more logically persuasive argument is that the numbers are becoming so high that they are unsustainable (Rubio-Marín, 2014; Ruhs, 2010; Ryan and Mitsilegas, 2010; Saadi et al., 2020; Samers, 2004; Sampson, Mitchell, and Bowring, 2011). This is partially due to the perceived benefits of living and working in certain countries such as the USA and UK (Ramji-Nogales, 2007; Rubio-Marín, 2014; Ruhs, 2010; Ryan and Mitsilegas, 2010; Saadi et al., 2020; Samers, 2004).

One of the more problematic segments of an immigrant population are those who are not regularized (Peberdy, 2001; Ramji-Nogales, 2007; Rubio-Marín, 2014; Ruhs, 2010; Ryan and Mitsilegas, 2010; Saadi et al., 2020; Samers, 2004). Not only are these immigrants breaking the laws of their host country, they may be also working in clandestine employment which does not bring in tax revenue for the state (Paz, 2016; Peberdy, 2001; Ramji-Nogales, 2007; Rubio-Marín, 2014; Ruhs, 2010; Ryan and Mitsilegas, 2010; Saadi et al., 2020). Going back to the question of sovereignty, the influx of undocumented immigrants means that the population of a given nation will be growing without the consent of the members of that community and without the oversight of the government (Ozdowski, 1985; Paz, 2016; Peberdy, 2001; Ramji-Nogales, 2007; Rubio-Marín, 2014; Ruhs, 2010; Ryan and Mitsilegas, 2010). Theoretically, there could even come a time when the migrant population exceeds the indigenous population (Orfanos, 2019; Ozdowski, 1985; Paz, 2016; Peberdy, 2001; Ramji-Nogales, 2007; Rubio-Marín, 2014; Ruhs, 2010). This is an argument that has been used in countries like the USA in order to stop any efforts to regularize the status of those without appropriate documentation (Oberman, 2016; Orfanos, 2019; Ozdowski, 1985; Paz, 2016; Peberdy, 2001; Ramji-Nogales, 2007; Rubio-Marín, 2014). Concerns about being replaced by foreigners remain a potent issue when deployed as a weapon against any reform that allows new immigrants in or even regularizes the status of those that are already in the country (Guild, 2001; Guild and Niessen, 1996; Hailbronner, 2000; Hayter, 2000; Heisler, 2000; Hernandez-Truyol and Johns, 1997).

A sizeable proportion of debates and discourses on immigration generally focus on the negative aspects of illegal immigration, with the presumption that most illegal immigrants are actually economic migrants that fail to make use of the normal routes of entry such as asylum, tourism, and family reunion (Newman, Proctor, and Dudley, 2013; Oberman, 2016; Orfanos, 2019; Ozdowski, 1985; Paz, 2016; Peberdy, 2001). The challenge is that the alternative routes of entry are practically closed off for economic migrants (Nethery and Holman, 2016; Newman, Proctor, and Dudley, 2013; Oberman, 2016; Orfanos, 2019; Ozdowski, 1985).

It is very rare for a government to ascertain that it can offer working visas for economic migrants, unless they represent highly specialized labor that is not readily available on the local scene (Motomura, 1999; Nethery and Holman, 2016; Newman, Proctor, and Dudley, 2013; Oberman, 2016; Orfanos, 2019). Even where countries like the USA have benefited from the influx of legal economic migrants, there is always negative sentiment towards their presence based on the notion that these expatriates tend to "steal" the jobs of local people (Morris, 2002, 2016; Motomura, 1999; Nethery and Holman, 2016; Newman, Proctor, and Dudley, 2013; Oberman, 2016).

Of course, when the situation is reversed and it is the host country sending immigrants abroad, they are automatically labeled as "expatriates" in order to drive the narrative that these immigrants are there to do some good and to develop the nation (Morris, 2002; Motomura, 1999; Nethery and Holman, 2016; Newman, Proctor, and Dudley, 2013; Oberman, 2016). It is a continuation of the colonial narratives in which people from the developing world were seen as being backward and therefore in need of the enlightening influence of missionaries and colonial administrators (Money, 1998; Morris, 2002, 2016; Motomura, 1999; Nethery and Holman, 2016; Newman, Proctor, and Dudley, 2013). The popular press tends to adopt xenophobic, racist, and jingoistic language when talking about immigrants from abroad (Molnar and Gill, 2018; Money, 1998; Morris, 2002, 2016; Motomura, 1999; Nethery and Holman, 2016). This can influence public opinion away from immigrants and stifle any attempts to engage in rational immigration reform (Miller, 2016; Molnar and Gill, 2018; Money, 1998; Morris, 2002, 2016; Motomura, 1999; Nethery and Holman, 2016).

The shortage of premium labor markets that has arisen following a number of global financial crises has increased the impetus to migrate in search of better opportunities (Miller, 2015, 2016; Molnar and Gill, 2018;

Money, 1998; Morris, 2002, 2016; Motomura, 1999; Nethery and Holman, 2016). At the same time on the domestic front, the popular destinations in Europe and North America are facing high unemployment levels which also dictate immigration policies must be tightened in order to protect domestic workers (Melis, 2001; Miller, 2015, 2016; Molnar and Gill, 2018; Money, 1998; Morris, 2002, 2016; Motomura, 1999). This creates a tension between the rising numbers of those wishing to come in and those that need the jobs within a shrinking labor market (Mehan, 1997; Melis, 2001; Miller, 2015, 2016; Molnar and Gill, 2018; Money, 1998; Morris, 2002, 2016).

It is also worth noting that other categories of immigrants can quickly end up becoming economic migrants once their status has been settled (Lorentzen, 2014; Mehan, 1997; Melis, 2001; Miller, 2015, 2016; Molnar and Gill, 2018; Money, 1998; Morris, 2016). Almost all refugees, for example, end up becoming productive members of their host nations regardless of the original reasons for their change of location (Lopez, 2005; Lorentzen, 2014; Mehan, 1997; Melis, 2001; Miller, 2015, 2016; Molnar and Gill, 2018; Money, 1998). That means that regardless of their categorization at the start of their immigration status, all these people end up becoming part of the workforce and causing the same pressures on the job market as other migrants (Guild and Niessen, 1996; Hailbronner, 2000; Hayter, 2000; Heisler, 2000; Hernandez-Truyol and Johns, 1997).

Businesses are an interest group when planning for economic migration since they are the primary employers of the new entrants (King, 2009; Lopez, 2005; Lorentzen, 2014; Mehan, 1997; Melis, 2001; Miller, 2015, 2016; Molnar and Gill, 2018). For example, enterprises have traditionally used migrants to balance out their workforce in terms of demography, competencies, and experience (Kelson and DeLaet, 1999; King, 2009; Lopez, 2005; Lorentzen, 2014; Mehan, 1997; Melis, 2001; Miller, 2015, 2016). Sometimes the costs of importing labor are much lower than the benefits of that labor (Kasimis, 2012; Kelson and DeLaet, 1999; King, 2009; Lopez, 2005; Lorentzen, 2014; Mehan, 1997; Melis, 2001; Miller, 2015). In those instances, businesses may express a preference for foreign workers (Joppke, 2010; Kasimis, 2012; Kelson and DeLaet, 1999; King, 2009; Lopez, 2005; Lorentzen, 2014; Mehan, 1997).

This can cause tension with the domestic labor force which may come to the conclusion that it is being de-populated out of the workforce; only to be replaced by cheaper foreign workers that can accept less than ideal working conditions (Joppke, 1999, 2010; Kasimis, 2012; Kelson and DeLaet, 1999;

King, 2009; Lopez, 2005; Lorentzen, 2014; Mehan, 1997). That is why the business community tends to favor migration because of the need of workers, particularly in the developed world which is also plagued by an aging population (Joppke, 1998, 1999, 2010; Kasimis, 2012; Kelson and DeLaet, 1999; King, 2009; Lopez, 2005; Lorentzen, 2014).

The issues of an aging population have inspired countries like Germany to import young people from troubled areas such as Syria and the Middle East in general (Johnson, 1996; Joppke, 1998, 1999, 2010; Kasimis, 2012; Kelson and DeLaet, 1999; King, 2009; Lopez, 2005). This is because many of the industrialized nations are reaping a demographic dividend in which people are living longer, taking early pensions, and collection those pensions for a longer period of time (Jacobson, 1996; Johnson, 1996; Joppke, 1998, 1999, 2010; Kasimis, 2012; Kelson and DeLaet, 1999). Besides, the birth rate among indigenous populations is declining (Hollifield, Martin, and Orrenius, 2014; Jacobson, 1996; Johnson, 1996; Joppke, 1998, 1999, 2010; Kasimis, 2012). That means that there is a potential crisis in the future where they could be far too many old people to be supported by a diminishing younger population (Hernandez-Truyol and Johns, 1997; Hollifield, Martin, and Orrenius, 2014; Jacobson, 1996; Johnson, 1996; Joppke, 1998).

Where the government decides to take a drastic step, such as importing workers; the response from the popular press is often negative (Heisler, 2000; Hernandez-Truyol and Johns, 1997; Hollifield, Martin, and Orrenius, 2014; Jacobson, 1996; Johnson, 1996). Some mask outright racism and xenophobia by talking about concerns to do with a "way of living" and the potential for "international terrorism" (Hayter, 2000; Heisler, 2000; Hernandez-Truyol and Johns, 1997; Hollifield, Martin, and Orrenius, 2014; Jacobson, 1996). Whereas, these are valid concerns in of themselves, they do not adequately address the issues of immigration from the standpoint of sustaining the economy (Hailbronner, 2000; Hayter, 2000; Heisler, 2000; Hernandez-Truyol and Johns, 1997; Hollifield, Martin, and Orrenius, 2014). The next section emphasis this standpoint.

1.3. ECONOMIC DEVELOPMENT AND MIGRATION PATTERNS

Migration patterns to follow economic development in as far as poorer people are likely to migrate to wealthier nations in order to find new opportunities (Frederking, 2012; Gilman, 2013; Guia, Koulish, and Mitsilegas, 2016; Guild, 2001; Guild and Niessen, 1996; Hailbronner, 2000). Research has shown that highly skilled and experienced migrants can improve the workforce generally in terms of productivity and overall efficiency. This is a key prerequisite for economic growth and development (Flynn, 2013; Frederking, 2012; Gilman, 2013; Guia, Koulish, and Mitsilegas, 2016; Guild, 2001; Guild and Niessen, 1996). Migrants can help to stimulate business development because they include entrepreneurs and potential consumers of end products (Fiske, 2016; Flynn, 2013; Frederking, 2012; Gilman, 2013; Guia, Koulish, and Mitsilegas, 2016; Guild, 2001; Guild and Niessen, 1996). In this way, it may be possible for migrants to create even more jobs than they take up (Exdell, 2009; Fiske, 2016; Flynn, 2013; Frederking, 2012; Gilman, 2013; Guia, Koulish, and Mitsilegas, 2016; Guild, 2001). The innovativeness and resilience of foreign businesspeople can significantly support the economy, particularly during economic downturns (Dunn, 2010; Exdell, 2009; Fiske, 2016; Flynn, 2013; Frederking, 2012; Gilman, 2013; Guia, Koulish, and Mitsilegas, 2016). The USA is an example of a country that has traditionally welcomed migrants, who now form a substantial portion of the working population (see Figure 1.3).

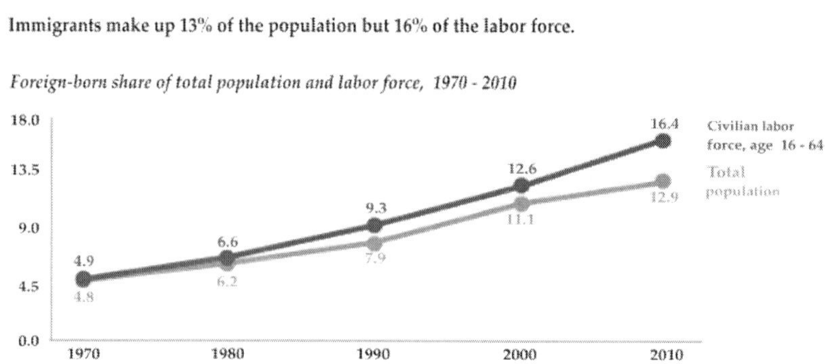

Figure 1.3: Migrants as growing segment of the US labor force.

Source: Brookings Institution.

Where migrants are allowed to contribute to social security systems, they can bridge the gaps that exist in developed nations which are aging in terms of their demography (Dunn, 2001, 2010; Exdell, 2009; Fiske, 2016; Flynn, 2013; Frederking, 2012; Gilman, 2013; Guia, Koulish, and Mitsilegas, 2016). This is besides the work that migrants do in key sectors such as health, jobs that might otherwise be shunned by the indigenous population because they are perceived to be undesirable (Dudley et al., 2012;

Dunn, 2001, 2010; Exdell, 2009; Fiske, 2016; Flynn, 2013; Frederking, 2012; Gilman, 2013). Through the use of migrant labor and innovators, it is possible to improve competitiveness in domestic sectors which may have fallen into complacency due to the protectionist policies of their home governments (Den Heijer, 2010; Dudley et al., 2012; Dunn, 2001, 2010; Exdell, 2009; Fiske, 2016; Flynn, 2013; Frederking, 2012). A case in point are the construction, agriculture, and services sectors that may be suffering from chronic inefficiency prior to the introduction of foreign firms and workers which shake up the market (Dauvergne, 2012; Den Heijer, 2010; Dudley et al., 2012; Dunn, 2001, 2010; Exdell, 2009; Fiske, 2016; Flynn, 2013). Indeed, part of the opposition to migrants may be inefficient home companies that do not want to be exposed to competition (Costello, 2012; Dauvergne, 2012; Den Heijer, 2010; Dudley et al., 2012; Dunn, 2001, 2010; Exdell, 2009; Fiske, 2016).

The ILO has undertaken a number of research projects that are implicitly aimed at demystifying the role of immigrant workers (Cornelisse, 2010; Costello, 2012; Dauvergne, 2012; Den Heijer, 2010; Dudley et al., 2012; Dunn, 2001, 2010). For example, research has shown that migrant workers in Southern Europe (as is the case in many other parts of the developed world), migrants mainly take jobs that local people will not take (Cornelisse, 2004, 2010; Costello, 2012; Dauvergne, 2012; Den Heijer, 2010; Dudley et al., 2012; Dunn, 2001). Unless there are migrant workers, whole industries would collapse due to a lack of a dependable workforce (Cook, 2003; Cornelisse, 2004, 2010; Costello, 2012; Dauvergne, 2012; Den Heijer, 2010; Dudley et al., 2012). One of the industries in Europe that is particularly dependent on migrant labor is that of picking strawberries and processing them (Chin, 1999; Cook, 2003; Cornelisse, 2004, 2010; Costello, 2012; Dauvergne, 2012; Den Heijer, 2010; Dudley et al., 2012). If the governments were to completely tighten all immigration routes, there is a real risk that these industries will eventually face difficulties in recruiting staff (Chavez, 2001; Chin, 1999; Cook, 2003; Cornelisse, 2004, 2010; Costello, 2012; Dauvergne, 2012; Den Heijer, 2010). Despite the fact that immigrants only compete in marginal sectors of the economy, they are often at the center of debates concerning unemployment (Brochmann and Hammar, 2020; Chavez, 2001; Chin, 1999; Cook, 2003; Cornelisse, 2004, 2010; Costello, 2012).

Some have argued that the ready availability of replacement immigration and welfare benefits create ideal circumstances for perpetual existence on social welfare rather than looking for a job (Brané and Lundholm,

2007; Brochmann and Hammar, 2020; Chavez, 2001; Chin, 1999; Cook, 2003; Cornelisse, 2004). However, such a view is belied by the individual experiences of indigenous people or legal residents who may not be able to work for any number of given reasons (Becerra, 2016; Brané and Lundholm, 2007; Brochmann and Hammar, 2020; Chavez, 2001; Chin, 1999; Cook, 2003). Besides, there is no guarantee that the skillset that employers are looking for will be available locally, hence the need to recruit elsewhere (Barak-Erez, 2008; Becerra, 2016; Brané and Lundholm, 2007; Brochmann and Hammar, 2020; Chavez, 2001; Chin, 1999). It is for this reason, that some fiscal Conservatives have philosophically re-orientated themselves towards the liberalization and eventual globalization of the labor market (Bangarth, 2003; Barak-Erez, 2008; Becerra, 2016; Brané and Lundholm, 2007; Brochmann and Hammar, 2020; Chavez, 2001). One of the resultant benefits for businesses is that they can price their wages competitively without having to rely on a very restricted domestic work pool (Baldwin-Edwards, 2006; Bangarth, 2003; Barak-Erez, 2008; Becerra, 2016; Brané and Lundholm, 2007; Brochmann and Hammar, 2020).

There may be certain characteristics that are associated with new migrants which make it easier for them to prosper in the new destinations (Bacon, 1996; Baldwin-Edwards, 2006; Bangarth, 2003; Barak-Erez, 2008; Becerra, 2016; Brané and Lundholm, 2007). A case in point is the well-established notion that immigrants are generally more entrepreneurial, innovative, and resilient than other members of a community that do not opt to leave one location to move to another (Aynsley-Green et al., 2012; Bacon, 1996; Baldwin-Edwards, 2006; Bangarth, 2003; Barak-Erez, 2008; Becerra, 2016). That means that when migrants get to new destinations that are conducive, such as the USA for example; they are likely to create new companies and open up new jobs that can help to offset the perceived impact that they have on the local job market (Adelman, 2002; Aynsley-Green et al., 2012; Bacon, 1996; Baldwin-Edwards, 2006; Bangarth, 2003; Barak-Erez, 2008). Countries like Spain and Portugal are particularly interested in working with migrants that are capable of developing such opportunities and will grant them preferential treatment whenever possible (Ackerman and Furman, 2014; Adelman, 2002; Aynsley-Green et al., 2012; Bacon, 1996; Baldwin-Edwards, 2006).

There is empirical evidence to support the notion that economic migrants specifically and migrants in general, have a positive impact on general income levels (Acer and Goodman, 2009; Ackerman and Furman, 2014; Adelman, 2002; Aynsley-Green et al., 2012; Bacon, 1996). A case in point is the United Kingdom, a historically international nation that has recently been overtaken by a parochial desire for independence from the European Union, partly in order to better control immigration (Dauvergne, 2012; Den Heijer, 2010; Dudley et al., 2012; Dunn, 2001, 2010; Exdell, 2009; Fiske, 2016; Flynn, 2013). The latest statistics indicate that although immigrants only account for just over 10% of the entire population in the UK, they own nearly 15% of small and medium sizes businesses in that country (Den Heijer, 2010; Dudley et al., 2012; Dunn, 2001, 2010; Exdell, 2009; Fiske, 2016; Flynn, 2013; Frederking, 2012). This figure could even be underestimated since many immigrants are reluctant to engage with authorities for fear of attracting negative attention from the popular press (Dudley et al., 2012; Dunn, 2001, 2010; Exdell, 2009; Fiske, 2016; Flynn, 2013; Frederking, 2012; Gilman, 2013). Getting rid of these immigrant entrepreneurs would have a devastating impact on the economy, yet there is no guarantee that the indigenous population would ably fill the gap that they leave behind (Dunn, 2001, 2010; Exdell, 2009; Fiske, 2016; Flynn, 2013; Frederking, 2012; Gilman, 2013; Guia, Koulish, and Mitsilegas, 2016).

Developed nations are facing a particular problem filling labor-intensive jobs that have been rejected by the local population as being undesirable (Dunn, 2010; Exdell, 2009; Fiske, 2016; Flynn, 2013; Frederking, 2012; Gilman, 2013; Guia, Koulish, and Mitsilegas, 2016). In the absence of appropriate mechanization, companies one of two options (Exdell, 2009; Fiske, 2016; Flynn, 2013; Frederking, 2012; Gilman, 2013; Guia, Koulish, and Mitsilegas, 2016; Guild, 2001). First, they can outsource the jobs but that might mean that the domestic government misses out on the revenue and demand arising out of these outsourced jobs (Fiske, 2016; Flynn, 2013; Frederking, 2012; Gilman, 2013; Guia, Koulish, and Mitsilegas, 2016; Guild, 2001; Guild and Niessen, 1996). The second option is to take advantage of immigrants that are already within the borders of the host country, as well as being willing and able to do those jobs (Flynn, 2013; Frederking, 2012; Gilman, 2013; Guia, Koulish, and Mitsilegas, 2016; Guild, 2001; Guild and Niessen, 1996). Indeed, this second option is much better than importing specialized expatriates because it does not involve additional transport costs (Frederking, 2012; Gilman, 2013; Guia, Koulish, and Mitsilegas, 2016; Guild, 2001; Guild and Niessen, 1996; Hailbronner, 2000).

Some shortages are so severe that the domestic consumers have literally imported workers to do jobs that would otherwise be neglected (Gilman, 2013; Guia, Koulish, and Mitsilegas, 2016; Guild, 2001; Guild and Niessen, 1996; Hailbronner, 2000; Hayter, 2000). Nowhere is this more visible than in the importation of domestic servants to the Middle East, an industry that is growing by the day (Guia, Koulish, and Mitsilegas, 2016; Guild, 2001; Guild and Niessen, 1996; Hailbronner, 2000; Hayter, 2000; Heisler, 2000). Such schemes have acquired a reputation for poor treatment of migrant workers and are therefore treated with suspicion by some policymakers or even human rights campaigners (Guild, 2001; Guild and Niessen, 1996; Hailbronner, 2000; Hayter, 2000; Heisler, 2000; Hernandez-Truyol and Johns, 1997). There are three characteristics of jobs that are associated with migrant labor, and they are known as the "3D Jobs." The abbreviation breaks down into **D**irty or **D**egrading, **D**angerous, and **D**ifficult jobs (Guild and Niessen, 1996; Hailbronner, 2000; Hayter, 2000; Heisler, 2000; Hernandez-Truyol and Johns, 1997). There is an entire cottage industry that has arisen out of the exploitation of migrant labor and many are engaged in work as agents and brokers to this effect (Hailbronner, 2000; Hayter, 2000; Heisler, 2000; Hernandez-Truyol and Johns, 1997; Hollifield, Martin, and Orrenius, 2014).

Employers exploit migrant workers because they can (Hayter, 2000; Heisler, 2000; Hernandez-Truyol and Johns, 1997; Hollifield, Martin, and Orrenius, 2014; Jacobson, 1996). First of all, the employee protections that generally exist, such as the minimum wage and paid leave are often restricted to domestic workers in practice (Heisler, 2000; Hernandez-Truyol and Johns, 1997; Hollifield, Martin, and Orrenius, 2014; Jacobson, 1996; Johnson, 1996). This occurs even where the enabling legislation has not explicitly excluded migrant workers (Hernandez-Truyol and Johns, 1997; Hollifield, Martin, and Orrenius, 2014; Jacobson, 1996; Johnson, 1996; Joppke, 1998). The second issue is the relative disadvantage of migrant workers that have no established social capital networks and are therefore largely reliant on their adopted home (Hollifield, Martin, and Orrenius, 2014; Jacobson, 1996; Johnson, 1996; Joppke, 1998, 1999, 2010; Kasimis, 2012). That means that they have nothing to fall back on if they lose their job and hence the impetus to maintain the job at any cost (Jacobson, 1996; Johnson, 1996; Joppke, 1998, 1999, 2010; Kasimis, 2012; Kelson and DeLaet, 1999). In effect, they have to continue working in certain degrading conditions even if they are not satisfied with their employment terms (Johnson, 1996; Joppke, 1998, 1999, 2010; Kasimis, 2012; Kelson and DeLaet, 1999; King, 2009; Lopez, 2005).

Those that are not regularized face even more huddles and can easily be exploited by unscrupulous business people in order to lower costs and increase their profits (Joppke, 1998, 1999, 2010; Kasimis, 2012; Kelson and DeLaet, 1999; King, 2009; Lopez, 2005; Lorentzen, 2014). Migrant laborers tend to dominate sectors which are highly competitive in terms of controlling costs; yet with lower unit prices (Joppke, 1999, 2010; Kasimis, 2012; Kelson and DeLaet, 1999; King, 2009; Lopez, 2005; Lorentzen, 2014; Mehan, 1997). That means that their employers are continuously under pressure to reduce marginal costs and will try to do so even if it means harming the migrant workers that help them to achieve this objective (Joppke, 2010; Kasimis, 2012; Kelson and DeLaet, 1999; King, 2009; Lopez, 2005; Lorentzen, 2014; Mehan, 1997). There is plenty of evidence showing migrants living and working in appalling conditions, yet seemingly unable to take the necessary steps to report that exploitation that they are facing (Kasimis, 2012; Kelson and DeLaet, 1999; King, 2009; Lopez, 2005; Lorentzen, 2014; Mehan, 1997; Melis, 2001; Miller, 2015).

Whereas the generalized lack of unionization among migrant workers is desirable for certain employers, it means that this segment of workers is open to exploitation (Bacon, 1996; Baldwin-Edwards, 2006; Bangarth, 2003; Barak-Erez, 2008; Becerra, 2016; Brané and Lundholm, 2007). For example, migrant workers may find it difficult to successfully complain about poor health and safety standards in the most hazardous jobs (Baldwin-Edwards, 2006; Bangarth, 2003; Barak-Erez, 2008; Becerra, 2016; Brané and Lundholm, 2007; Brochmann and Hammar, 2020). Indeed, the employer may have preferred migrant workers precisely because they are unlikely to raise complaints about health and safety issues (Bangarth, 2003; Barak-Erez, 2008; Becerra, 2016; Brané and Lundholm, 2007; Brochmann and Hammar, 2020; Chavez, 2001). Besides, migrant workers get few opportunities for training and development since many of the schemes available are restricted to legal residents and citizens of the host nation (Barak-Erez, 2008; Becerra, 2016; Brané and Lundholm, 2007; Brochmann and Hammar, 2020; Chavez, 2001; Chin, 1999). The implication is that migrant workers rarely progress beyond the enjoy jobs that they first applied for (Becerra, 2016; Brané and Lundholm, 2007; Brochmann and Hammar, 2020; Chavez, 2001; Chin, 1999; Cook, 2003).

The management of migrant workers leaves a lot to be desired in terms of controlling their entry and providing them protections once employed in the host countries (Brané and Lundholm, 2007; Brochmann and Hammar, 2020; Chavez, 2001; Chin, 1999; Cook, 2003; Cornelisse, 2004). For example, the government continues to collect taxes and social contributions from immigrants despite the fact that they are in effect discriminated against when it comes to workplace benefits in general, critically including health and safety matters (Brochmann and Hammar, 2020; Chavez, 2001; Chin, 1999; Cook, 2003; Cornelisse, 2004, 2010; Costello, 2012). There has even been research showing that clandestine workers were paying some form of tax that ended up in the government coffers despite the fact that this was a population that had been deemed to be without any legitimate right to be in the country (Chavez, 2001; Chin, 1999; Cook, 2003; Cornelisse, 2004, 2010; Costello, 2012; Dauvergne, 2012; Den Heijer, 2010). Because these contributions are often automatically withheld from the payslip, immigrants have limited control over where they end up and have limited evidence to support their substantial economic contributions to the destination country (Chin, 1999; Cook, 2003; Cornelisse, 2004, 2010; Costello, 2012; Dauvergne, 2012; Den Heijer, 2010; Dudley et al., 2012).

The paradox here is that the government is in effect benefitting from immigrant workers without acknowledging their contribution (Cook, 2003; Cornelisse, 2004, 2010; Costello, 2012; Dauvergne, 2012; Den Heijer, 2010; Dudley et al., 2012). It is the hypocrisy that has rendered the debates on immigration too emotionally charged for rational decision-making in some countries. The politicians are reluctant to put a complete stop to immigration despite the outcries from local communities that are looking to exclude outsiders. This is because many government officials understand the devastating effect it would have on the economy if they chose to completely and comprehensively excluded any form of immigration (Cornelisse, 2004, 2010; Costello, 2012; Dauvergne, 2012; Den Heijer, 2010; Dudley et al., 2012; Dunn, 2001). At the same time, the governments are not willing or able to make a coherent and persuasive case for migration. This leaves space for inaccurate and damaging debates to dominate the immigration arena. In some cases, the end result can be poor policy formulation and implementation. In the next section, we consider the impact of net migration on the sending countries.

1.4. IMPACT OF EMIGRATION ON SENDING COUNTRIES

It is customary to speak of immigrants in terms of the costs and benefits that are accrued by the hosting country (Costello, 2012; Dauvergne, 2012; Den Heijer, 2010; Dudley et al., 2012; Dunn, 2001, 2010; Exdell, 2009; Fiske, 2016). In reality, the country that the emigrant is leaving behind will also have benefits and costs that are associated with this phenomenon (Wexler, 2007; Wilcox, 2009; Zúñiga and Hernández-León, 2005; Zwi and

Mares, 2015). From the perspective of the country of origin, emigrants can send remittances that sustain poor families (Welch, 2002; Wexler, 2007; Wilcox, 2009; Zúñiga and Hernández-León, 2005; Zwi and Mares, 2015). If they ever return, these emigrants will bring new skills, competencies, and exposure to the local populace (Webber, 2012; Welch, 2002; Wexler, 2007; Wilcox, 2009; Zúñiga and Hernández-León, 2005; Zwi and Mares, 2015). Moreover, the fact that many young people are leaving for greener pastures may somewhat alleviate the unemployment pressures that the economy is facing at a given moment in time (Thym, 2008; Webber, 2012; Welch, 2002; Wexler, 2007; Wilcox, 2009; Zúñiga and Hernández-León, 2005; Zwi and Mares, 2015).

In Figure 1.4, we see some of the merits and demerits of international migration from the perspectives of both the sender and receiving communities. One of the startling findings of recent research is that the vast majority of migrants settle in the developing world (Taylor, 2000; Thym, 2008; Webber, 2012; Welch, 2002; Wexler, 2007; Wilcox, 2009; Zúñiga and Hernández-León, 2005). Yet, the loudest voices expressing concerning about migration are the most industrialized nations which take up a very small portion of migrants (Spijkerboer and Van Walsum, 2007; Taylor, 2000; Thym, 2008; Webber, 2012; Welch, 2002; Wexler, 2007; Wilcox, 2009). In effect, the poorest nations are willing to share the little that they have while the richest nations are not willing to share even a portion of the largesse that they have (Soysal, 2012; Spijkerboer and Van Walsum, 2007; Taylor, 2000; Thym, 2008; Webber, 2012; Welch, 2002; Wexler, 2007). Such arguments are not properly articulated when developing discourses on international immigration, instead preferring to sustain the narratives that the most developed nations are swamped by illegal immigrants (Smith, 2014; Soysal, 2012; Spijkerboer and Van Walsum, 2007; Taylor, 2000; Thym, 2008; Webber, 2012; Welch, 2002).

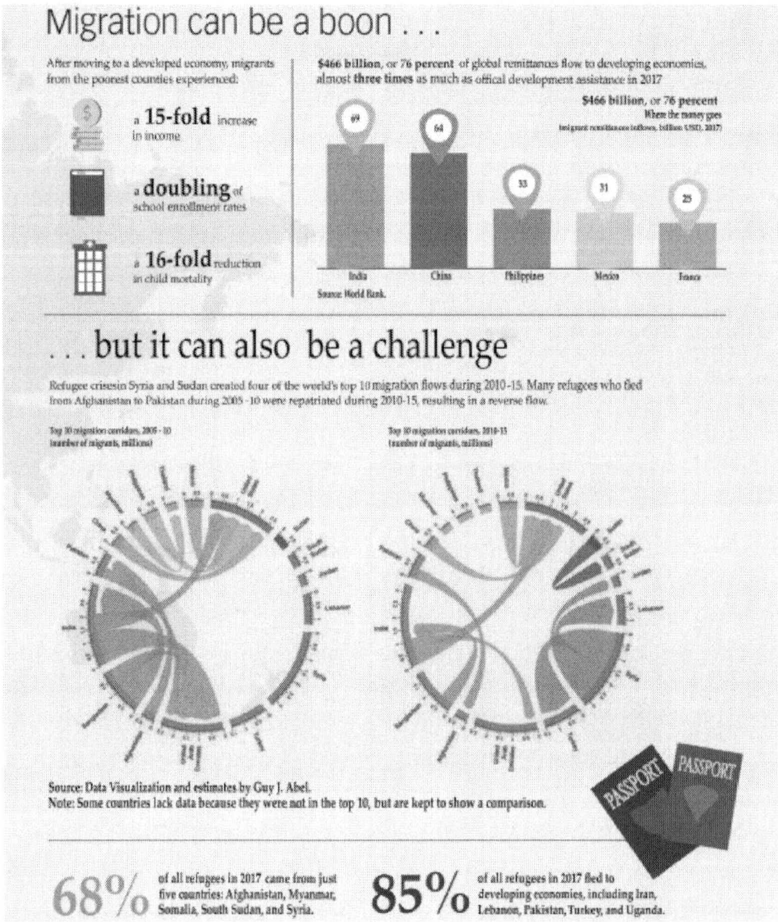

Figure 1.4: Immigration as a boon and challenge.

Source: GJ Abel via IMF.

Many developing countries are facing the exact opposite of the demographic dividend that developed countries are benefitting from (Shohamy and McNamara, 2009; Smith, 2014; Soysal, 2012; Spijkerboer and Van Walsum, 2007; Taylor, 2000; Thym, 2008). For example, the population in developing countries is younger, poorer, less education, and with a high reproductive rate (Sassen, 1997; Shohamy and McNamara, 2009; Smith, 2014; Soysal, 2012; Spijkerboer and Van Walsum, 2007). That implies significant population pressures that makes high youth unemployment an inevitable consequence (Sassen, 1996, 1997; Shohamy and McNamara, 2009; Smith, 2014; Soysal, 2012; Spijkerboer and Van Walsum, 2007). One way of reducing these pressures is for younger people to migrate to other countries for alternative opportunities (Sanggaran, Haire, and Zion, 2016; Sassen, 1996, 1997; Shohamy and McNamara, 2009; Smith, 2014). Besides, wages in developing countries are chronically low, and there are very few protections for workers in general (Sampson, Mitchell, and Bowring, 2011; Sanggaran, Haire, and Zion, 2016; Sassen, 1996, 1997; Shohamy and McNamara, 2009). That makes industrialized nations an attractive proposition, particularly if these young people can gain some form of legal status (Samers, 2004; Sampson, Mitchell, and Bowring, 2011; Sanggaran, Haire, and Zion, 2016; Sassen, 1996, 1997). The so-called "surplus labor" that exists in developing countries continues to grow during times of political instability, economic crises, and significant social change (Saadi et al., 2020; Samers, 2004; Sampson, Mitchell, and Bowring, 2011; Sanggaran, Haire, and Zion, 2016; Sassen, 1996).

The fact that young people have left a country to work abroad may on the face of it appear to be a loss of productive labor (Ryan and Mitsilegas, 2010; Saadi et al., 2020; Samers, 2004; Sampson, Mitchell, and Bowring, 2011; Sanggaran, Haire, and Zion, 2016). However, the remittances that these young people send can help in supporting the local community (Ruhs, 2010; Ryan and Mitsilegas, 2010; Saadi et al., 2020; Samers, 2004; Sampson, Mitchell, and Bowring, 2011). They are particularly important for supplementing the meager social support systems that exist in developing countries (Rubio-Marín, 2014; Ruhs, 2010; Ryan and Mitsilegas, 2010; Saadi et al., 2020; Samers, 2004; Sampson, Mitchell, and Bowring, 2011). Besides, the remittances may be used for developmental activities that contribute to the economic growth of the sending nation (Ramji-Nogales, 2007; Rubio-Marín, 2014; Ruhs, 2010; Ryan and Mitsilegas, 2010; Saadi et al., 2020; Samers, 2004). These are significant financial in-flows from the developed world through remittances to developing countries (Peberdy, 2001; Ramji-Nogales, 2007; Rubio-Marín, 2014; Ruhs, 2010; Ryan and Mitsilegas, 2010; Saadi et al., 2020; Samers, 2004).

One of the emerging debates concerns the costs of sending remittances (Paz, 2016; Peberdy, 2001; Ramji-Nogales, 2007; Rubio-Marín, 2014; Ruhs, 2010; Ryan and Mitsilegas, 2010; Saadi et al., 2020). Some estimates indicate that the costs of sending remittances can be as high as 10% of the total value of the transaction (Ozdowski, 1985; Paz, 2016; Peberdy, 2001; Ramji-Nogales, 2007; Rubio-Marín, 2014; Ruhs, 2010; Ryan and Mitsilegas, 2010). These costs were even higher when transferring funds to regions with poor technological and financial coverage, such as Sub-

Saharan Africa. Ironically, these are the poorest regions on earth and it is where remittances are needed most (Orfanos, 2019; Ozdowski, 1985; Paz, 2016; Peberdy, 2001; Ramji-Nogales, 2007; Rubio-Marín, 2014; Ruhs, 2010). However, due to poor infrastructure and vested interests throughout the supply chain, the costs of sending money are inordinately high. Besides, the available avenues for sending and receiving remittances are severely restricted (Oberman, 2016; Orfanos, 2019; Ozdowski, 1985; Paz, 2016; Peberdy, 2001; Ramji-Nogales, 2007; Rubio-Marín, 2014). The widespread use of the internet has somewhat helped in providing a wider choice to people that wish to send money to developing countries (Newman, Proctor, and Dudley, 2013; Oberman, 2016; Orfanos, 2019; Ozdowski, 1985; Paz, 2016; Peberdy, 2001). However, recently there has also been a problem of unreliable internet connection and the surreptitious anti-money laundering laws which are in reality designed to ensure that local people do not have access to funds to potentially overthrow the dictatorships in that part of the world (Nethery and Holman, 2016; Newman, Proctor, and Dudley, 2013; Oberman, 2016; Orfanos, 2019; Ozdowski, 1985).

Some governments in the developing world once suggested that they could regulate these

remittances so that they could be directed towards developmental activities (Motomura, 1999; Nethery and Holman, 2016; Newman, Proctor, and Dudley, 2013; Oberman, 2016; Orfanos, 2019). However, such a suggestion was strongly resisted; not least because these are private funds that should not be used by the government in order to meet its national budgetary obligations (Morris, 2002, 2016; Motomura, 1999; Nethery and Holman, 2016; Newman, Proctor, and Dudley, 2013; Oberman, 2016). A much more amenable approach was to support the transfer of so-called “social remittances” including professional skills, values, ideas, practices, and knowledge that would otherwise not be available domestically (Morris, 2002; Motomura, 1999; Nethery and Holman, 2016; Newman, Proctor, and Dudley, 2013; Oberman, 2016). Moreover, research has shown that migrants can significantly improve the livelihoods of the families and friends that they leave at home (Money, 1998; Morris, 2002, 2016; Motomura, 1999; Nethery and Holman, 2016; Newman, Proctor, and Dudley, 2013).

From a sustainable development perspective, immigration can act as an enabling factor for achieving inclusive social development (Aynsley-Green et al., 2012; Bacon, 1996; Baldwin-Edwards, 2006; Bangarth, 2003; Barak-Erez, 2008; Becerra, 2016). Those that are left behind in the national planning may end up getting a second chance through the people that immigrate and bring capital back into the economy (Bacon, 1996; Baldwin-Edwards, 2006; Bangarth, 2003; Barak-Erez, 2008; Becerra, 2016; Brané and Lundholm, 2007). That goal or potential benefit has to be counterbalanced with the reality that the exit of young and dynamic people might mean that the national pool of workers is depleted of skills and experiences (Baldwin-Edwards, 2006; Bangarth, 2003; Barak-Erez, 2008; Becerra, 2016; Brané and Lundholm, 2007; Brochmann and Hammar, 2020). This is particularly important if the national resources have been expended in training and developing these people (Bangarth, 2003; Barak-Erez, 2008; Becerra, 2016; Brané and Lundholm, 2007; Brochmann and Hammar, 2020; Chavez, 2001).

Quite often, there are high level academics who never return to their homeland when they go to study abroad (Barak-Erez, 2008; Becerra, 2016; Brané and Lundholm, 2007; Brochmann and Hammar, 2020; Chavez, 2001; Chin, 1999). This is a great loss for the home nation that will have invested significant resources in educating that person (Becerra, 2016; Brané and Lundholm, 2007; Brochmann and Hammar, 2020; Chavez, 2001; Chin, 1999; Cook, 2003). Meanwhile the receiving country has the considerable advantage of merely skimming off an already finished product (Brané and Lundholm, 2007; Brochmann and Hammar, 2020; Chavez, 2001; Chin, 1999; Cook, 2003; Cornelisse, 2004). The "brain drain" is no longer merely a cliché to excuse the failure to invest in human capital development programs within the developing nations (Brochmann and Hammar, 2020; Chavez, 2001; Chin, 1999; Cook, 2003; Cornelisse, 2004, 2010; Costello, 2012). Instead, it is a real problem with real consequences for those countries that have witnessed the mass exodus of their best to the more industrialized nations (Chavez, 2001; Chin, 1999; Cook, 2003; Cornelisse, 2004, 2010; Costello, 2012; Dauvergne, 2012; Den Heijer, 2010).

Large-scale migration abroad can weaken national economies. It does this by draining the local labor forces of skills and essential vitality for industrial competitiveness (Chin, 1999; Cook, 2003; Cornelisse, 2004, 2010; Costello, 2012; Dauvergne, 2012; Den Heijer, 2010; Dudley et al., 2012). This phenomenon is particularly damaging to small countries which already have limited resources such as a relatively small population when compared to the economic giants of China, the European Union, and the USA (Cook, 2003; Cornelisse, 2004, 2010; Costello, 2012; Dauvergne, 2012; Den Heijer, 2010; Dudley et al., 2012). Hence, the long-term reliance on sending nationals for employment abroad ought to be counterbalanced with efforts to create decent jobs at home. In this way, it is possible to raise living standards for everyone in a given community (Cornelisse, 2004, 2010; Costello, 2012; Dauvergne, 2012; Den Heijer, 2010; Dudley et al., 2012; Dunn, 2001). It is one of the goals of sustainable development which recognizes the fact that some parts of the economy get an unfair advantage over others and that the distribution of national resources is not always equitable (Cornelisse, 2010; Costello, 2012; Dauvergne, 2012; Den Heijer, 2010; Dudley et al., 2012; Dunn, 2001, 2010). It is important to remember that there are many vulnerable people and communities in the developing world which could not survive without the support of the remittances that are sent by migrants who are working away from home (Costello, 2012; Dauvergne, 2012; Den Heijer, 2010; Dudley et al., 2012; Dunn, 2001, 2010; Exdell, 2009; Fiske, 2016). In recognition of the contribution that migrants play in their home countries, there are some nations that have taken steps to increase their protection (Wexler, 2007; Wilcox, 2009; Zúñiga and Hernández-León, 2005; Zwi and Mares, 2015). A case in point are the developing countries that are increasingly demanding for licenses and other verification checks. These are undertaken before migrants can be taken to other countries for work. The system is designed to weed out those that either do not have the right credentials or are alternatively looking to take advantage of vulnerable migrants (Welch, 2002; Wexler, 2007; Wilcox, 2009; Zúñiga and Hernández-León, 2005; Zwi and Mares, 2015). Moreover, if those workers face problems there are consulate and diplomatic resources that can be used to assist them. These can be in the form of either repatriation or further support if they remain in the host country (Webber, 2012; Welch, 2002; Wexler, 2007; Wilcox, 2009; Zúñiga and Hernández-León, 2005; Zwi and Mares, 2015). However, the level of support is determined by the relative wealth and influence of the home nation (Thym, 2008; Webber, 2012; Welch, 2002; Wexler, 2007; Wilcox, 2009; Zúñiga and Hernández-León, 2005; Zwi and Mares, 2015). For example, China is able to protect its nationals abroad more than other countries because of its economic clout (Taylor, 2000; Thym, 2008; Webber, 2012; Welch, 2002; Wexler, 2007; Wilcox, 2009; Zúñiga and Hernández-León, 2005). A case in point are the visa waivers for certain categories of Chinese travelers, an achievement that still eludes many developing countries that often ignore their citizens when they are being denied entry into other countries (Spijkerboer and Van Walsum, 2007; Taylor, 2000; Thym, 2008; Webber, 2012; Welch, 2002; Wexler, 2007; Wilcox, 2009). The global hegemony in political, economic, and social terms is reflected in the migration patterns and the ways in which migrants are treated when they arrive on the receiving shores. For the most part, immigration from developing to developed countries is strongly discouraged while visitors from the developed world can travel virtually anywhere that they choose. Immigration in this case is strongly linked to economic strength and influence. The next section explores the role of global crises in driving migration patterns.

1.5. LINKS BETWEEN MIGRATION AND GLOBAL CRISES

The impacts of economic crises can become exponential over time in ways that may not be initially anticipated. One of the effects is the desire by young people to move to other countries for more opportunities and to escape the harsh conditions of their home countries (Smith, 2014; Soysal, 2012; Spijkerboer and Van Walsum, 2007; Taylor, 2000; Thym, 2008; Webber, 2012; Welch, 2002). That does not mean that migration only happens during an economic downturn (Shohamy and McNamara, 2009; Smith, 2014; Soysal, 2012; Spijkerboer and Van Walsum, 2007; Taylor, 2000; Thym, 2008). Indeed, there are indicators that during an economic boom, people may migrate because they have the means to do so. Moreover, during an economic boom across the globe the potential receiving countries are in need of specific labor categories in order to meet the increasing demand for goods and services (Sassen, 1997; Shohamy and McNamara, 2009; Smith, 2014; Soysal, 2012; Spijkerboer and Van Walsum, 2007).

Economic downturns can be particularly hard for migrants who are then relegated to second class applications in their new destinations (Sassen, 1996, 1997; Shohamy and McNamara, 2009; Smith, 2014; Soysal, 2012; Spijkerboer and Van Walsum, 2007). At the same time, the prospect of returning home to a low paying job is not an attractive one given the effort that is invested in escaping the first time (Sanggaran, Haire, and Zion, 2016; Sassen, 1996, 1997; Shohamy and McNamara, 2009; Smith, 2014). It is therefore pertinent to consider how each stage of the business cycle or economic cycle impacts on migratory patterns across the globe, bearing in mind that different countries will have different levels of economic prosperity (Sampson, Mitchell, and Bowring, 2011; Sanggaran, Haire, and Zion, 2016; Sassen, 1996, 1997; Shohamy and McNamara, 2009). Figure 1.5 is an example of how skilled migration is linked to the business cycle in South Africa.

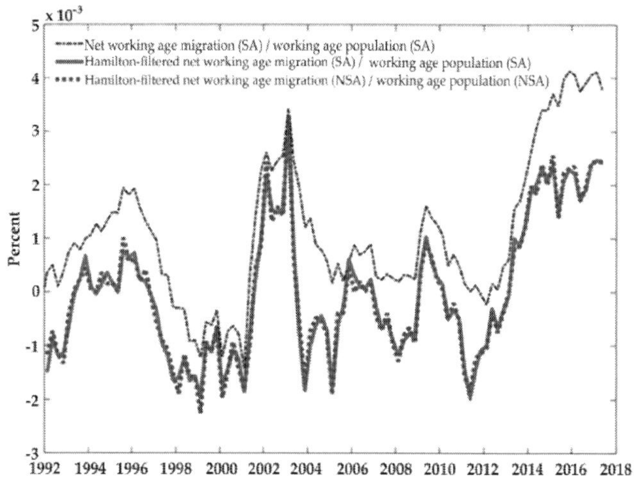

Figure 1.5: Linking skilled migration and the business cycle in South Africa.

Source: Science Direct.

Migrant labor is often used as a "cyclical buffer" for economies that are both developed and developing. In these cases, migrant labor covers some of the problems that would others be prevalent at various stages of the business cycle (Samers, 2004; Sampson, Mitchell, and Bowring, 2011; Sanggaran, Haire, and Zion, 2016; Sassen, 1996, 1997). Indeed, there are governments that use immigrants (particularly the highly skilled ones) in much the same way as other macroeconomic policies in order to correct structural problems within their economic setup or policy framework (Saadi et al., 2020; Samers, 2004; Sampson, Mitchell, and Bowring, 2011; Sanggaran, Haire, and Zion, 2016; Sassen, 1996). In this classification, migrant workers are an instrumentality of economic policy that is aimed at maximizing economic growth and minimizing unemployment (Ryan and Mitsilegas, 2010; Saadi et al., 2020; Samers, 2004; Sampson, Mitchell, and Bowring, 2011; Sanggaran, Haire, and Zion, 2016).

Migrant workers are often the last to be hired and the first to be fired because they have limited employment rights or privileges by definition (Ruhs, 2010; Ryan and Mitsilegas, 2010; Saadi et al., 2020; Samers, 2004; Sampson, Mitchell, and Bowring, 2011). Employers may prefer to hire migrant workers because their employment relationships are frequently non-standard and outside the minimum standards for that jurisdiction. The jobs that are dominated by migrant workers are precarious in nature and poorly regulated because they are not given national priority when planning for the labor force (Rubio-Marín, 2014; Ruhs, 2010; Ryan and Mitsilegas, 2010; Saadi et al., 2020; Samers, 2004; Sampson, Mitchell, and Bowring, 2011). Indeed, there have been complaints that the uncontrolled presence of migrant workers can significantly reduce the working conditions for the rest of the population. Such results happen because employers now have a cheap and convenient alternative to indigenous workers. Exploitative employers specifically take advantage of these situations in order to maximize their profits (Ramji-Nogales, 2007; Rubio-Marín, 2014; Ruhs, 2010; Ryan and Mitsilegas, 2010; Saadi et al., 2020; Samers, 2004).

The impact of the financial crisis and economic recession on migrant workers is not fully understood, not least because the crises themselves are quite complex. Nevertheless, it is generally believed that migrant workers are likely to get the worst of the crises since they do not benefit from the economy's in-built protection mechanisms such as a social safety net, social capital, and legal recourse (Peberdy, 2001; Ramji-Nogales, 2007; Rubio-Marín, 2014; Ruhs, 2010; Ryan and Mitsilegas, 2010; Saadi et al., 2020; Samers, 2004). Data compiled by the ILO has confirmed several widely experienced impacts of the financial crisis and subsequent economic downturn on migrant workers (Paz, 2016; Peberdy, 2001; Ramji-Nogales, 2007; Rubio-Marín, 2014; Ruhs, 2010; Ryan and Mitsilegas, 2010; Saadi et al., 2020). For example, migrant workers and other foreigners were disproportionately disadvantaged in the labor market correction measures such as layoffs and involuntary redundancies (Ozdowski, 1985; Paz, 2016; Peberdy, 2001; Ramji-Nogales, 2007; Rubio-Marín, 2014; Ruhs, 2010; Ryan and Mitsilegas, 2010). The sectors dominated by migrant workers are sensitive to the economic cycle than those that are dominated by indigenous workers (Orfanos, 2019; Ozdowski, 1985; Paz, 2016; Peberdy, 2001; Ramji-Nogales, 2007; Rubio-Marín, 2014; Ruhs, 2010). These sectors included traditional migrant strongholds such as construction and manufacturing (Oberman, 2016; Orfanos, 2019; Ozdowski, 1985; Paz, 2016; Peberdy, 2001; Ramji-Nogales, 2007; Rubio-Marín, 2014).

Other research has revealed a differentiated impact on male and female migrant workers, hence raising the possibility of a gendered process during economy recovery (Newman, Proctor, and Dudley, 2013; Oberman, 2016; Orfanos, 2019; Ozdowski, 1985; Paz, 2016; Peberdy, 2001). This is because male migrant workers predominate in construction which receives government subsidies in a financial crisis and is considered to be relatively non-controversial case for bailouts. By contrast, female migrant workers are often overrepresented in manufacturing particularly in the less desirable categories such as garment production and textile industries which may struggle to receive bailouts in case there is a serious financial crisis (Nethery and Holman, 2016; Newman, Proctor, and Dudley, 2013; Oberman, 2016; Orfanos, 2019; Ozdowski, 1985). Migrant workers who stayed employed during financial crises such as the credit crunch were often affected by reductions in pay or working time. These migrant workers additionally have to deal with deteriorating working conditions or even the potential loss of their job when the economy recovers and they are no longer employees of the first resort (Motomura, 1999; Nethery and Holman, 2016; Newman, Proctor, and Dudley, 2013; Oberman, 2016; Orfanos, 2019). Migrant workers have less access to social safety net support than do national workers and this means that they can be exploited by their employers (Morris, 2002, 2016; Motomura, 1999; Nethery and Holman, 2016; Newman, Proctor, and Dudley, 2013; Oberman, 2016). This is especially true for migrant workers in an irregular situation in terms of not having the right to live and work in their host country, where the employer is safe in the knowledge that it is highly unlikely that the migrant worker will ever complain to the authorities (Morris, 2002; Motomura, 1999; Nethery and Holman, 2016; Newman, Proctor, and Dudley, 2013; Oberman, 2016).

Despite all these challenges, migrant workers persisted in travel far and wide in order to extend their job opportunities (Money, 1998; Morris, 2002, 2016; Motomura, 1999; Nethery and Holman, 2016; Newman, Proctor, and Dudley, 2013). Despite the devastating effects of various global financial crises, many migrant workers did not return home but continued working in the destination countries (Molnar and Gill, 2018; Money, 1998; Morris, 2002, 2016; Motomura, 1999; Nethery and Holman, 2016). The exceptions were those that were forcibly expelled once the policies on employment were tightened to weed out migrant workers or alternatively, they had been discovered by the authorities (Miller, 2016; Molnar and Gill, 2018; Money, 1998; Morris, 2002, 2016; Motomura, 1999; Nethery and Holman, 2016). It can therefore be argued that even when migrants were being offered financial incentives to depart voluntarily, they were happy to remain in the country of destination (Melis, 2001; Miller, 2015, 2016; Molnar and Gill, 2018; Money, 1998; Morris, 2002, 2016; Motomura, 1999). The primary reason for this pattern of behavior was the fact that conditions in home countries were even worse during a financial crisis (Miller, 2015, 2016; Molnar and Gill, 2018; Money, 1998; Morris, 2002, 2016; Motomura, 1999; Nethery and Holman, 2016). While there may be opportunities for some kind of work in host countries, there were simply none at all at home (Mehan, 1997; Melis,

2001; Miller, 2015, 2016; Molnar and Gill, 2018; Money, 1998; Morris, 2002, 2016).

During the financial crises, migrant workers are compelled to take whatever work they can find given the shrinking job market and the focus on citizens or legal permanent residents (Lorentzen, 2014; Mehan, 1997; Melis, 2001; Miller, 2015, 2016; Molnar and Gill, 2018; Money, 1998; Morris, 2016). In these instances, migrants are forced to accept even more substandard pay and abusive conditions than before (Lopez, 2005; Lorentzen, 2014; Mehan, 1997; Melis, 2001; Miller, 2015, 2016; Molnar and Gill, 2018; Money, 1998). This raises important policy challenges and implications in terms of governance and for stabilization of labor markets. It is very hard to maintain good working conditions when there is a second-class category of workers that are recruited by employers who are looking to further maximize their profits (King, 2009; Lopez, 2005; Lorentzen, 2014; Mehan, 1997; Melis, 2001; Miller, 2015, 2016; Molnar and Gill, 2018).

Scapegoating of migrants and xenophobic violence against foreigners tends to increase during times of distress when the populace becomes more focused on self-interest. This is particularly damaging to the case of migrants if they have been taking up jobs amidst generalized high employment. During the emotionality of the immigration debates, few people are able to successfully argue that migrants are doing jobs which the local populace is not doing or refuses to do. Even when such an argument is advanced, the counter is that it is better to get citizens off the welfare system and force them into doing the jobs that are currently being done by migrant labor (Kelson and DeLaet, 1999; King, 2009; Lopez, 2005; Lorentzen, 2014; Mehan, 1997; Melis, 2001; Miller, 2015, 2016). This anti-migrant animus may be expressed through the murder or lynching of migrants in some countries where there was a generalized anti-foreigner sentiment (Kasimis, 2012; Kelson and DeLaet, 1999; King, 2009; Lopez, 2005; Lorentzen, 2014; Mehan, 1997; Melis, 2001; Miller, 2015). A notable example are the xenophobic attacks on black migrants in South Africa, a situation that was considered even worse than the rise of the far-right in Europe and North America.

Part of the reason for the anti-migrant sentiment is the hostile political discourse that is taking place in developing and developed nations alike (Joppke, 2010; Kasimis, 2012; Kelson and DeLaet, 1999; King, 2009; Lopez, 2005; Lorentzen, 2014; Mehan, 1997). For example, the popular press regularly makes calls to exclude migrants from labor markets and social protection benefits (Joppke, 1999, 2010; Kasimis, 2012; Kelson and DeLaet, 1999; King, 2009; Lopez, 2005; Lorentzen, 2014; Mehan, 1997). Others continuously present misinterpreted statistics to show that somehow immigrants are about to overrun the indigenous population and overturn the social order (Joppke, 1998, 1999, 2010; Kasimis, 2012; Kelson and DeLaet, 1999; King, 2009; Lopez, 2005; Lorentzen, 2014). In response, many countries have reduced the quotas for admission of foreign workers, including the highly skilled ones, if only to quieten nationalistic fervor against all foreigners generally. Europe with its particular history during Nazi Germany is very sensitive to any accusations of widespread racism and xenophobia (Johnson, 1996; Joppke, 1998, 1999, 2010; Kasimis, 2012; Kelson and DeLaet, 1999; King, 2009; Lopez, 2005). Additionally, some governments have embarked on policies to deliberately exclude and expel migrant workers in a very unsympathetic and dehumanizing way (Jacobson, 1996; Johnson, 1996; Joppke, 1998, 1999, 2010; Kasimis, 2012; Kelson and DeLaet, 1999).

While the presence of migrant workers in an irregular situation is often tolerated in economic boom times, pressures to expel them from the country is likely to increase during downturns when the focus must be on finding jobs for local people (Hollifield, Martin, and Orrenius, 2014; Jacobson, 1996; Johnson, 1996; Joppke, 1998, 1999, 2010; Kasimis, 2012). There are knock-on effects on some of the benefits that might otherwise have accrued through migrant labor to "home countries," which are in most cases developing countries (Hernandez-Truyol and Johns, 1997; Hollifield, Martin, and Orrenius, 2014; Jacobson, 1996; Johnson, 1996; Joppke, 1998). For example, migrant remittances to home countries are likely to decline during periods of economic distress, such as the recent COVID-19 pandemic. In fact, this is a double tragedy when considering the deteriorated situations in some home countries which render remittances an even more crucial lifeline for families and communities (Heisler, 2000; Hernandez-Truyol and Johns, 1997; Hollifield, Martin, and Orrenius, 2014; Jacobson, 1996; Johnson, 1996).

Over time, remittances may recover despite the negative impact of financial crises. However, that does not mean that they necessarily return to the pre-crisis state (Hayter, 2000; Heisler, 2000; Hernandez-Truyol and Johns, 1997; Hollifield, Martin, and Orrenius, 2014; Jacobson, 1996). Moreover, research shows that these financial flows continue to vary, primarily depending on the extent to which employment will have improved in destination countries following a recession or financial crisis

(Hailbronner, 2000; Hayter, 2000; Heisler, 2000; Hernandez-Truyol and Johns, 1997; Hollifield, Martin, and Orrenius, 2014). A case in point is how employment opportunities may shrink in countries of origin. The implication is that there are fewer options for persons returning from abroad (Guild and Niessen, 1996; Hailbronner, 2000; Hayter, 2000; Heisler, 2000; Hernandez-Truyol and Johns, 1997). Such a pattern has the effect of posing additional challenges to labor market stability and social cohesion in some countries (Guild, 2001; Guild and Niessen, 1996; Hailbronner, 2000; Hayter, 2000; Heisler, 2000; Hernandez-Truyol and Johns, 1997).

These consequences of the crisis on migration and migrant workers in particular underline the urgency of government action in every country affected by migration (Guia, Koulish, and Mitsilegas, 2016; Guild, 2001; Guild and Niessen, 1996; Hailbronner, 2000; Hayter, 2000; Heisler, 2000). Such an imperative includes those countries of origin, transit as well as destination (Gilman, 2013; Guia, Koulish, and Mitsilegas, 2016; Guild, 2001; Guild and Niessen, 1996; Hailbronner, 2000; Hayter, 2000). While not all such problems can necessarily be solved solely by a human rights-based approach, all of them have a human rights component which can be addressed from a legislative and administrative point of view (Frederking, 2012; Gilman, 2013; Guia, Koulish, and Mitsilegas, 2016; Guild, 2001; Guild and Niessen, 1996; Hailbronner, 2000). Parliaments and governments can play a role by elaborating and implementing measures to combat racism and xenophobia (Flynn, 2013; Frederking, 2012; Gilman, 2013; Guia, Koulish, and Mitsilegas, 2016; Guild, 2001; Guild and Niessen, 1996). It is not enough to merely enact anti-discrimination provisions; these rules must be enforced and become part of the culture of work (Fiske, 2016; Flynn, 2013; Frederking, 2012; Gilman, 2013; Guia, Koulish, and Mitsilegas, 2016; Guild, 2001; Guild and Niessen, 1996). The crisis and the rhetoric of some political groups has led to the belief that migrants are taking away the jobs of nationals (Exdell, 2009; Fiske, 2016; Flynn, 2013; Frederking, 2012; Gilman, 2013; Guia, Koulish, and Mitsilegas, 2016; Guild, 2001). Such rhetoric must be vigorously challenged by presenting factual information so that citizens can make informed decision (Dunn, 2010; Exdell, 2009; Fiske, 2016; Flynn, 2013; Frederking, 2012; Gilman, 2013; Guia, Koulish, and Mitsilegas, 2016). Changes in cultural attitudes and practices can play a role in tackling racist and xenophobic behavior in the workplace as well as other instances multiple discrimination (Dunn, 2001, 2010; Exdell, 2009; Fiske, 2016; Flynn, 2013; Frederking, 2012; Gilman, 2013; Guia, Koulish, and Mitsilegas, 2016).

Another important arm of the intervention is the reinforcement of the social safety and its coverage so that indigenous people are not left on the margins following globalization (Dudley et al., 2012; Dunn, 2001, 2010; Exdell, 2009; Fiske, 2016; Flynn, 2013; Frederking, 2012; Gilman, 2013). This should be expressly addressed to both nationals and migrants. Special attention should be given to those migrants in an irregular situation (Den Heijer, 2010; Dudley et al., 2012; Dunn, 2001, 2010; Exdell, 2009; Fiske, 2016; Flynn, 2013; Frederking, 2012). This is because of the inherent vulnerability of this group to exploitation (Dauvergne, 2012; Den Heijer, 2010; Dudley et al., 2012; Dunn, 2001, 2010; Exdell, 2009; Fiske, 2016; Flynn, 2013). Illegal immigrants are more likely to fall outside the coverage of national health, social protection, and social security systems as a case in point (Costello, 2012; Dauvergne, 2012; Den Heijer, 2010; Dudley et al., 2012; Dunn, 2001, 2010; Exdell, 2009; Fiske, 2016). Moreover, access to social protection can make it easier to re-enter the labor market (Cornelisse, 2010; Costello, 2012; Dauvergne, 2012; Den Heijer, 2010; Dudley et al., 2012; Dunn, 2001, 2010).

There ought to be a reinforcement of labor inspections to ensure that standards are maintained (Cornelisse, 2004, 2010; Costello, 2012; Dauvergne, 2012; Den Heijer, 2010; Dudley et al., 2012; Dunn, 2001). The crisis induces employers to offer and migrants to take jobs that fail to meet minimum labor standards (Cook, 2003; Cornelisse, 2004, 2010; Costello, 2012; Dauvergne, 2012; Den Heijer, 2010; Dudley et al., 2012). Labor inspection targeted at sectors where migrants may be prevalent is an important means of reducing abuse and supporting a "level playing field," where national and foreign workers benefit from equivalent conditions and protection (Chin, 1999; Cook, 2003; Cornelisse, 2004, 2010; Costello, 2012; Dauvergne, 2012; Den Heijer, 2010; Dudley et al., 2012). Governments should adopt measures aimed at promoting social dialog in a mutually respectful and supportive way (Chavez, 2001; Chin, 1999; Cook, 2003; Cornelisse, 2004, 2010; Costello, 2012; Dauvergne, 2012; Den Heijer, 2010). In adopting legislation to deal with crises, social dialog can provide a means of ensuring non-discrimination and equality of treatment and opportunity (Brochmann and Hammar, 2020; Chavez, 2001; Chin, 1999; Cook, 2003; Cornelisse, 2004, 2010; Costello, 2012). Generally speaking, policy formulators and implementers should emphasize additional vigilance when monitoring the implementation and enforcement of laws in times of financial and economic crisis (Brané and Lundholm, 2007; Brochmann and Hammar, 2020; Chavez, 2001; Chin, 1999; Cook, 2003; Cornelisse, 2004).

CHAPTER 1 SUMMARY

This chapter has explored some of the contextual issues that are relevant to international immigration. For example, the chapter has discussed how uncontrolled immigration can be perceived to be a threat to national sovereignty. Emphasis is placed on economically productive migrants who bring benefits to both their home and destination countries. The chapter closes with a look at how global financial crises can fuel anti-immigrant sentiment and the associated multiple discrimination. The next chapter explores ways in which rationality and equity can be brought to the immigration debates.

CHAPTER 2

EQUITY AND RATIONALITY IN MIGRATION POLICY

CONTENTS

This second chapter explores the possibilities and limitations of bringing rationality and equity to the policy on immigration. The first section examines the ways in which migrants can become agents of social change. In the second section, we explore the possibilities and impetus for gender sensitivity when formulating immigration policies. The third section adopts an internationalist perspective of migration. The fourth section explores some of the ways in which domestic laws can be amended in order to account for the realities of migration numbers and patterns. The chapter will close by summarizing some human rights aspects that must be considered when developing a policy on immigration.

2.1. MIGRANTS AS AGENTS OF SOCIAL CHANGE

Research has shown that when migrants travel from country to country, they tend to adopt many of the societal norms and values of their host nations. To some extent, this happens to all migrants regardless of the strength of their home ties (Becerra, 2016; Brané and Lundholm, 2007; Brochmann and Hammar, 2020; Chavez, 2001; Chin, 1999; Cook, 2003). When these migrants engage with the home populace, they can bring about social change through the contagion of exchange (Barak-Erez, 2008; Becerra, 2016; Brané and Lundholm, 2007; Brochmann and Hammar, 2020; Chavez, 2001; Chin, 1999). A case in point is the desire for certain standards of living that may not be readily available in the home countries (Bangarth, 2003; Barak-Erez, 2008; Becerra, 2016; Brané and Lundholm, 2007; Brochmann and Hammar, 2020; Chavez, 2001).

The migrants may also be active members of the social safety net through the remittances that they send (Baldwin-Edwards, 2006; Bangarth, 2003; Barak-Erez, 2008; Becerra, 2016; Brané and Lundholm, 2007; Brochmann and Hammar, 2020). Indeed, those countries that do not have an institutionalized welfare system have come to rely on migrants through remittances in order to look after some of the most vulnerable members of society (Bacon, 1996; Baldwin-Edwards, 2006; Bangarth, 2003; Barak-Erez, 2008; Becerra, 2016; Brané and Lundholm, 2007). Even relatively insular countries like Russia (see Figure 2.1 for an illustration) have a significant contingent of immigrants in their workforce. Some have speculated about the potential transformative influence of those immigrants on their home countries as well as their host destinations (Aynsley-Green et al., 2012; Bacon, 1996; Baldwin-Edwards, 2006; Bangarth, 2003; Barak-Erez, 2008; Becerra, 2016).

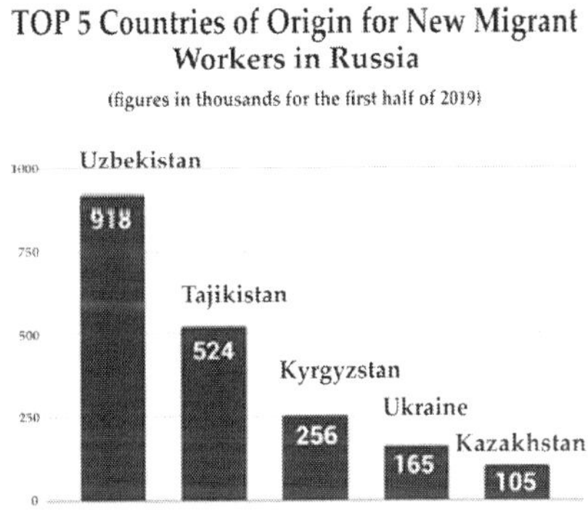

Figure 2.1: Distribution of migrant workers in Russia.

Source: FSB Border Service via The Moscow Times.

Through emigration and immigration, it is possible to subtly change the ways in which people live, believe, and behave (Adelman, 2002; Aynsley-Green et al., 2012; Bacon, 1996; Baldwin-Edwards, 2006; Bangarth, 2003; Barak-Erez, 2008). There is a form of social contagion from the various countries that immigrants visit (Ackerman and Furman, 2014; Adelman, 2002; Aynsley-Green et al., 2012; Bacon, 1996; Baldwin-Edwards, 2006). It is from that perspective that the notion of "social remittances" has emerged in existing literature in order to counter and enrich the pre-existing narratives about monetary remittances (Acer and Goodman, 2009; Ackerman and Furman, 2014; Adelman, 2002; Aynsley-Green et al., 2012; Bacon, 1996). Social remittances comprise sets of ideas, know-how, norms, values, knowledge, behavior, practices, and skills which migrants acquire from the communities that host them (Dauvergne, 2012; Den Heijer, 2010; Dudley et al., 2012; Dunn, 2001, 2010; Exdell, 2009; Fiske, 2016; Flynn, 2013). The migrants then bring or send these social remittances. These social remittances can promote or deter development in home countries depending on how they are received and utilized (Den Heijer, 2010; Dudley et al., 2012; Dunn, 2001, 2010; Exdell, 2009; Fiske, 2016; Flynn, 2013; Frederking, 2012).

Some researchers are of the view that social remittances are more important than financial remittances in terms of creating social change in communities (Dudley et al., 2012; Dunn, 2001, 2010; Exdell, 2009; Fiske, 2016; Flynn, 2013; Frederking, 2012; Gilman, 2013). There are four major types of social remittances that are transferred from migrants to their home countries, including new norms, practices, identities, and social capital

(Dunn, 2001, 2010; Exdell, 2009; Fiske, 2016; Flynn, 2013; Frederking, 2012; Gilman, 2013; Guia, Koulish, and Mitsilegas, 2016). Some of the social remittances may be updates to pre-existing norms, values, behaviors, and identities (Dunn, 2010; Exdell, 2009; Fiske, 2016; Flynn, 2013; Frederking, 2012; Gilman, 2013; Guia, Koulish, and Mitsilegas, 2016). The social capital that migrants expand can be particularly important in business cycles where communities have to seek alternatives to the traditional job market (Exdell, 2009; Fiske, 2016; Flynn, 2013; Frederking, 2012; Gilman, 2013; Guia, Koulish, and Mitsilegas, 2016; Guild, 2001).

Social remittances can be diffused by migrants as well as by refugees (Fiske, 2016; Flynn, 2013; Frederking, 2012; Gilman, 2013; Guia, Koulish, and Mitsilegas, 2016; Guild, 2001; Guild and Niessen, 1996). These social influences are transferred when migrants return or visit their home countries (Flynn, 2013; Frederking, 2012; Gilman, 2013; Guia, Koulish, and Mitsilegas, 2016; Guild, 2001; Guild and Niessen, 1996). They can also occur when non-migrants visit their family and friends in the destination countries (Frederking, 2012; Gilman, 2013; Guia, Koulish, and Mitsilegas, 2016; Guild, 2001; Guild and Niessen, 1996; Hailbronner, 2000). Others are transmitted in the non-physical form, including communication and electronic correspondence as the migrants try to maintain contact with the people that they have left at home (Gilman, 2013; Guia, Koulish, and Mitsilegas, 2016; Guild, 2001; Guild and Niessen, 1996; Hailbronner, 2000; Hayter, 2000). As we shall see later in the book, diasporas are growing in strength and influence, while at the same time enriching the communities in which they are hosted. Indeed, there have instances where a distinct diaspora culture has emerged to challenge and complement the dominant culture within the home country.

Social remittances do not only affect family relations because they can have an impact on the economic and social well-being. For example, migrants will come in with new ideas about gender roles, class, and race which are very different from the ones that they originally shared with the people and communities from their country of origin (Guia, Koulish, and Mitsilegas, 2016; Guild, 2001; Guild and Niessen, 1996; Hailbronner, 2000; Hayter, 2000; Heisler, 2000). Social remittances could also have a substantial impact on political, social, cultural, economic, and religious participation within the receiving community and the sending communities (Guild, 2001; Guild and Niessen, 1996; Hailbronner, 2000; Hayter, 2000; Heisler, 2000; Hernandez-Truyol and Johns, 1997).

Migrants have been known to adopt progressive or regressive ideas when compared to both the host and sending communities. They can challenge people's ideas, beliefs, and views about a range of phenomena in ways that were not originally envisaged when they left. Such critical voices have a knock-on effect on other aspects of community life. For example, they may involve the re-evaluation of existing norms and values so that they can either be reinterpreted or replaced depending on the prevailing social mood. The influence of migrants can be seen in a range of areas because they remain part of the sending and hosting communities. Some of their spheres of influence include health, democracy, religion, politics, science, institutions, culture, society, technology, business, economics, education, and perspectives on gender issues (Guild and Niessen, 1996; Hailbronner, 2000; Hayter, 2000; Heisler, 2000; Hernandez-Truyol and Johns, 1997). That is why some conservative voices are wary of these social remittances since they can lead to revolutions or an overturning of the social order (Hailbronner, 2000; Hayter, 2000; Heisler, 2000; Hernandez-Truyol and Johns, 1997; Hollifield, Martin, and Orrenius, 2014). Generally speaking, returning migrants are enlightened and may not accept the restrictive norms and values that exist in traditional societies (Hayter, 2000; Heisler, 2000; Hernandez-Truyol and Johns, 1997; Hollifield, Martin, and Orrenius, 2014; Jacobson, 1996).

At the same time, incoming immigrants can challenge the pre-existing norms and values of a society, leading to significant social change. This happens regardless of whether or not the society that is being impacted considers these changes to be appropriate and valuable (Heisler, 2000; Hernandez-Truyol and Johns, 1997; Hollifield, Martin, and Orrenius, 2014; Jacobson, 1996; Johnson, 1996). This is most felt among the younger generation that is typically most amenable to change in both the sending and host communities (Hernandez-Truyol and Johns, 1997; Hollifield, Martin, and Orrenius, 2014; Jacobson, 1996; Johnson, 1996; Joppke, 1998). A significant case in point is how migration patterns can impact on the empowerment of women (Hollifield, Martin, and Orrenius, 2014; Jacobson, 1996; Johnson, 1996; Joppke, 1998, 1999, 2010; Kasimis, 2012). First of all, women that are returning after having worked and earned a substantial income, will not be willing to put up with the traditional role of a subservient wife or daughter (Jacobson, 1996; Johnson, 1996; Joppke, 1998, 1999, 2010; Kasimis, 2012; Kelson and DeLaet, 1999). Secondly, incoming immigrants will challenge local gender norms and values in such ways as to empower and liberate women (Johnson, 1996; Joppke, 1998, 1999, 2010; Kasimis,

2012; Kelson and DeLaet, 1999; King, 2009; Lopez, 2005). This could lead to a revolution that overturns the traditional institution of patriarchy and some societies are resistant to such changes because they de-privilege those that have been traditionally privileged (Joppke, 1998, 1999, 2010; Kasimis, 2012; Kelson and DeLaet, 1999; King, 2009; Lopez, 2005; Lorentzen, 2014).

There is evidence to suggest that migration to countries with higher political empowerment for women significantly increases the share of women in parliament in the home country (Joppke, 1999, 2010; Kasimis, 2012; Kelson and DeLaet, 1999; King, 2009; Lopez, 2005; Lorentzen, 2014; Mehan, 1997). That means that the effects of social change may be far-reaching than the immediate act of someone leaving their country in search of greener pastures (Joppke, 2010; Kasimis, 2012; Kelson and DeLaet, 1999; King, 2009; Lopez, 2005; Lorentzen, 2014; Mehan, 1997). The destination-specific effect of emigration on women empowerment is very important, not least because of the potentially transformative power that it is imbued with (Kasimis, 2012; Kelson and DeLaet, 1999; King, 2009; Lopez, 2005; Lorentzen, 2014; Mehan, 1997; Melis, 2001; Miller, 2015). A case in point is how Turkish emigration to the West encourages women's empowerment in Turkey, a trend that has been noted by researchers and through anecdotal evidence. This trend has been one of the cornerstones of the argument made for ascension to the European Union in as far as it is portrayed as an example of a Muslim-majority country, but with significantly more liberal approaches to community life than other Muslim-majority countries. More specifically, a 1% increase in migration to the EU and OECD countries increases the share of women in the Turkish parliament by 7% in the long run.

The migration of women from socially conservative countries to the more liberal ones conveys certain values, norms, and practices that contribute to women's empowerment (Kelson and DeLaet, 1999; King, 2009; Lopez, 2005; Lorentzen, 2014; Mehan, 1997; Melis, 2001; Miller, 2015, 2016). This change can be as high as that contribution made by the sheer mass education of women in order to empower them for a new world in which they are socially, politically, and economically active members of society (King, 2009; Lopez, 2005; Lorentzen, 2014; Mehan, 1997; Melis, 2001; Miller, 2015, 2016; Molnar and Gill, 2018). In contrast, emigration to socially conservative countries (such as the ones in the Middle East) elicits comparatively less impact on women's empowerment since those countries have already very strong conservative roots that are very difficult to change or influence (Lopez, 2005; Lorentzen, 2014; Mehan, 1997; Melis,

2001; Miller, 2015, 2016; Molnar and Gill, 2018; Money, 1998). Indeed, emigrants to socially conservative countries are more likely to support the religious parties and their ideologies in their home countries, meaning that the contagion is reversed (Lorentzen, 2014; Mehan, 1997; Melis, 2001; Miller, 2015, 2016; Molnar and Gill, 2018; Money, 1998; Morris, 2016). That means that emigrants can end up becoming more conservative and even radicalized when they return home (Mehan, 1997; Melis, 2001; Miller, 2015, 2016; Molnar and Gill, 2018; Money, 1998; Morris, 2002, 2016). Interestingly, the radicalization that has led to terrorism in Europe tends to happen at home with migrants coming from more conservative countries who eventually recruit home participants (Melis, 2001; Miller, 2015, 2016; Molnar and Gill, 2018; Money, 1998; Morris, 2002, 2016; Motomura, 1999). It is for such reasons that some countries monitor and even bar migration from certain Muslim-majority countries that are perceived to be socially conservative (Miller, 2015, 2016; Molnar and Gill, 2018; Money, 1998; Morris, 2002, 2016; Motomura, 1999; Nethery and Holman, 2016).

Even more troubling is the notion that socially unacceptable practices such as child marriage, genital mutilation, gender-based violence, and forced marriage can be imported into otherwise liberal countries (Miller, 2016; Molnar and Gill, 2018; Money, 1998; Morris, 2002, 2016; Motomura, 1999; Nethery and Holman, 2016). A case in point are Western European countries that are grappling with the problem of Muslim immigrants that are demanding for the adoption of aspects of Shariat law into domestic law (Molnar and Gill, 2018; Money, 1998; Morris, 2002, 2016; Motomura, 1999; Nethery and Holman, 2016). Some of these practices has led to the abuse and exploitation of women who are effectively imprisoned in their own homes, whilst living countries that are deemed to be democratic and fairly liberal (Money, 1998; Morris, 2002, 2016; Motomura, 1999; Nethery and Holman, 2016; Newman, Proctor, and Dudley, 2013). This has led to a crackdown on Muslim-based practices such as covering the head and face, most notably in France where the Burqa was controversially banned (Morris, 2002, 2016; Motomura, 1999; Nethery and Holman, 2016; Newman, Proctor, and Dudley, 2013; Oberman, 2016). It seems that European countries are coming to the conclusion that the protection of their norms and values necessitates some controls on immigrants that are coming from socially conservative countries (Morris, 2002; Motomura, 1999; Nethery and Holman, 2016; Newman, Proctor, and Dudley, 2013; Oberman, 2016).

There are many ways in which the empowering social remittances from immigration and emigration can be used in order to facilitate the liberation of women and other oppressed groups (Motomura, 1999; Nethery and Holman, 2016; Newman, Proctor, and Dudley, 2013; Oberman, 2016; Orfanos, 2019). For example, researchers and pro-immigration advocates argue that migration and the resultant social remittances should be accepted as an important component in development for both sending and destination countries (Nethery and Holman, 2016; Newman, Proctor, and Dudley, 2013; Oberman, 2016; Orfanos, 2019; Ozdowski, 1985). Migrant women's organization or migrants' organization that seek to empower women in the destination countries should be supported and encouraged by destination country governments (Newman, Proctor, and Dudley, 2013; Oberman, 2016; Orfanos, 2019; Ozdowski, 1985; Paz, 2016; Peberdy, 2001). Ideally, these organization should be linked to organizations in the home countries by the sending country governments (Oberman, 2016; Orfanos, 2019; Ozdowski, 1985; Paz, 2016; Peberdy, 2001; Ramji-Nogales, 2007; Rubio-Marín, 2014).

Additionally, there could be more formal dialogs through conferences, seminars, and workshops should be established and strengthened between migrants and non-migrant communities (Orfanos, 2019; Ozdowski, 1985; Paz, 2016; Peberdy, 2001; Ramji-Nogales, 2007; Rubio-Marín, 2014; Ruhs, 2010). This objective can be achieved by working with both sending and destination country governments and NGOs (Ozdowski, 1985; Paz, 2016; Peberdy, 2001; Ramji-Nogales, 2007; Rubio-Marín, 2014; Ruhs, 2010; Ryan and Mitsilegas, 2010). It is advisable that the social, political, and cultural problems of the sending countries should be investigated and better understood by destination countries in order to allow for a more seamless resettlement framework (Paz, 2016; Peberdy, 2001; Ramji-Nogales, 2007; Rubio-Marín, 2014; Ruhs, 2010; Ryan and Mitsilegas, 2010; Saadi et al., 2020). This will allow for easier and more durable integration of new immigrants into the hosting communities (Peberdy, 2001; Ramji-Nogales, 2007; Rubio-Marín, 2014; Ruhs, 2010; Ryan and Mitsilegas, 2010; Saadi et al., 2020; Samers, 2004).

When it comes to the perspective of policymakers and implementer; migrants should be understood as a central element in understanding of social problems that exist in both the sending and receiving countries (Ramji-Nogales, 2007; Rubio-Marín, 2014; Ruhs, 2010; Ryan and Mitsilegas, 2010; Saadi et al., 2020; Samers, 2004). Such investigations and interactions offer solutions as well as contributing to non-migrant communities in the home countries through ideas and knowledge (Guild, 2001; Miller, 2016; Ryan and Mitsilegas, 2010; Wexler, 2007; Wilcox, 2009). One of the instrumentalities for this type of work are the norms and values accumulated in host countries

(Den Heijer, 2010; Miller, 2015; Ruhs, 2010; Welch, 2002; Zwi and Mares, 2015).

Looking at the progress of most developing countries, it is safe to state that social remittances do impact the lives of migrants, their families, and societies at large (Dauvergne, 2012; Hernandez-Truyol and Johns, 1997; Molnar and Gill, 2018; Zúñiga and Hernández-León, 2005). After living in a developed country and adapting to its lifestyle, a migrant will often try to replicate a similar way of life in his or her home country (Costello, 2012; Guia, Koulish, and Mitsilegas, 2016; Melis, 2001; Rubio-Marín, 2014; Webber, 2012). Basic hygiene, sanitation, and infrastructure facilities are the first changes that migrants make towards social development, back home (Cornelisse, 2010; Gilman, 2013; Kelson and DeLaet, 1999; Orfanos, 2019; Thym, 2008). Living in foreign countries, migrants observe the various skill sets required for different kinds of jobs and services (Brochmann and Hammar, 2020; Frederking, 2012; Kasimis, 2012; Oberman, 2016; Taylor, 2000). They impart this knowledge to their families and friends (who are aspiring migrants) and persuade them to attain higher education and enhance their skills, which will in turn benefit them while they seek jobs abroad (Brané and Lundholm, 2007; Flynn, 2013; Joppke, 2010; Newman, Proctor, and Dudley, 2013; Sassen, 1997). On a macro level, this benefits the economy of the country in terms of the number of remittances coming into the country which is directly proportional to the number of migrants moving abroad (Becerra, 2016; Fiske, 2016; Joppke, 1999; Nethery and Holman, 2016; Sassen, 1996). On the other hand, migrants who have sought advanced training abroad, return home to set up their own businesses, thus also creating employment opportunities in the country (Barak-Erez, 2008; Exdell, 2009; Joppke, 1998; Motomura, 1999; Sanggaran, Haire, and Zion, 2016). The next section focuses on gender sensitivity in migration policy formulation.

2.2. GENDER-SENSITIVE IMMIGRATION POLICY

There are certain gendered patterns in the experiences of migration (Bangarth, 2003; Dunn, 2010; Johnson, 1996; Morris, 2002; Sampson, Mitchell, and Bowring, 2011). Women comprise about 50% of all migrants and yet there is no specific policy that addresses some of the issues of social exclusion, exploitation, and discrimination that they may face as immigrants (Baldwin-Edwards, 2006; Dunn, 2001; Jacobson, 1996; Morris, 2016; Samers, 2004). At the same time, there is limited consideration of the impact of women immigrants on the receiving communities; regardless of whether or not that impact is positive (Aynsley-Green et al., 2012; Cornelisse, 2004; Heisler, 2000; Mehan, 1997; Ramji-Nogales, 2007; Spijkerboer and Van Walsum, 2007). Nevertheless, existing research seems to indicate that migration has become increasingly feminized and that has implications for the ways in which migrants are treated generally when they reach their countries of destination (Adelman, 2002; Cook, 2003; Hayter, 2000; Lorentzen, 2014; Peberdy, 2001; Soysal, 2012). The feminization of migration arises because many women are now migrating on their own. This is a different pattern from when women were traveling as dependents of their husbands and other male family members (Ackerman and Furman, 2014; Chin, 1999; Hailbronner, 2000; Lopez, 2005; Paz, 2016; Smith, 2014). Hence, there are specific needs and issues that affect women migrants which must be addressed in the policy formulation process (Acer and Goodman, 2009; Chavez, 2001; Guild and Niessen, 1996; King, 2009; Ozdowski, 1985; Shohamy and McNamara, 2009). Currently, other issues such as race and education (see for an example of a statistical breakdown of immigrants by their education level and race) do not take on a gender-sensitive lens. In effect, that can lead to serious gaps within the policy response to immigration generally (Figure 2.2).

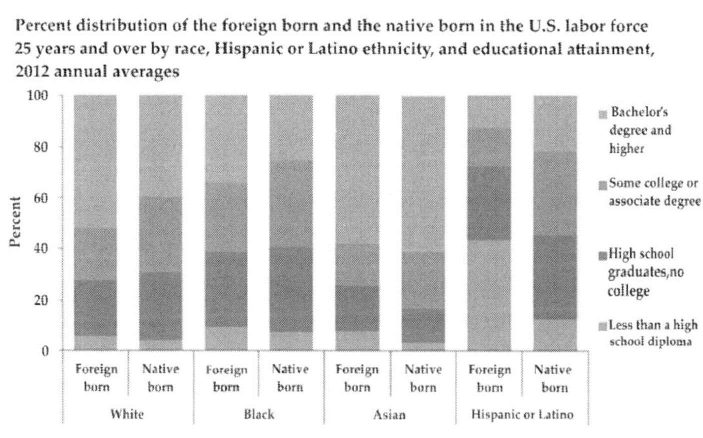

Figure 2.2: Labor force, ethnicity, and education levels in the USA.

Source: US Bureau of Labor Statistics.

After moving abroad, women migrants can gain insights and opportunities that would otherwise be denied to them in their home country, primarily because of their gender (Rubio-Marín, 2014; Ruhs, 2010; Ryan and Mitsilegas, 2010; Saadi et al., 2020; Samers, 2004; Sampson, Mitchell, and Bowring, 2011). When those women return to their home countries, they are no longer willing to accept some of the stifling gender norms that exist in their own societies particularly if those societies are culturally conservative (Ruhs, 2010, Ryan and Mitsilegas, 2010; Saadi et al., 2020; Samers, 2004; Sampson, Mitchell, and Bowring, 2011). At the same time, the receiving communities have to consider the possibilities of integrating women that come from societies that are more conservative and therefore have a more restrictive view of women's rights (Ryan and Mitsilegas, 2010; Saadi et al., 2020; Samers, 2004; Sampson, Mitchell, and Bowring, 2011; Sanggaran, Haire, and Zion, 2016).

Europe and parts of North America have been struggling with this problem. For example, women who have been oppressed in their home countries continue being oppressed when they join local communities that are derived from their homelands. These sub-communities comprise mainly conservative diaspora living in otherwise liberal societies (Saadi et al., 2020; Samers, 2004; Sampson, Mitchell, and Bowring, 2011; Sanggaran, Haire, and Zion, 2016; Sassen, 1996). Some of the restrictions that are within these socially isolated migrant communities are explicitly or implicitly contrary to the laws and values of the receiving countries. If no harmonization takes place, there is inevitably a clash of cultures which sometimes calls for the intervention of the courts (Samers, 2004; Sampson, Mitchell, and Bowring, 2011; Sanggaran, Haire, and Zion, 2016; Sassen, 1996, 1997). In that sense, immigration has raised important questions about cultural relativity and tolerance in modern societies that welcome a variety of migrants from all walks of life across the globe who must then live together in a modicum of harmoniousness (Sampson, Mitchell, and Bowring, 2011; Sanggaran, Haire, and Zion, 2016; Sassen, 1996, 1997; Shohamy and McNamara, 2009). That does not mean that migration is necessarily a negative for women or the host communities (Sanggaran, Haire, and Zion, 2016; Sassen, 1996, 1997; Shohamy and McNamara, 2009; Smith, 2014). This is because women can bring important contributions to both the home and receiving communities in terms of social capital, financial capital, new norms, and new values (Sassen, 1996, 1997; Shohamy and McNamara, 2009; Smith, 2014; Soysal, 2012; Spijkerboer and Van Walsum, 2007).

In moving for work abroad, many women gain opportunities they would not have at home and are thus economically empowered by migration (Sassen, 1997; Shohamy and McNamara, 2009; Smith, 2014; Soysal, 2012; Spijkerboer and Van Walsum, 2007). This has the effect of enabling women to make constructive contributions to destination countries in ways that are often ignored in virulent immigration debates (Shohamy and McNamara, 2009; Smith, 2014; Soysal, 2012; Spijkerboer and Van Walsum, 2007; Taylor, 2000; Thym, 2008). Women also send remittances home (both social and financial) which contribute to the well-being of their families in countries of origin (Smith, 2014; Soysal, 2012; Spijkerboer and Van Walsum, 2007; Taylor, 2000; Thym, 2008; Webber, 2012; Welch, 2002). The impact of women's remittances can be wide because of their key responsibilities in the family and in the community as a whole, as well as their propensity to traditionally care for others within their communities (Soysal, 2012; Spijkerboer and Van Walsum, 2007; Taylor, 2000; Thym, 2008; Webber, 2012; Welch, 2002; Wexler, 2007). However, women migrants are particularly at risk of discrimination because gender-insensitivity exists in even the most advanced of countries (Spijkerboer and Van Walsum, 2007; Taylor, 2000; Thym, 2008; Webber, 2012; Welch, 2002; Wexler, 2007; Wilcox, 2009).

Women migrants may face specific and pernicious forms of abuse and exploitative treatment when they are migrant workers (Taylor, 2000; Thym, 2008; Webber, 2012; Welch, 2002; Wexler, 2007; Wilcox, 2009; Zúñiga and Hernández-León, 2005). While migration presents new opportunities for women and maybe a means for their economic empowerment through wider participation, it may also place their human rights and security at risk (Thym, 2008; Webber, 2012; Welch, 2002; Wexler, 2007; Wilcox, 2009; Zúñiga and Hernández-León, 2005; Zwi and Mares, 2015). One of the problematic areas of migrations has been the export of young women from Sub-Saharan Africa and the Philippines to work as maids in the Middle East (Webber, 2012; Welch, 2002; Wexler, 2007; Wilcox, 2009; Zúñiga and Hernández-León, 2005; Zwi and Mares, 2015). Invariably, these women come back with stories of harrowing abuse which is partly driven by a cultural disrespect of womanhood as well as aspects of racism and xenophobia (Welch, 2002; Wexler, 2007; Wilcox, 2009; Zúñiga and Hernández-León, 2005; Zwi and Mares, 2015). These are real qualitative experiences that are not always fully explored in the policy formulation process (Wexler, 2007; Wilcox, 2009; Zúñiga and Hernández-León, 2005; Zwi and Mares, 2015).

Although immigration control remains an exclusive right of sovereign states, there are certain international standards on gender equality which ought to be considered (Acer and Goodman, 2009; Chavez, 2001; Guild and Niessen, 1996; King, 2009; Ozdowski, 1985; Shohamy and McNamara, 2009). This certainly holds true for all those countries that are signatories to international agreements on gender equality (Ackerman and Furman, 2014;

Chin, 1999; Hailbronner, 2000; Lopez, 2005; Paz, 2016; Smith, 2014). While individual countries and regional bodies are entitled to control their borders and regulate migration, they must do so in full compliance with their obligations as parties to the human rights treaties they have ratified or acceded to (Adelman, 2002; Cook, 2003; Hayter, 2000; Lorentzen, 2014; Peberdy, 2001; Soysal, 2012). That includes the promotion of safe migration procedures and the obligation to respect, protect, and fulfill the human rights of women throughout the migration cycle (Aynsley-Green et al., 2012; Cornelisse, 2004; Heisler, 2000; Mehan, 1997; Ramji-Nogales, 2007; Spijkerboer and Van Walsum, 2007). Those obligations must be undertaken in recognition of the social and economic contributions of women migrant workers to their own countries and countries of destination (Bacon, 1996; Dudley et al., 2012; Hollifield, Martin, and Orrenius, 2014; Money, 1998; Saadi et al., 2020). Such roles may be achieved in a range of activities such as through caregiving and domestic work (Baldwin-Edwards, 2006; Dunn, 2001; Jacobson, 1996; Morris, 2016; Samers, 2004).

Although both men and women migrate, migration is not always a gender-neutral phenomenon (Bangarth, 2003; Dunn, 2010; Johnson, 1996; Morris, 2002; Sampson, Mitchell, and Bowring, 2011). For example, the position of female migrants is different from that of male migrants in terms of legal migration channels, treatment, experiences, and responses (Barak-Erez, 2008; Exdell, 2009; Joppke, 1998; Motomura, 1999; Sanggaran, Haire, and Zion, 2016). There is also a gender divide in the sectors into which people migrate, with women occupying increasingly feminized low-paying and low-status jobs (Becerra, 2016; Fiske, 2016; Joppke, 1999; Nethery and Holman, 2016; Sassen, 1996). Moreover, the forms of abuse that migrants suffer and the consequences of those abuses can be gendered with women facing pernicious restrictions on their work and the rewards that they subsequently secure (Brané and Lundholm, 2007; Flynn, 2013; Joppke, 2010; Newman, Proctor, and Dudley, 2013; Sassen, 1997). These differences in experience across genders may mean that a generic policy that is gender-blind will not adequately address the needs and expectations of women migrants (Brochmann and Hammar, 2020; Frederking, 2012; Kasimis, 2012; Oberman, 2016; Taylor, 2000). This is how women migrants end up falling through the cracks despite the significant contributions that they make to both the sending and host countries in the migration chain (Cornelisse, 2010; Gilman, 2013; Kelson and DeLaet, 1999; Orfanos, 2019; Thym, 2008). Once they reach their destinations, women migrant workers may encounter multiple forms of de jure and de facto discrimination

(Costello, 2012; Guia, Koulish, and Mitsilegas, 2016; Melis, 2001; Rubio-Marín, 2014; Webber, 2012). Their status as migrants means that they are not in a strong position to advocate for their own rights, a situation made even worse by systemic gender-based discrimination and gender-based violence (Dauvergne, 2012; Hernandez-Truyol and Johns, 1997; Molnar and Gill, 2018; Zúñiga and Hernández-León, 2005). There are countries whose governments sometimes impose restrictions or bans on women's employment in particular sectors because of cultural and practical reasons, regardless of the inclinations and capabilities of the women in question (Den Heijer, 2010; Miller, 2015; Ruhs, 2010; Welch, 2002; Zwi and Mares, 2015). Whatever the situation, women migrant workers face additional hazards compared to men because of gender-insensitive environments that do not allow mobility for women (Guild, 2001; Miller, 2016; Ryan and Mitsilegas, 2010; Wexler, 2007; Wilcox, 2009). There are also cultural and practical barriers that give women little access to relevant information about their rights and entitlements (Guild and Niessen, 1996; Hailbronner, 2000; Hayter, 2000; Heisler, 2000; Hernandez-Truyol and Johns, 1997). Others may be reluctant to push the issue of their rights because culturally they are expected to be completely malleable and subservient.

Research has shown that women migrants are often trapped in ignorance. This means that they cannot easily escape the restrictions that are placed on them (Den Heijer, 2010; Miller, 2015; Ruhs, 2010; Welch, 2002; Zwi and Mares, 2015). Those that have been trafficked are particularly vulnerable because they do not have the right immigration status or papers for that matter (Cornelisse, 2010; Costello, 2012; Dauvergne, 2012; Den Heijer, 2010; Dudley et al., 2012; Dunn, 2001, 2010). Gendered notions of appropriate work for women abound in many conservative countries. This means that job opportunities that are available for migrant women reflect familial and service functions ascribed to women. Such attitudes and practices are particularly prevalent in the informal sector, where many migrant women operate out of necessity (Bangarth, 2003; Dunn, 2010; Johnson, 1996; Morris, 2002; Sampson, Mitchell, and Bowring, 2011). These are typically low status and low paying jobs that have very limited protection for workers generally, even more so those that are migrants and women (King, 2009; Lopez, 2005; Lorentzen, 2014; Mehan, 1997; Melis, 2001; Miller, 2015, 2016; Molnar and Gill, 2018). Under such circumstances, occupations in which women dominate are systematically associated with poor working conditions. Examples include domestic work and certain forms of entertainment, as well as the sex industry (Nethery and Holman, 2016; Newman, Proctor, and Dudley, 2013; Oberman, 2016; Orfanos, 2019; Ozdowski, 1985).

Because of discrimination on the basis of sex and gender, women migrant workers may receive lower wages than men who do similar or commensurate work (Sassen, 1996, 1997; Shohamy and McNamara, 2009; Smith, 2014, Soysal, 2012; Spijkerboer and Van Walsum, 2007). Others may experience non-payment of wages which makes it difficult for them to meet their basic needs, let alone send financial remittances at home (Den Heijer, 2010; Dudley et al., 2012; Dunn, 2001, 2010; Exdell, 2009; Fiske, 2016; Flynn, 2013; Frederking, 2012). The payments made to migrant women workers are often delayed until departure which puts them in a vulnerable position in terms of complaining about any mistreatment that they face during their work assignments (Shohamy and McNamara, 2009; Smith, 2014; Soysal, 2012; Spijkerboer and Van Walsum, 2007; Taylor, 2000; Thym, 2008). Others are required to transfer all their wages into bank accounts that are inaccessible to them, meaning that they are at risk of being defrauded and even losing all their wages over time (Ozdowski, 1985; Paz, 2016; Peberdy, 2001; Ramji-Nogales, 2007; Rubio-Marín, 2014; Ruhs, 2010; Ryan and Mitsilegas, 2010).

Some employers insist that domestic workers are required to deposit their wages into an account in the employer's name which is an invasion of privacy and a high risk of exploitation (Baldwin-Edwards, 2006; Bangarth, 2003; Barak-Erez, 2008; Becerra, 2016; Brané and Lundholm, 2007; Brochmann and Hammar, 2020). If a woman and her spouse both have worker status, her wages may be paid into an account in the name of her spouse which further removes her personal agency concerning the management of her finances (Wexler, 2007; Wilcox, 2009; Zúñiga and Hernández-León, 2005; Zwi and Mares, 2015). All these are violations of the right to work for a wage (Dudley et al., 2012; Dunn, 2001, 2010; Exdell, 2009; Fiske, 2016; Flynn, 2013; Frederking, 2012; Gilman, 2013). Certain pre-existing gender inequalities such as unequal pay may be transferred to migrant women workers and may even affect them in more severe ways than local women workers (Melis, 2001; Miller, 2015, 2016; Molnar and Gill, 2018; Money, 1998; Morris, 2002, 2016; Motomura, 1999).

Women migrant workers often suffer from inequalities that threaten their health and general well-being (Aynsley-Green et al., 2012; Cornelisse, 2004; Heisler, 2000; Mehan, 1997; Ramji-Nogales, 2007; Spijkerboer and Van Walsum, 2007). They may be unable to access health services, including reproductive health services (Adelman, 2002; Cook, 2003; Hayter, 2000; Lorentzen, 2014; Peberdy, 2001; Soysal, 2012). This is because insurance or national health schemes are not available to them by virtue of their status as migrants (Hayter, 2000; Heisler, 2000; Hernandez-Truyol and Johns, 1997; Hollifield, Martin, and Orrenius, 2014; Jacobson, 1996). Others may have to pay unaffordable fees, a situation made worse if they have not contributed to insurance schemes for long enough to qualify for significant discounts (Bacon, 1996; Dudley et al., 2012; Hollifield, Martin, and Orrenius, 2014; Money, 1998; Saadi et al., 2020).

As women have health needs different from those of men, this aspect requires special attention (Cook, 2003; Cornelisse, 2004, 2010; Costello, 2012; Dauvergne, 2012; Den Heijer, 2010; Dudley et al., 2012). Women migrant workers are sometimes subjected to sex-discriminatory mandatory HIV/AIDS testing or testing for other infections without their consent (Adelman, 2002; Cook, 2003; Hayter, 2000; Lorentzen, 2014; Peberdy, 2001; Soysal, 2012). This is followed by the provision of test results to agents and employers rather than to the worker herself which further dehumanizes and stigmatizes the woman (Den Heijer, 2010; Dudley et al., 2012; Dunn, 2001, 2010; Exdell, 2009; Fiske, 2016; Flynn, 2013; Frederking, 2012). This may result in loss of job or deportation if test results are positive for a contagious disease such as HIV/AIDS and Hepatitis (Acer and Goodman, 2009; Ackerman and Furman, 2014; Adelman, 2002; Aynsley-Green et al., 2012; Bacon, 1996). At the same time, the loss of privacy and control over their medical records is dehumanizing to women migrant workers may have long term psychological effects on them (Spijkerboer and Van Walsum, 2007; Taylor, 2000; Thym, 2008; Webber, 2012; Welch, 2002; Wexler, 2007; Wilcox, 2009).

Discrimination may be especially acute in relation to pregnancy or women of a child bearing age (Nethery and Holman, 2016; Newman, Proctor, and Dudley, 2013; Oberman, 2016; Orfanos, 2019; Ozdowski, 1985). Women migrant workers may face mandatory pregnancy tests followed by deportation if the test is positive (Paz, 2016; Peberdy, 2001; Ramji-Nogales, 2007; Rubio-Marín, 2014; Ruhs, 2010; Ryan and Mitsilegas, 2010; Saadi et al., 2020). Migrant women may be subjected to coercive abortion or lack of access to safe reproductive health and abortion services (Becerra, 2016; Fiske, 2016; Joppke, 1999; Nethery and Holman, 2016; Sassen, 1996). Others receive substandard healthcare, which puts their lives at risk (Saadi et al., 2020; Samers, 2004; Sampson, Mitchell, and Bowring, 2011; Sanggaran, Haire, and Zion, 2016; Sassen, 1996). Then there are problems of dealing with pregnancies following sexual assault, particularly if the assailant is in a position of power such as the husband of the employer (Saadi et al., 2020; Samers, 2004; Sampson, Mitchell, and Bowring, 2011; Sanggaran, Haire, and Zion, 2016). There is a reported absence of, or inadequate, maternity leave and benefits and absence of affordable obstetric care for migrant women workers which results in serious health risks for this category of workers (Dunn, 2010; Exdell, 2009; Fiske, 2016; Flynn, 2013; Frederking, 2012; Gilman, 2013; Guia, Koulish, and Mitsilegas, 2016). The next section introduces an internationalist perspective that may implicitly address some of the abuses that migrant workers (including women) face.

2.3. IMMIGRATION FROM AN INTERNATIONALIST PERSPECTIVE

An internationalist perspective is generally more welcoming to immigration than one which is nationalist and parochial (Acer and Goodman, 2009; Chavez, 2001; Guild and Niessen, 1996; King, 2009; Ozdowski, 1985; Shohamy and McNamara, 2009). That is why some researchers have suggested that an internationalist perspective will help in eliminating some of the obstacles to immigration generally, and economic migrants in particular (Flynn, 2013; Frederking, 2012; Gilman, 2013; Guia, Koulish, and Mitsilegas, 2016; Guild, 2001; Guild and Niessen, 1996). If we see the globe as an interconnected and interdependent space, it no longer makes sense to put excessive restrictions on the movement of people (Hollifield, Martin, and Orrenius, 2014; Jacobson, 1996; Johnson, 1996; Joppke, 1998, 1999, 2010; Kasimis, 2012).

Nevertheless, many governments are increasing migration restrictions rather than reducing them (Costello, 2012; Dauvergne, 2012; Den Heijer, 2010; Dudley et al., 2012; Dunn, 2001, 2010; Exdell, 2009). Part of this is a reaction of populist movements that threaten to unseat any politician that shows even the slightest interest in immigration reform which might increase the number of immigrants (Costello, 2012; Guia, Koulish, and Mitsilegas, 2016; Melis, 2001; Rubio-Marín, 2014; Webber, 2012). Instead, there is a generalized demand for some extreme measures such as forcible deportations of even those that already have a right to remain (Lorentzen, 2014; Mehan, 1997; Melis, 2001; Miller, 2015, 2016; Molnar and Gill, 2018; Money, 1998; Morris, 2016). There is a disconnect between the nationalist pressures from the community and the internationalist stance that many countries wish to project to the rest of the world (Ryan and Mitsilegas, 2010; Saadi et al.,

as regular, irregular, documented, and undocumented (Sassen, 1996, 1997; Shohamy and McNamara, 2009; Smith, 2014; Soysal, 2012; Spijkerboer and Van Walsum, 2007). Their human rights are not isolated from the rights of others despite the fact that they are no citizen (Thym, 2008; Webber, 2012; Welch, 2002; Wexler, 2007; Wilcox, 2009; Zúñiga and Hernández-León, 2005; Zwi and Mares, 2015). There is one notable exception in terms of the right to enter another country and to vote and stand for election to political office (Miller, 2015, 2016; Molnar and Gill, 2018; Money, 1998; Morris, 2002, 2016; Motomura, 1999). Ideally, migrants should enjoy the same human and labor rights as nationals (Jacobson, 1996; Johnson, 1996; Joppke, 1998, 1999, 2010; Kasimis, 2012; Kelson and DeLaet, 1999). The reality is very much removed from this ideal because most countries always explicitly and implicitly prioritize their own citizens over migrants (Sanggaran, Haire, and Zion, 2016; Sassen, 1996, 1997; Shohamy and McNamara, 2009; Smith, 2014). Others completely ignore migrants as if they were not part of the workforce (Orfanos, 2019; Ozdowski, 1985; Paz, 2016; Peberdy, 2001; Ramji-Nogales, 2007; Rubio-Marín, 2014; Ruhs, 2010).

In extreme cases, the state may even support local residents as they exploit immigrants (Joppke, 1999, 2010; Kasimis, 2012; Kelson and DeLaet, 1999; King, 2009; Lopez, 2005; Lorentzen, 2014; Mehan, 1997). A case in point is the summary deportation procedure which is feared by migrants and hence makes it very difficult for them to report any abuse that they may have been suffering (Cornelisse, 2010; Gilman, 2013; Kelson and DeLaet, 1999; Orfanos, 2019; Thym, 2008). The local citizenry may recognize the fact that migrants have limited rights and will therefore attempt to exploit them in terms of providing cheap or even free labor (Costello, 2012; Dauvergne, 2012; Den Heijer, 2010; Dudley et al., 2012; Dunn, 2001, 2010; Exdell, 2009; Fiske, 2016). There are immigrants that have in effect become captive in their host countries because all their travel documents are held by their exploiters and their diplomatic services are unable to or unwilling to help (Guia, Koulish, and Mitsilegas, 2016; Guild, 2001; Guild and Niessen, 1996; Hailbronner, 2000; Hayter, 2000; Heisler, 2000). Such vulnerable immigrants tend to be overwhelmingly from the developing world and female (Brochmann and Hammar, 2020; Frederking, 2012; Kasimis, 2012; Oberman, 2016; Taylor, 2000).

International law recognizes the right of everyone to leave any country, including their own, and to return to their own country (Webber, 2012; Welch, 2002; Wexler, 2007; Wilcox, 2009; Zúñiga and Hernández-León, 2005; Zwi and Mares, 2015). However, it does not establish a right of entry to another country as a matter of course. In fact, international law upholds the sovereign prerogative of states to decide on criteria for the admission and expulsion of non-nationals. The categories that are explicitly covered by these sovereign rights and privileges include the right to include and exclude migrants at will, save for those that quality for asylum (Brané and Lundholm, 2007; Flynn, 2013; Joppke, 2010; Newman, Proctor, and Dudley, 2013; Sassen, 1997). Nevertheless, states are prohibited from returning anyone to countries where they would face torture. No deportations should take place if they result in other serious human rights violations or persecution. The specifics of the criterion are set out in the 1951 Geneva Convention Relating to the Status of Refugees. Another important reference is the 1967 Protocol (Fiske, 2016; Flynn, 2013; Frederking, 2012; Gilman, 2013; Guia, Koulish, and Mitsilegas, 2016; Guild, 2001). The challenge is that each country has its own standards of what consists a genuine fear of persecution (Johnson, 1996; Joppke, 1998, 1999, 2010; Kasimis, 2012; Kelson and DeLaet, 1999; King, 2009; Lopez, 2005).

The closed alternative legal avenues for economic migration mean that many claim asylum statuses when in fact they are economic migrants (Motomura, 1999; Nethery and Holman, 2016; Newman, Proctor, and Dudley, 2013; Oberman, 2016; Orfanos, 2019). Hence, a significant number of resources that are routinely expended in trying to weed out the economic migrants from the genuine refugees (Ramji-Nogales, 2007; Rubio-Marín, 2014; Ruhs, 2010; Ryan and Mitsilegas, 2010; Saadi et al., 2020; Samers, 2004). Those who are denied status end up looking for alternative ways of remaining in their chosen country (Guild and Niessen, 1996; Hailbronner, 2000; Hayter, 2000; Heisler, 2000; Hernandez-Truyol and Johns, 1997). Countries are expected to provide due process in removal or deportation proceedings and to avoid collective expulsions. However, that happens in as far as policy considerations may outweigh the individual merits of each case (Spijkerboer and Van Walsum, 2007; Taylor, 2000; Thym, 2008; Webber, 2012; Welch, 2002; Wexler, 2007; Wilcox, 2009). In reality, even the most developed countries sometimes break these rules under public pressure to control immigration (Kasimis, 2012; Kelson and DeLaet, 1999; King, 2009; Lopez, 2005; Lorentzen, 2014; Mehan, 1997; Melis, 2001; Miller, 2015).

The general interpretation of international law also stipulates that there are certain unacceptable grounds of discrimination, such as race, sex, religion, or health status concerning who may be admitted. However, countries have often ended discriminating against immigrants in this way even if that is not the intention that is explicitly mentioned when an immigration policy is launched (Oberman, 2016; Orfanos, 2019; Ozdowski, 1985; Paz, 2016; Peberdy, 2001; Ramji-Nogales, 2007; Rubio-Marín, 2014). However, these rules are often flaunted, and the state is not always vigilant in bringing the culprits to book (Hailbronner, 2000; Hayter, 2000; Heisler, 2000; Hernandez-Truyol and Johns, 1997; Hollifield, Martin, and Orrenius, 2014). A case in point is the real or perceived HIV status which the USA used to deny entry to migrants in the 1980s and 1990s (Dauvergne, 2012; Den Heijer, 2010; Dudley et al., 2012; Dunn, 2001, 2010; Exdell, 2009; Fiske, 2016; Flynn, 2013). During the COVID-19 pandemic, it became quite clear that these were criterion that the public expected to consider, and many who are considered to have a high risk of COVID face being turned away. The next section explores the possibilities of harmonizing both domestic and international law, a task that has so far eluded the international community as a whole.

2.4. HARMONIZING DOMESTIC LAWS WITH MIGRATION REALITIES

In order to successfully achieve harmony and broad consensus on immigration policy, it is appropriate to consider the possibilities and limitations of harmonizing domestic and international law (Cornelisse, 2004, 2010; Costello, 2012; Dauvergne, 2012; Den Heijer, 2010; Dudley et al., 2012; Dunn, 2001). Migration policies and practices can only be viable and effective when they are based on a firm foundation of legal norms, and thus operate under the rule of law (Frederking, 2012; Gilman, 2013; Guia, Koulish, and Mitsilegas, 2016; Guild, 2001; Guild and Niessen, 1996; Hailbronner, 2000). One of the practical problems that governments have to face is the rejection of low skilled and low paying jobs that have to be covered through immigration (Joppke, 1998, 1999, 2010; Kasimis, 2012; Kelson and DeLaet, 1999; King, 2009; Lopez, 2005; Lorentzen, 2014). See Figure 2.4 for the example of the USA.

At the same time, the laws that are applied must be consistent with the norms, values, and expectations of the host community as well as the community that is sending in immigrants (Brochmann and Hammar, 2020; Chavez, 2001; Chin, 1999; Cook, 2003; Cornelisse, 2004, 2010). To obtain credibility and ensure enforceability, migration governance needs to be based on a public legal framework established by a formal legislative process (Smith, 2014; Soysal, 2012; Spijkerboer and Van Walsum, 2007; Taylor, 2000; Thym, 2008; Webber, 2012; Welch, 2002).

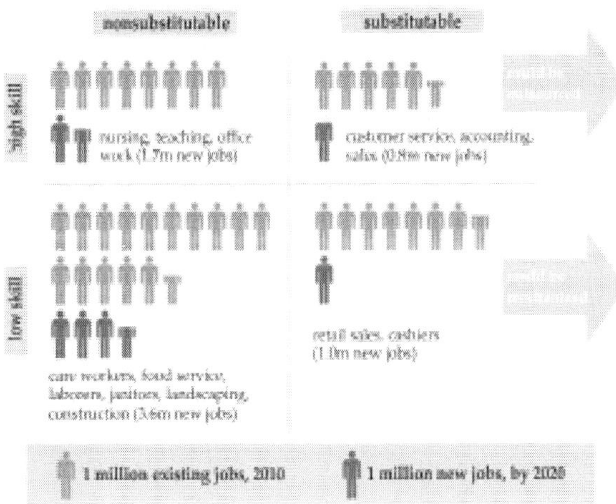

Figure 2.4: Rejection of low skilled and low paying jobs in the USA.

Source: Center for Global Development.

This tends to happen in a parliament and is then administered under law by the executive branch of government (Hernandez-Truyol and Johns, 1997; Hollifield, Martin, and Orrenius, 2014; Jacobson, 1996; Johnson, 1996; Joppke, 1998). Such rules, laws, and regulations can be reviewed and enforced by the judiciary as the arbitrating part of the government (Money, 1998; Morris, 2002, 2016; Motomura, 1999; Nethery and Holman, 2016; Newman, Proctor, and Dudley, 2013). The rule of law stipulates that in all circumstances, all communities, states, and international relations are governed by a system of rules and guidelines which apply to all people and in all circumstances. Nevertheless, it is important to recognize the inherent inequalities in community life (Sampson, Mitchell, and Bowring, 2011; Sanggaran, Haire, and Zion, 2016; Sassen, 1996, 1997; Shohamy and McNamara, 2009).

Immigration laws are based on a framework that is usually set up or endorsed by a legislative process which represents the local community (Samers, 2004; Sampson, Mitchell, and Bowring, 2011; Sanggaran, Haire, and Zion, 2016; Sassen, 1996, 1997). The resultant laws are then enforced through a set of institutions and mechanisms under the authority of states or government in power (Morris, 2002, 2016; Motomura, 1999; Nethery and Holman, 2016; Newman, Proctor, and Dudley, 2013; Oberman, 2016). There are certain essential principles are that out to underpin immigration policy formulation and implementation. The extent of the exact application of these laws, rules, and regulations is contested with reference to some states (Becerra, 2016; Brané and Lundholm, 2007; Brochmann and Hammar, 2020; Chavez, 2001; Chin, 1999; Cook, 2003).

First, no person, collective or institution is above the law. However, the reality is that those who are well-connected can obtain visas without going through the normal process (Ozdowski, 1985; Paz, 2016; Peberdy, 2001; Ramji-Nogales, 2007; Rubio-Marín, 2014; Ruhs, 2010; Ryan and Mitsilegas, 2010). Secondly, it is argued that no individual or body can be punished by the state or any other entity except for a breach of the law (Baldwin-Edwards, 2006; Dunn, 2001; Jacobson, 1996; Morris, 2016; Samers, 2004). In reality, some of the burdens that are placed on immigrants are a form of punishment which is outside the law and dependent on the proclivities of the people that handle these immigrants (Welch, 2002; Wexler, 2007; Wilcox, 2009; Zúñiga and Hernández-León, 2005; Zwi and Mares, 2015). A case in point are the rampant abuses that happen in detention centers and during the forcible deportation process (Brochmann and Hammar, 2020; Chavez, 2001; Chin, 1999; Cook, 2003; Cornelisse, 2004, 2010; Costello, 2012). The third principle is that no one can be convicted of breaching the law except in the manner set forth by the law itself (Aynsley-Green et al., 2012; Bacon, 1996; Baldwin-Edwards, 2006; Bangarth, 2003; Barak-Erez, 2008; Becerra, 2016). The saga of the Guantanamo detainees demonstrates the limitations of both domestic and international law when it comes to reigning the excesses of powerful countries (Bangarth, 2003; Barak-Erez, 2008; Becerra, 2016; Brané and Lundholm, 2007; Brochmann and Hammar, 2020; Chavez, 2001).

A key step aspect when establishing the governance (and by extension the governability) of migration is the establishment of national law based on and in compliance with international law (Molnar and Gill, 2018; Money, 1998; Morris, 2002, 2016; Motomura, 1999; Nethery and Holman, 2016). This is usually accomplished through ratification by states of relevant international human rights instruments (Chavez, 2001; Chin, 1999; Cook, 2003; Cornelisse, 2004, 2010; Costello, 2012; Dauvergne, 2012; Den Heijer, 2010). Critically, the immigration law should be consistent with international labor standards or even exceed them whenever and wherever possible (Guild, 2001; Miller, 2016; Ryan and Mitsilegas, 2010; Wexler, 2007; Wilcox, 2009). At the same time, the enactment of these laws should be followed by their effective implementation in order to ensure that the policy goals of immigration management are achieved (Kelson and DeLaet, 1999; King, 2009; Lopez, 2005; Lorentzen, 2014; Mehan, 1997; Melis, 2001; Miller, 2015, 2016).

The nations that are failing to control their immigration are likely to be failing at one or more of the steps that are provided above (Kasimis, 2012; Kelson and DeLaet, 1999; King, 2009; Lopez, 2005; Lorentzen, 2014; Mehan, 1997; Melis, 2001; Miller, 2015). For example, there are countries that are still reliant on old colonial laws that make little sense in the modern context (Soysal, 2012; Spijkerboer and Van Walsum, 2007; Taylor, 2000; Thym, 2008; Webber, 2012; Welch, 2002; Wexler, 2007). Others feel that they are restricted by supra-laws that are enacted at the regional level without considering the needs and expectations of the local population (Brané and Lundholm, 2007; Brochmann and Hammar, 2020; Chavez, 2001; Chin, 1999; Cook, 2003; Cornelisse, 2004). One such instance was the unhappiness of the UK justice administration team on the interference from the European Union on the grounds of the Human Rights laws that have been invariably enacted in that part of the world.

Such interference would lead to patently absurd decisions such as having to accommodate international terrorists that had harmed the local population and were vehemently opposed to the local way of life (Lopez, 2005; Lorentzen, 2014; Mehan, 1997; Melis, 2001; Miller, 2015, 2016; Molnar and Gill, 2018; Money, 1998). All that these terrorists had to do was sustain a human rights claim, even on the most flippant of excuses (Smith, 2014; Soysal, 2012; Spijkerboer and Van Walsum, 2007; Taylor, 2000; Thym, 2008; Webber, 2012; Welch, 2002). Meanwhile, the local populace was left seething with resentment at their perceived loss of independence, and that is why when the opportunity arose, the UK decided to abandon the European Union through a referendum. National legislatures are an important safeguard against the general perception that the country is no longer in charge of its own immigration policy or that there are outside forces with an undue influence over the conduct of immigration policy (Molnar and Gill, 2018; Money, 1998; Morris, 2002, 2016; Motomura, 1999; Nethery and Holman, 2016).

Parliaments usually play an important role in ratifying international treaties, including international human rights and labor conventions (Morris, 2002, 2016; Motomura, 1999; Nethery and Holman, 2016; Newman, Proctor, and Dudley, 2013; Oberman, 2016). In this way, they provide democratic scrutiny and legitimacy to the resultant laws (Acer and Goodman, 2009; Chavez, 2001; Guild and Niessen, 1996; King, 2009; Ozdowski, 1985; Shohamy and McNamara, 2009). Rules and procedures differ from country to country, albeit with reference to certain universal human rights and conventional practices (Hernandez-Truyol and Johns,

1997; Hollifield, Martin, and Orrenius, 2014; Jacobson, 1996; Johnson, 1996; Joppke, 1998). In most cases, the national executive (comprising the presidency or a government minister) proposes the ratification of a treaty or convention, bearing in mind its political implications (Dunn, 2001, 2010; Exdell, 2009; Fiske, 2016; Flynn, 2013; Frederking, 2012; Gilman, 2013; Guia, Koulish, and Mitsilegas, 2016).

Parliament must give its consent before the executive can register it (Mehan, 1997; Melis, 2001; Miller, 2015, 2016; Molnar and Gill, 2018; Money, 1998; Morris, 2002, 2016). However, there have been examples of the executive pushing the very limits of its discretion when running immigration policy to the extent that the parliament may be kept in the dark about what is really happening (Guild, 2001; Guild and Niessen, 1996; Hailbronner, 2000; Hayter, 2000; Heisler, 2000; Hernandez-Truyol and Johns, 1997). The effects of such actions can be devastating to the reputation of the country as well as the immigrants themselves (Bangarth, 2003; Dunn, 2010; Johnson, 1996; Morris, 2002; Sampson, Mitchell, and Bowring, 2011). Recently, the USA has been involved in a scandal where immigration officials were forcibly separating children from their parents and placing them in so-called "cages" in order to put pressure on the parents to accept deportation.

The legislature may also initiate ratification by asking the government about its plans for ratification of a particular treaty or convention (Barak-Erez, 2008; Exdell, 2009; Joppke, 1998; Motomura, 1999; Sanggaran, Haire, and Zion, 2016). International law pertaining to migration can be complex and emerges in incremental patterns. Part of the challenge for governments is to ensure that current laws are coherent and do not create undesirable precedents (Motomura, 1999; Nethery and Holman, 2016; Newman, Proctor, and Dudley, 2013; Oberman, 2016; Orfanos, 2019). A key concern will be the treatment and management of economic migrants (Adelman, 2002; Aynsley-Green et al., 2012; Bacon, 1996; Baldwin-Edwards, 2006; Bangarth, 2003; Barak-Erez, 2008). International human rights instruments, including those relating to fundamental rights at work, and international labor standards are essentially sets of minimum legal provisions drawn up at international conferences to provide guidance (Rubio-Marín, 2014; Ruhs, 2010; Ryan and Mitsilegas, 2010; Saadi et al., 2020; Samers, 2004; Sampson, Mitchell, and Bowring, 2011). These must then be reinterpreted for a national audience and then incorporated into domestic law (Guia, Koulish, and Mitsilegas, 2016; Guild, 2001; Guild and Niessen, 1996; Hailbronner, 2000; Hayter, 2000; Heisler, 2000).

The international conventions on migrant rights are often prepared in specific language, which is important for national legislation, policy, and practice. International instruments comprise both conventions and declarations (Gilman, 2013; Guia, Koulish, and Mitsilegas, 2016; Guild, 2001; Guild and Niessen, 1996; Hailbronner, 2000; Hayter, 2000). However, declarations are usually not binding unless they represent customary international law (Exdell, 2009; Fiske, 2016; Flynn, 2013; Frederking, 2012; Gilman, 2013; Guia, Koulish, and Mitsilegas, 2016; Guild, 2001). For example, the UDHR of 1948 and the International Labor Organization (ILO) Declaration of Fundamental Principles and Rights at Work of 1998 are not legally binding treaties (Fiske, 2016; Flynn, 2013; Frederking, 2012; Gilman, 2013; Guia, Koulish, and Mitsilegas, 2016; Guild, 2001). However, they express widely accepted principles and rights found in the legally binding instruments of international human rights and international labor law (Sampson, Mitchell, and Bowring, 2011; Sanggaran, Haire, and Zion, 2016; Sassen, 1996, 1997; Shohamy and McNamara, 2009). Many of the resultant legal practices are also recognized as customary international law (Soysal, 2012; Spijkerboer and Van Walsum, 2007; Taylor, 2000; Thym, 2008; Webber, 2012; Welch, 2002; Wexler, 2007).

Whereas most states will try to follow the international conventions, political pressure at home may require them to diverge away from those laws (Gilman, 2013; Guia, Koulish, and Mitsilegas, 2016; Guild, 2001; Guild and Niessen, 1996; Hailbronner, 2000; Hayter, 2000). Indeed, there have been cases where politicians have expressly campaigned on the promise of taking back control over borders in express contravention of international conventions (Chin, 1999; Cook, 2003; Cornelisse, 2004, 2010; Costello, 2012; Dauvergne, 2012; Den Heijer, 2010; Dudley et al., 2012). This highlights the difficulty of having an international standard that is applied in a fairly uniform way (Ackerman and Furman, 2014; Adelman, 2002; Aynsley-Green et al., 2012; Bacon, 1996; Baldwin-Edwards, 2006). Some have argued that the most appropriate approach is to acknowledge the individual diversities of legal regimes, but instead advocate for a human rights approach to migration law and enforcement (Newman, Proctor, and Dudley, 2013; Oberman, 2016; Orfanos, 2019; Ozdowski, 1985; Paz, 2016; Peberdy, 2001).

There are certain instruments that are binding on member nations and these have sometimes been used as the foundation for a more human immigration policy (Chin, 1999; Cook, 2003; Cornelisse, 2004, 2010; Costello, 2012; Dauvergne, 2012; Den Heijer, 2010; Dudley et al., 2012). A case in point is the 1966 UN International Covenant on Civil and Political Rights (Ackerman and Furman, 2014; Adelman, 2002; Aynsley-Green et al., 2012; Bacon, 1996; Baldwin-Edwards, 2006). Additionally, the 1966 International Covenant on Economic, Social, and Cultural Rights is binding on its signatories (Newman, Proctor, and Dudley, 2013; Oberman, 2016; Orfanos, 2019; Ozdowski, 1985; Paz, 2016; Peberdy, 2001). These have more force than the recommendations of the ILO which can be ignored by sovereign nations without any serious consequences (Cook, 2003; Cornelisse, 2004, 2010; Costello, 2012; Dauvergne, 2012; Den Heijer, 2010; Dudley et al., 2012).

These instruments of international law are responsible for providing non-binding guidance which is often referenced as best practice (Costello, 2012; Guia, Koulish, and Mitsilegas, 2016; Melis, 2001; Rubio-Marín, 2014; Webber, 2012). A unique (and some argue fortuitous) characteristic of international labor standards is that these are designed not only by governments but also by employers' and workers' representatives (Dudley et al., 2012; Dunn, 2001, 2010; Exdell, 2009; Fiske, 2016; Flynn, 2013; Frederking, 2012; Gilman, 2013). These external contributors are important for ensuring a tripartite structure that is more inclusive than the design of other international law instruments (Baldwin-Edwards, 2006; Bangarth, 2003; Barak-Erez, 2008; Becerra, 2016; Brané and Lundholm, 2007). In that way, a range of perspectives contributes towards defining what best practice actually is in a range of contexts.

The general comments and recommendations adopted by the human rights treaty bodies provide guidance to States Parties on the implementation of their treaty obligations under the core international human rights treaties (Sassen, 1996, 1997; Shohamy and McNamara, 2009; Smith, 2014; Soysal, 2012; Spijkerboer and Van Walsum, 2007). These instruments usually define the rights and entitlements of the persons and populations concerned, which in these cases they are mainly asylum-seekers and migrant workers (Brochmann and Hammar, 2020; Chavez, 2001; Chin, 1999; Cook, 2003; Cornelisse, 2004, 2010; Costello, 2012). In many instances, they may also establish their obligations as well.

Included are specific guidelines for states and provisions for implementing rights and obligations (Dauvergne, 2012; Hernandez-Truyol and Johns, 1997; Molnar and Gill, 2018; Zúñiga and Hernández-León, 2005). Others specific the mechanisms for application and supervision (Acer and Goodman, 2009; Ackerman and Furman, 2014; Adelman, 2002; Aynsley-

Green et al., 2012; Bacon, 1996). In some areas, such as international migration, international instruments may provide for specific measures and mechanisms of international consultation and cooperation to implement basic principles regarding rights, obligations, and governance mechanisms (Nethery and Holman, 2016; Newman, Proctor, and Dudley, 2013; Oberman, 2016; Orfanos, 2019; Ozdowski, 1985). This chapter will conclude with a section on the human rights aspects of migration management.

2.5. HUMAN RIGHTS ASPECTS OF MIGRATION

Advocates of migrants have argued that only through acknowledging its human rights aspects, can immigration be managed in an effective, fair, and equitable way (Taylor, 2000; Thym, 2008; Webber, 2012; Welch, 2002; Wexler, 2007; Wilcox, 2009; Zúñiga and Hernández-León, 2005; Zwi and Mares, 2015). There is a significant body of international human rights law that can be referenced, depending of course on how the local authorities interpret its provisions (Adelman, 2002; Aynsley-Green et al., 2012; Bacon, 1996; Baldwin-Edwards, 2006; Bangarth, 2003; Barak-Erez, 2008). For example, some countries see human rights as inalienable aspects that must always be considered in the legislative process (Ruhs, 2010; Ryan and Mitsilegas, 2010; Saadi et al., 2020; Samers, 2004; Sampson, Mitchell, and Bowring, 2011). Protecting the rights of migrants makes sense given the important role they play in the economy (Guild and Niessen, 1996; Hailbronner, 2000; Hayter, 2000; Heisler, 2000; Hernandez-Truyol and Johns, 1997). For example, Figure 2.5 highlights the important role the migrants play in the health sector among OECD countries.

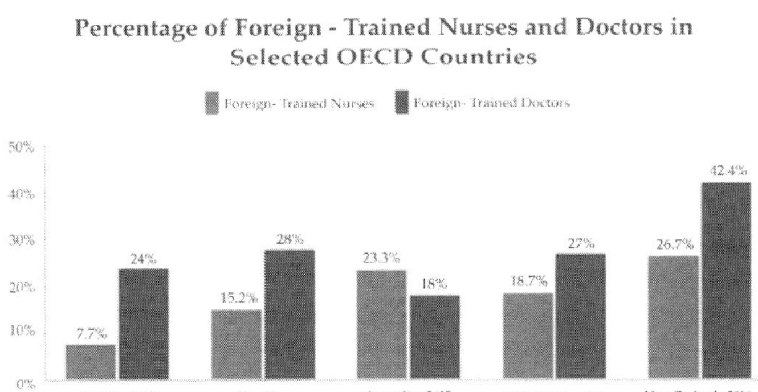

Figure 2.5: Role of foreign workers in health services among OECD countries.

Source: WENR World Education Services.

Others see international human rights legislation as alien and therefore an infringement on their national sovereignty (Miller, 2015, 2016; Molnar and Gill, 2018; Money, 1998; Morris, 2002, 2016; Motomura, 1999; Nethery and Holman, 2016). Depending on the nature of interpretation, the outcomes for migrants can be markedly different (Lorentzen, 2014; Mehan, 1997; Melis, 2001; Miller, 2015, 2016; Molnar and Gill, 2018; Money, 1998; Morris, 2016). Getting a visa to Norway is considerably more straightforward than one to Iran, despite the fact that the former is one of the most developed nations on earth with a generous benefits system for migrants and their families (Paz, 2016; Peberdy, 2001; Ramji-Nogales, 2007; Rubio-Marín, 2014; Ruhs, 2010; Ryan and Mitsilegas, 2010). The latter has been acknowledged as a human rights pariah that regularly detains visitors and those that trespass, regardless of how minor the infringement is.

International human rights are enshrined in international law as a form of guidance and a framework that can be referenced when managing immigration (Baldwin-Edwards, 2006; Bangarth, 2003; Barak-Erez, 2008; Becerra, 2016; Brané and Lundholm, 2007; Brochmann and Hammar, 2020). These international laws on human rights establish unequivocally that migrants and members of their families are first and foremost human beings (Fiske, 2016; Flynn, 2013; Frederking, 2012; Gilman, 2013; Guia, Koulish, and Mitsilegas, 2016; Guild, 2001; Guild and Niessen, 1996). This was in response to the insidious dehumanization of migrants in order to socially isolate them from the receiving community (Thym, 2008; Webber, 2012; Welch, 2002; Wexler, 2007; Wilcox, 2009; Zúñiga and Hernández-León, 2005; Zwi and Mares, 2015). Immigrants and their families then become the holders of universal human rights whose dignity and security require specific protection (Webber, 2012; Welch, 2002; Wexler, 2007; Wilcox, 2009; Zúñiga and Hernández-León, 2005; Zwi and Mares, 2015).

Consequently, immigrants and their families enjoy the protection of international human rights law like anyone else (Samers, 2004; Sampson, Mitchell, and Bowring, 2011; Sanggaran, Haire, and Zion, 2016; Sassen, 1996, 1997). This holds true even if they are in an irregular situation, as can be the case with migrants (Barak-Erez, 2008; Becerra, 2016; Brané and Lundholm, 2007; Brochmann and Hammar, 2020; Chavez, 2001; Chin, 1999). The only exceptions relate to political rights, with specific reference to the right to vote, to stand in elections and to enter and stay in a country (Cornelisse, 2010; Costello, 2012; Dauvergne, 2012; Den Heijer, 2010; Dudley et al., 2012; Dunn, 2001, 2010). These rights are restricted to citizens and are exercised at the discretion of the state (Jacobson, 1996; Johnson,

1996; Joppke, 1998, 1999, 2010; Kasimis, 2012; Kelson and DeLaet, 1999). However, the right to enter and stay in a country may also apply to foreign nationals with permanent or secure residence in the country (Bacon, 1996; Baldwin-Edwards, 2006; Bangarth, 2003; Barak-Erez, 2008; Becerra, 2016; Brané and Lundholm, 2007).

International human rights law prescribes what governments and other stakeholders have agreed ought to be done concerning migrants and their families (Peberdy, 2001; Ramji-Nogales, 2007; Rubio-Marín, 2014; Ruhs, 2010; Ryan and Mitsilegas, 2010; Saadi et al., 2020; Samers, 2004). It contains norms that address wider human rights questions affecting all migrants, as well as specific standards that deal directly with migrant workers and their families (Sassen, 1997; Shohamy and McNamara, 2009; Smith, 2014; Soysal, 2012; Spijkerboer and Van Walsum, 2007). There may be local values and norms that exceed or fall below these international standards which could be adopted by countries that wish to go an extra mile in protecting human rights (Morris, 2002; Motomura, 1999; Nethery and Holman, 2016; Newman, Proctor, and Dudley, 2013; Oberman, 2016). Other countries have such a significant culture of human rights that their societal processes far exceed any standards that international organizations might recommend. A case in point is Norway, where access to high-speed internet is taken to be a human right, whereas some countries routinely limit access to the internet. However, there is an underlying principle that international law is supposed to promote best practice and encourage all governments who are signatories to follow suit (Paz, 2016; Peberdy, 2001; Ramji-Nogales, 2007; Rubio-Marín, 2014; Ruhs, 2010; Ryan and Mitsilegas, 2010; Saadi et al., 2020). Regardless of whether it is a highly liberal and industrialized nation or a conservative and less developed nations; these principles become red lines that must not be crossed.

There is a host of protocols, rules, regulations, and even laws that are supposed to put human rights at the heart of immigration policy (Aynsley-Green et al., 2012; Bacon, 1996; Baldwin-Edwards, 2006; Bangarth, 2003; Barak-Erez, 2008; Becerra, 2016). It is, however, not always the case that these rules and regulations are followed. If they are followed, it is sometimes done in a perfunctory way that does not maximize the possibilities for a human rights approach to immigration. Migrants are supposed to enjoy the human rights available to all persons under UN and ILO conventions, even though that is not always the case (Baldwin-Edwards, 2006; Dunn, 2001; Jacobson, 1996; Morris, 2016; Samers, 2004). Migrants are also protected under regional human rights instruments, some receiving particular attention because of their circumstances (Frederking, 2012; Gilman, 2013; Guia, Koulish, and Mitsilegas, 2016; Guild, 2001; Guild and Niessen, 1996; Hailbronner, 2000). A case in point are those migrants that are fleeing from political persecution who seek asylum and may eventually become refugees upon acceptance (Hollifield, Martin, and Orrenius, 2014; Jacobson, 1996; Johnson, 1996; Joppke, 1998, 1999, 2010). The world of work is of particular interest to the ILO because it has far reaching economic implications. Right from its origin, ILO resolved that migrant workers deserve special attention (Kasimis, 2012; Kelson and DeLaet, 1999; King, 2009; Lopez, 2005; Lorentzen, 2014; Mehan, 1997; Melis, 2001).

Indeed, the protection of migrant workers is enshrined in the Preamble to the ILO Constitution (Cornelisse, 2004, 2010; Costello, 2012; Dauvergne, 2012; Den Heijer, 2010; Dudley et al., 2012; Dunn, 2001). It is referenced as one of the areas where an improvement in labor conditions is seen as urgent (Joppke, 2010; Kasimis, 2012; Kelson and DeLaet, 1999; King, 2009; Lopez, 2005; Lorentzen, 2014; Mehan, 1997). The international instruments recognize the fact that if there is injustice in the labor market, the resultant hardship and privation may lead to social unrest and this has sometimes been expressed in the form of anti-migrant sentiment (Joppke, 1998, 1999, 2010; Kasimis, 2012; Kelson and DeLaet, 1999; King, 2009; Lopez, 2005; Lorentzen, 2014). Even more serious is the possibility that such unrest negatively impacts on peace and harmony throughout the world (Dauvergne, 2012; Den Heijer, 2010; Dudley et al., 2012; Dunn, 2001, 2010; Exdell, 2009; Fiske, 2016; Flynn, 2013).

Typically, political agitation based on labor rights comes from domestic forces which are entrenched and powerful. In such instances, migrants are only a marginal concern (Miller, 2016; Molnar and Gill, 2018; Money, 1998; Morris, 2002, 2016; Motomura, 1999; Nethery and Holman, 2016). Indeed, there are instances where migrants are the target of such activism and are used as a scapegoat for all the problems that pre-exist their entry into a given society (Fiske, 2016; Flynn, 2013; Frederking, 2012; Gilman, 2013; Guia, Koulish, and Mitsilegas, 2016; Guild, 2001; Guild and Niessen, 1996). An example is where local trade unions are adamant that jobs should be ring-fenced to members rather than allowing foreign labor to act as a replacement (Brochmann and Hammar, 2020; Frederking, 2012; Kasimis, 2012; Oberman, 2016; Taylor, 2000). There can be a certain amount of tension between local workers and migrant workers which can lead to strife or even the gross violation of the human rights of the migrant workers (Saadi et al., 2020; Samers, 2004; Sampson, Mitchell, and Bowring, 2011; Sanggaran,

Haire, and Zion, 2016). A case in point are the xenophobic attacks against black migrant workers in South Africa.

Some countries try to diffuse tensions by generally overseeing an improvement in the working conditions of the entire labor force (Chin, 1999; Cook, 2003; Cornelisse, 2004, 2010; Costello, 2012; Dauvergne, 2012; Den Heijer, 2010; Dudley et al., 2012). Others prioritize their "home" workers and leave the migrants to take up the subprime job opportunities (Brochmann and Hammar, 2020; Chavez, 2001; Chin, 1999; Cook, 2003; Cornelisse, 2004, 2010). Nevertheless, the issue of exploitation in the workforce is one that needs to be addressed even as economic migration is being tackled (Costello, 2012; Dauvergne, 2012; Den Heijer, 2010; Dudley et al., 2012; Dunn, 2001, 2010; Exdell, 2009). Some unscrupulous businesses prefer to hire foreign workers in the belief (that is often justified by experience) that foreign workers are more likely to accept less than ideal working conditions (Ramji-Nogales, 2007; Rubio-Marín, 2014; Ruhs, 2010; Ryan and Mitsilegas, 2010; Saadi et al., 2020; Samers, 2004). The overall effect on the labor market is to lower standards since businesses always have the option of cheap and unquestioning foreign labor (Money, 1998; Morris, 2002, 2016; Motomura, 1999; Nethery and Holman, 2016; Newman, Proctor, and Dudley, 2013).

There may be some concern that overtly improving working conditions in one country will attract workers from other parts of the world that are looking to enjoy similar benefits (Oberman, 2016; Orfanos, 2019; Ozdowski, 1985; Paz, 2016; Peberdy, 2001; Ramji-Nogales, 2007; Rubio-Marín, 2014). One of the causes of this phenomenon happened within the European Union where new members from Eastern Europe experienced a significant rise in emigrants to Western Europe in search of better working conditions (Miller, 2016; Molnar and Gill, 2018; Money, 1998; Morris, 2002, 2016; Motomura, 1999; Nethery and Holman, 2016). Specifically, the United Kingdom reported that there was a lot of immigration from the European Union (Cornelisse, 2010; Gilman, 2013; Kelson and DeLaet, 1999; Orfanos, 2019; Thym, 2008). Since membership of the Union prevented any controls on the free movement of people, these economic migrants were all legal (Orfanos, 2019; Ozdowski, 1985; Paz, 2016; Peberdy, 2001; Ramji-Nogales, 2007; Rubio-Marín, 2014; Ruhs, 2010). The local population in England particularly reacted with a renewed interest in nationalism (Acer and Goodman, 2009; Ackerman and Furman, 2014; Adelman, 2002; Aynsley-Green et al., 2012; Bacon, 1996). Eventually, this became of the main contributing factors for Britain's exit from the union (Mehan, 1997;

Melis, 2001; Miller, 2015, 2016; Molnar and Gill, 2018; Money, 1998; Morris, 2002, 2016). There is a regulatory requirement to achieve the goals of a human rights-based approach to immigration management (Acer and Goodman, 2009; Ackerman and Furman, 2014; Adelman, 2002; Aynsley-Green et al., 2012; Bacon, 1996). This is because many businesses will try to take advantage of any loopholes in the system as well as creating new ones if they do not currently exist (Ackerman and Furman, 2014; Chin, 1999; Hailbronner, 2000; Lopez, 2005; Paz, 2016; Smith, 2014). A framework for regulating the job market may cover aspects such as termination, working hours, leave, pay, labor supply, retirement benefits, sick pay, and protection of people with disabilities (Flynn, 2013; Frederking, 2012; Gilman, 2013; Guia, Koulish, and Mitsilegas, 2016; Guild, 2001; Guild and Niessen, 1996). Of course, those that are against regulation argue that this can increase the costs of doing business and therefore call for complete liberalization (Sanggaran, Haire, and Zion, 2016; Sassen, 1996, 1997; Shohamy and McNamara, 2009; Smith, 2014). Hence, there is a real risk of companies abandoning those jurisdictions that are serious about controlling working conditions and moving to ones that appear to be de-regulated (Peberdy, 2001; Ramji-Nogales, 2007; Rubio-Marín, 2014; Ruhs, 2010; Ryan and Mitsilegas, 2010; Saadi et al., 2020; Samers, 2004).

To some extent, the human rights approach has been critiqued for having a utopian view of migration realities (Bangarth, 2003; Barak-Erez, 2008; Becerra, 2016; Brané and Lundholm, 2007; Brochmann and Hammar, 2020; Chavez, 2001). For example, the idea that all migrants have either to apply for asylum or risk being denied entry is an implicit reality of immigration systems particularly as they relate to those people that are coming from the developing world into the developed world (Nethery and Holman, 2016; Newman, Proctor, and Dudley, 2013; Oberman, 2016; Orfanos, 2019; Ozdowski, 1985). Secondly, national governments always prioritize their citizenry because it is the one that puts them in power and failure to do so will lead to political suicide (Aynsley-Green et al., 2012; Cornelisse, 2004; Heisler, 2000; Mehan, 1997; Ramji-Nogales, 2007; Spijkerboer and Van Walsum, 2007). This is particularly true of democracies in which the wrong choice about immigration can end a political career (Brané and Lundholm, 2007; Flynn, 2013; Joppke, 2010; Newman, Proctor, and Dudley, 2013; Sassen, 1997). That is why politicians are very cautious about making any policy changes that are perceived to be benefitting immigrants (Paz, 2016; Peberdy, 2001; Ramji-Nogales, 2007; Rubio-Marín, 2014; Ruhs, 2010; Ryan and Mitsilegas, 2010). Thirdly, many of the so-called democracies have popularized Rightwing anti-immigrant sentiments which are now creeping into the policy formulation process (Sassen, 1996, 1997; Shohamy and McNamara, 2009; Smith, 2014; Soysal, 2012; Spijkerboer and Van Walsum, 2007). The battle cry of "protecting borders" is a testament to the fact that many people in the developed world support stricter immigration controls (Taylor, 2000; Thym, 2008; Webber, 2012; Welch, 2002; Wexler, 2007; Wilcox, 2009; Zúñiga and Hernández-León, 2005).

CHAPTER 2 SUMMARY

In this second chapter, we have explored the possibilities and limitations of trying to bring rationality and equity to the management of immigration. Some of the issues that have been discussed include the positive and negative social changes that migrants bring to both their home countries on return and on the receiving country on arrival. The chapter has explored the limitations of migration policy in terms of achieving a gender-sensitive operational framework. Although the chapter explores the positive aspects of an internationalist view of migration, it also acknowledges the fact that there is inconsistent application of international law on migration. The chapter suggests that harmonization of domestic and international law might provide some answers. It concludes by portraying a human rights approach as being an ideal that many governments are failing to fully achieve when developing policies of immigration control. The next chapter focuses on the consequences and nature of migration patterns.

CHAPTER 3

THE NATURE AND CONSEQUENCES OF HUMAN MIGRATIONS

CONTENTS

This third chapter considers the nature of human migration and the resultant consequences. The first section attempts to conceptualize human migration to develop an understanding of its meaning in the modern context. The second section considers how the history of migration is necessarily patterned and the impact of those patterns on the construction of migration histories. The third section briefly introduces some typologies of human migration. In the fourth section, we develop a theoretical basis for migration, including its determinants, mediators, and outcomes. The final section of this chapter will highlight the social-scientific perspectives on human migration. As a starting point to this chapter, we must attempt to conceptualize human migration.

3.1. THE PROCESS OF CONCEPTUALIZING MIGRATION

The most basic definition of migration is the movement of people from one geographical space. The reasons for these moves may include the search for sanctuary, work-related transfers, the desire to achieve family reunions, and to enjoy tourism experiences (Barak-Erez, 2008; Exdell, 2009; Joppke, 1998; Motomura, 1999; Sanggaran, Haire, and Zion, 2016). Human migration can therefore be both permanent and transient depending on its motivations and modalities (Hollifield, Martin, and Orrenius, 2014; Jacobson, 1996; Johnson, 1996; Joppke, 1998, 1999, 2010). In most cases, the permanent and semi-permanent type of human migration is most important because it is the most consequential (Sassen, 1997; Shohamy and McNamara, 2009; Smith, 2014; Soysal, 2012; Spijkerboer and Van Walsum, 2007). The intentions of those people might change along the way or after they arrive at their destination because migration patterns are not always linear (Guild and Niessen, 1996; Hailbronner, 2000; Hayter, 2000; Heisler, 2000; Hernandez-Truyol and Johns, 1997). For example, someone may come as a visitor and then end up remaining as a permanent resident.

It is appropriate to decipher the motivations of those that move from their homeland. Moreover, it is important to compare and contrast their experiences in order to learn lessons about policy options on immigration (Morris, 2002; Motomura, 1999; Nethery and Holman, 2016; Newman, Proctor, and Dudley, 2013; Oberman, 2016). Given the overall harassment that migrants face, it is very hard to get accurate and up-to-date data about this vulnerable population (Ackerman and Furman, 2014; Adelman, 2002; Aynsley-Green et al., 2012; Bacon, 1996; Baldwin-Edwards, 2006). Most of the data available comprise anecdotes and stories from those that may be already prejudiced against immigration and its effects (Becerra, 2016; Fiske, 2016; Joppke, 1999; Nethery and Holman, 2016; Sassen, 1996). Studies have shown that there is a gap between the reality of migration and public perceptions of it in most countries, particularly ones that report an "immigration problem" (Dunn, 2001, 2010; Exdell, 2009; Fiske, 2016; Flynn, 2013; Frederking, 2012; Gilman, 2013; Guia, Koulish, and Mitsilegas, 2016). A case in point is the assumption by many in the developing world that people are running to their shores to reap welfare benefits (Rubio-Marín, 2014; Ruhs, 2010; Ryan and Mitsilegas, 2010; Saadi et al., 2020; Samers, 2004; Sampson, Mitchell, and Bowring, 2011). These misunderstandings have real consequences because they can foster anti-immigrant sentiment, which can possibly turn violent (Oberman, 2016; Orfanos, 2019; Ozdowski, 1985; Paz, 2016; Peberdy, 2001; Ramji-Nogales, 2007; Rubio-Marín, 2014).

There are many issues that can be linked to immigration which have to be dealt with at the local, national, regional, and international level (Guild, 2001; Guild and Niessen, 1996; Hailbronner, 2000; Hayter, 2000; Heisler, 2000; Hernandez-Truyol and Johns, 1997). One of the emerging concerns about human migration is the failure to control it or to account for issues such as gendered patterns of immigration impacts (Johnson, 1996; Joppke, 1998, 1999, 2010; Kasimis, 2012; Kelson and DeLaet, 1999; King, 2009; Lopez, 2005). A case in point is the increasing role of women in migration (see Figure 3.1).

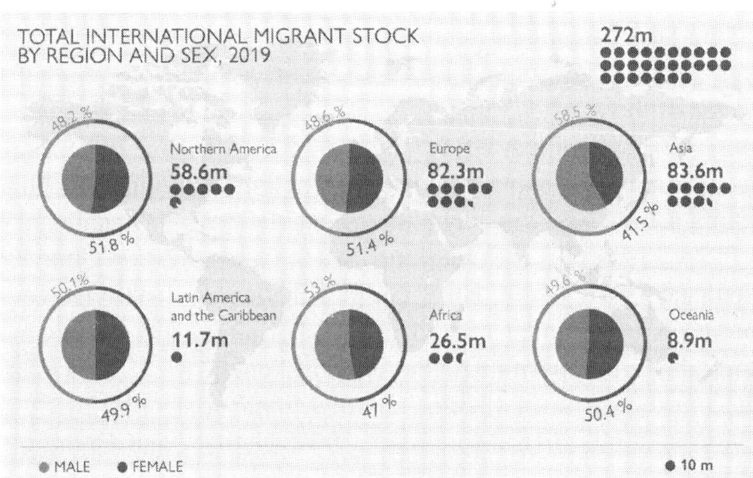

Figure 3.1: Gender and migration stock by region.

Source: Migration Data Portal via UN DESA 2019.

Many descriptions of political, religious, or any another form of persecution are necessarily subjective and culturally bounded (Dauvergne, 2012; Hernandez-Truyol and Johns, 1997; Molnar and Gill, 2018; Zúñiga and Hernández-León, 2005). This means that countries often prefer migrants that are more in line with the existing culture than those who come from parts of the world that are markedly different in terms of the way that they perceive, live, and behave (Brochmann and Hammar, 2020; Chavez, 2001; Chin, 1999; Cook, 2003; Cornelisse, 2004, 2010; Costello, 2012). The recent moves against migrants from Muslim-majority countries into Europe and North America reflect this trend of fearing the unfamiliar because it might possibly disrupt existing cultural norms (Sassen, 1996, 1997; Shohamy and McNamara, 2009; Smith, 2014; Soysal, 2012; Spijkerboer and Van Walsum, 2007). At the same time, there is public concern that migrants sometimes import their own prejudices (examples including sexism, homophobia, racism, religious intolerance, and xenophobia) into countries that like to consider themselves as open liberal democracies (Baldwin-Edwards, 2006; Bangarth, 2003; Barak-Erez, 2008; Becerra, 2016; Brané and Lundholm, 2007).

Several negative stereotypes have arisen surrounding asylum seekers (Dudley et al., 2012; Dunn, 2001, 2010; Exdell, 2009; Fiske, 2016; Flynn, 2013; Frederking, 2012; Gilman, 2013). Before they are granted full refugee status, they are often not allowed to work even though many of them would like to work and lead independent lives (Costello, 2012; Guia, Koulish, and Mitsilegas, 2016; Melis, 2001; Rubio-Marín, 2014; Webber, 2012). The communities in the receiving countries then use this as justification to label asylum seekers as welfare dependents that wish to take out of a system that they did not contribute to in a significant way (Cook, 2003; Cornelisse, 2004, 2010; Costello, 2012; Dauvergne, 2012; Den Heijer, 2010; Dudley et al., 2012). In the worst-case scenario, these anti-migrant stereotypes and language have inspired a violent backlash against migrants (Newman, Proctor, and Dudley, 2013; Oberman, 2016; Orfanos, 2019; Ozdowski, 1985; Paz, 2016; Peberdy, 2001). At other times, the backlash is in the form of harsh rules that target those that support migrants. There were times in which organizations that work with migrants could be prosecuted for aiding and abetting illegal immigrants (Ackerman and Furman, 2014; Adelman,

2002; Aynsley-Green et al., 2012; Bacon, 1996; Baldwin-Edwards, 2006). All these factors increase the vulnerabilities of asylum seekers and limit the options that they have for getting out of their predicament (Chin, 1999; Cook, 2003; Cornelisse, 2004, 2010; Costello, 2012; Dauvergne, 2012; Den Heijer, 2010; Dudley et al., 2012). The next section examines some of the patterns of immigration and their implications for policies on immigration management.

3.2. PATTERNED MIGRATION SEQUENCES AND HISTORIES

The patterning of migration can include time and spaces which are preferred by migrants over others (Gilman, 2013; Guia, Koulish, and Mitsilegas, 2016; Guild, 2001; Guild and Niessen, 1996; Hailbronner, 2000; Hayter, 2000). It can also cover the demographic characteristics and statuses of the migrants who are in the process of changing location (Soysal, 2012; Spijkerboer and Van Walsum, 2007; Taylor, 2000; Thym, 2008; Webber, 2012; Welch, 2002; Wexler, 2007). To rationalize the system and prevent abuse, there are specializations that are designed to deal with each pattern aspect of migration (Sampson, Mitchell, and Bowring, 2011; Sanggaran, Haire, and Zion, 2016; Sassen, 1996, 1997; Shohamy and McNamara, 2009). For example, the management of young asylum seekers from active warzones differs from the management of guest workers (Fiske, 2016; Flynn, 2013; Frederking, 2012; Gilman, 2013; Guia, Koulish, and Mitsilegas, 2016; Guild, 2001). As Figure 3.2 shows, OECD countries remain popular destinations because of their perceived affluence compared to developing countries. However, in the case of the United Arab Emirates (UAE), migrants can make up as much as 88% of the population and could therefore easily overturn existing politics if they were granted the right to vote. Whereas the USA accepts the most migrants (over 46 million per year according to some estimates), they make up only 14.5% of the population and can therefore be much more easily controlled.

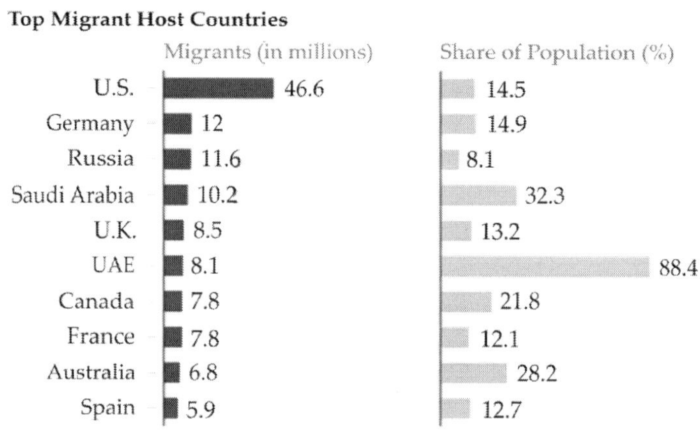

Figure 3.2: Popular host countries for migrant workers.

Source: US News and World Report.

In contemporary times, migration governance has necessarily become closely associated with state sovereignty because of the fear among nations that they could lose control over their population numbers (Exdell, 2009; Fiske, 2016; Flynn, 2013; Frederking, 2012; Gilman, 2013; Guia, Koulish, and Mitsilegas, 2016; Guild, 2001). Underpinning this protection of sovereignty is the fear that too many migrants might be able to change the course of a given nation without substantially contributing to it and not belonging to the citizenry (Gilman, 2013; Guia, Koulish, and Mitsilegas, 2016; Guild, 2001; Guild and Niessen, 1996; Hailbronner, 2000; Hayter, 2000). A case in point is the USA, where conservatives worry that the wholesale importation of South American immigrants will change the political landscape and turn it more leftwing. Part of the solution is to keep migrants in small enough numbers so that residents do not feel intimidated by their presence (Guia, Koulish, and Mitsilegas, 2016; Guild, 2001; Guild and Niessen, 1996; Hailbronner, 2000; Hayter, 2000; Heisler, 2000). An education and sensitization program might also be used to challenge some of the racist and xenophobic aspects of the prevailing immigration debates (Rubio-Marín, 2014; Ruhs, 2010; Ryan and Mitsilegas, 2010; Saadi et al., 2020; Samers, 2004; Sampson, Mitchell, and Bowring, 2011).

States retain the power of deciding on the entry and stay of non-nationals because migration directly affects some of the defining elements of a State (Adelman, 2002; Aynsley-Green et al., 2012; Bacon, 1996; Baldwin-Edwards, 2006; Bangarth, 2003; Barak-Erez, 2008). This is even truer of democratic and welfare states were the population size impacts on voting patterns as well as welfare entitlements (Motomura, 1999; Nethery and Holman, 2016; Newman, Proctor, and Dudley, 2013; Oberman, 2016; Orfanos, 2019). Many developed countries are already sounding the alarm on unfunded and ultimately unsustainable entitlements which are made that much more expensive by immigrants who are not officially allowed to work (Barak-Erez, 2008; Exdell, 2009; Joppke, 1998; Motomura, 1999; Sanggaran, Haire, and Zion, 2016). One of the policy options considered is that of denying new immigrants any welfare benefits or voting rights for a significant period before they are naturalized and can access them like other legal permanent residents (Bangarth, 2003; Dunn, 2010; Johnson, 1996; Morris, 2002; Sampson, Mitchell, and Bowring, 2011).

The challenge in that is that migrants take up other services such as housing, education, and health well beyond what the original plans were for the local citizenry (Guild, 2001; Guild and Niessen, 1996; Hailbronner, 2000; Hayter, 2000; Heisler, 2000; Hernandez-Truyol and Johns, 1997). Besides, migrants may not be denied certain services such as health on humanitarian grounds (Mehan, 1997; Melis, 2001; Miller, 2015, 2016; Molnar and Gill, 2018; Money, 1998; Morris, 2002, 2016). In the end, many states have just accepted the "cat and mouse" game of trying to prevent, catch, and return migrants (Dunn, 2001, 2010; Exdell, 2009; Fiske, 2016; Flynn, 2013; Frederking, 2012; Gilman, 2013; Guia, Koulish, and Mitsilegas, 2016). Meanwhile, unscrupulous elements are exploiting the system to traffic migrants and even assist them in maintaining an irregular stay (Hernandez-Truyol and Johns, 1997; Hollifield, Martin, and Orrenius, 2014; Jacobson, 1996; Johnson, 1996; Joppke, 1998). It has been suggested that a better way of stemming the tide is to target those who facilitate migration to put them out of business (Acer and Goodman, 2009; Chavez, 2001; Guild and Niessen, 1996; King, 2009; Ozdowski, 1985; Shohamy and McNamara, 2009). Alternatively, the migration crisis can be tackled from the source by discouraging rogue regimes that mismanage economies and persecute their citizenry (Morris, 2002, 2016; Motomura, 1999; Nethery and Holman, 2016; Newman, Proctor, and Dudley, 2013; Oberman, 2016).

Depending on the goal and reason for relocation, persons who migrate can be divided into three categories: migrants, refugees, and asylum seekers (Molnar and Gill, 2018; Money, 1998; Morris, 2002, 2016; Motomura, 1999; Nethery and Holman, 2016). Each category is defined broadly as the mixed circumstances might occur and motivate a person to change their location (Smith, 2014; Soysal, 2012; Spijkerboer and Van Walsum, 2007; Taylor,

2000; Thym, 2008; Webber, 2012; Welch, 2002). In the traditional sense, migrants are traditionally described as persons who change the country of their residence for general reasons and purposes (Lopez, 2005; Lorentzen, 2014; Mehan, 1997; Melis, 2001; Miller, 2015, 2016; Molnar and Gill, 2018; Money, 1998). Over time, this definition has become sophisticated enough to account for different motivations for immigration such as health tourism (Brané and Lundholm, 2007; Brochmann and Hammar, 2020; Chavez, 2001; Chin, 1999; Cook, 2003; Cornelisse, 2004). The definitions not only categorize the migrants, but also implicitly prescribe some of the ways that they may be treated (Soysal, 2012; Spijkerboer and Van Walsum, 2007; Taylor, 2000; Thym, 2008; Webber, 2012; Welch, 2002; Wexler, 2007). For example, tourists are welcome guests, but asylum seekers are treated as burdensome charity cases (Kasimis, 2012; Kelson and DeLaet, 1999; King, 2009; Lopez, 2005; Lorentzen, 2014; Mehan, 1997; Melis, 2001; Miller, 2015).

The definition of migrants may also be overtaken by local prejudices against race and class (Kelson and DeLaet, 1999; King, 2009; Lopez, 2005; Lorentzen, 2014; Mehan, 1997; Melis, 2001; Miller, 2015, 2016). For example, in South Africa, poor black immigrants from the rest of Africa are perceived to be problematic scroungers that take away the jobs that ought to belong to the indigenous people (Guild, 2001; Miller, 2016; Ryan and Mitsilegas, 2010; Wexler, 2007; Wilcox, 2009). However, wealth white immigrants are referred to as expatriates and tourists that are necessary for the economic development of South Africa (Chavez, 2001; Chin, 1999; Cook, 2003; Cornelisse, 2004, 2010; Costello, 2012; Dauvergne, 2012; Den Heijer, 2010). This represents a paradox in a country that has had a long history of a white minority government oppressing the black majority based on race.

These perceptions may not be borne out by reality, but they have real impacts on the reception that various migrants receive when they arrive on the shores of a foreign country (Molnar and Gill, 2018; Money, 1998; Morris, 2002, 2016; Motomura, 1999; Nethery and Holman, 2016). Indeed, recently a president of the USA was elected on a platform of anti-migrant sentiment and actions. However, they are other powerful incentives for anti-immigrant sentiments (Bangarth, 2003; Barak-Erez, 2008; Becerra, 2016; Brané and Lundholm, 2007; Brochmann and Hammar, 2020; Chavez, 2001). The issues can also act as a wedge issue that ensures immigrants cannot organize together as a vulnerable group (Aynsley-Green et al., 2012; Bacon, 1996; Baldwin-Edwards, 2006; Bangarth, 2003; Barak-Erez, 2008;

Becerra, 2016). Moreover, the policy framework for welcoming immigrants will fail if the local population does not accept the premises under which such programs are run (Brochmann and Hammar, 2020; Chavez, 2001; Chin, 1999; Cook, 2003; Cornelisse, 2004, 2010; Costello, 2012). One of the merging problems is where migrants perceive their own unique personalized identities as precluding them from joining the wider migrant support groups. Those that do not wish for any migration to be allowed will exploit these divisions to ensure that no immigrant group is treated well.

Some scholars have argued that anti-immigrant sentiment is born out of intellectual incuriosity and the desire for simplistic solutions. It is much easier to define immigrants as the "undesirable other" than to describe the potential benefits that migrants bring to a community (Welch, 2002; Wexler, 2007; Wilcox, 2009; Zúñiga and Hernández-León, 2005; Zwi and Mares, 2015). The circumstances under which people migrate may also impact on their behavior (Baldwin-Edwards, 2006; Dunn, 2001; Jacobson, 1996; Morris, 2016; Samers, 2004). For example, refugees are usually associated with people who must unwillingly relocate as fast as possible (Ozdowski, 1985; Paz, 2016; Peberdy, 2001; Ramji-Nogales, 2007; Rubio-Marín, 2014; Ruhs, 2010; Ryan and Mitsilegas, 2010). Hence, such migrants will likely relocate undocumented and will be fearful of government agencies (Becerra, 2016; Brané and Lundholm, 2007; Brochmann and Hammar, 2020; Chavez, 2001; Chin, 1999; Cook, 2003). One of the worst things that can happen to them is to be handed back to their home countries with an alert that they have ever claimed asylum (Morris, 2002, 2016; Motomura, 1999; Nethery and Holman, 2016; Newman, Proctor, and Dudley, 2013; Oberman, 2016). There are countries that have been accused of pursuing refugees right up to their destination countries to assassinate them or take some other revenge on them (Samers, 2004; Sampson, Mitchell, and Bowring, 2011; Sanggaran, Haire, and Zion, 2016; Sassen, 1996, 1997).

Asylum seekers are associated with persons who leave their country unwillingly, yet there is an assumption that many (if not all) of asylum seekers are seeking a better life (Sampson, Mitchell, and Bowring, 2011; Sanggaran, Haire, and Zion, 2016; Sassen, 1996, 1997; Shohamy and McNamara, 2009). In some instances, asylum seekers have left comfortable lives and are forced to start again in a new country where they are treated with disdain as well as a host of other forms of discrimination (Money, 1998; Morris, 2002, 2016; Motomura, 1999; Nethery and Holman, 2016; Newman, Proctor, and Dudley, 2013). To transition from an asylum seeker into a bona fide refugee, someone must show that they left their homeland under oppressing circumstances such as war or death threats (Hernandez-Truyol and Johns, 1997; Hollifield, Martin, and Orrenius, 2014; Jacobson, 1996; Johnson, 1996; Joppke, 1998). This requires undergoing an intimidating immigration interview in which the first instinct of the interview is to disbelieve the interviewee (Smith, 2014; Soysal, 2012; Spijkerboer and Van Walsum, 2007; Taylor, 2000; Thym, 2008; Webber, 2012; Welch, 2002). Others are subjected to humiliating tests of credibility which border on the violation of their rights (Barak-Erez, 2008; Becerra, 2016; Brané and Lundholm, 2007; Brochmann and Hammar, 2020; Chavez, 2001; Chin, 1999).

The motivation to leave the country for asylum seekers might involve an unstable economic or political situation in the country. Others may decide to migrate to move away from high rates of crime in their home communities (Joppke, 1998, 1999, 2010; Kasimis, 2012; Kelson and DeLaet, 1999; King, 2009; Lopez, 2005; Lorentzen, 2014). Thus, asylum seekers relocate predominantly to escape the degradation of the quality of their lives, a natural desire among human beings and even animals (Brochmann and Hammar, 2020; Chavez, 2001; Chin, 1999; Cook, 2003; Cornelisse, 2004, 2010). Nevertheless, upon arrival asylum seekers may face further degradation as they are considered with suspicion and even fear (Frederking, 2012; Gilman, 2013; Guia, Koulish, and Mitsilegas, 2016; Guild, 2001; Guild and Niessen, 1996; Hailbronner, 2000).

It is also important to consider the trauma that asylum seekers may have gone through prior to and during their journey (Cornelisse, 2004, 2010; Costello, 2012; Dauvergne, 2012; Den Heijer, 2010; Dudley et al., 2012; Dunn, 2001). For example, women who are victims of domestic violence or gender-based violence may be unwilling to tell the entirety of their story for fear and shame (Dauvergne, 2012; Den Heijer, 2010; Dudley et al., 2012; Dunn, 2001, 2010; Exdell, 2009; Fiske, 2016; Flynn, 2013). Yet, the authorities may require a detailed account of the person's experience to ascertain the veracity of their claim (Hailbronner, 2000; Hayter, 2000; Heisler, 2000; Hernandez-Truyol and Johns, 1997; Hollifield, Martin, and Orrenius, 2014). Besides, the assessor may rely on country reports that are either inaccurate or do not adequately cover the exact issues that the person is facing (Oberman, 2016; Orfanos, 2019; Ozdowski, 1985; Paz, 2016; Peberdy, 2001; Ramji-Nogales, 2007; Rubio-Marín, 2014).

There are other migrations that do not fit into the traditional asylum process, a case in point being nomadic movements. These nomadic movements are normally not regarded as migrations under international and national immigration law (Kasimis, 2012; Kelson and DeLaet, 1999; King, 2009; Lopez, 2005; Lorentzen, 2014; Mehan, 1997; Melis, 2001; Miller, 2015). This is because the movement is generally seasonal and that means that the travelers may soon return to their homes or move on to other places (Spijkerboer and Van Walsum, 2007; Taylor, 2000; Thym, 2008; Webber, 2012; Welch, 2002; Wexler, 2007; Wilcox, 2009). In fact, research has shown that in seasonal migration, there is no intention to settle in the new place at all. Instead, the nomads are looking for access to seasonal natural resources such as grass and water (Guild and Niessen, 1996; Hailbronner, 2000; Hayter, 2000; Heisler, 2000; Hernandez-Truyol and Johns, 1997). However, only a few people have retained this form of lifestyle in modern times and therefore it cannot be included in the types of migrations that have the potential to fundamentally transform a nation (Ramji-Nogales, 2007; Rubio-Marín, 2014; Ruhs, 2010; Ryan and Mitsilegas, 2010; Saadi et al., 2020; Samers, 2004).

Nevertheless, seasonal migrants can be damaging to the economy as well as the living standards of the local community (Motomura, 1999; Nethery and Holman, 2016; Newman, Proctor, and Dudley, 2013; Oberman, 2016; Orfanos, 2019). For example, in rural areas the entrance of nomads with their cattle can bring diseases and deforestation which makes it difficult to engage in further agricultural activities (Johnson, 1996; Joppke, 1998, 1999, 2010; Kasimis, 2012; Kelson and DeLaet, 1999; King, 2009; Lopez, 2005). Other nomads can become unruly and engage in criminal behavior, which breaks down the fabric of society. They do this knowing that they are not likely to be staying for long in any given place where they can be apprehended. In other words, the nomads become a lawless community (Fiske, 2016; Flynn, 2013; Frederking, 2012; Gilman, 2013; Guia, Koulish, and Mitsilegas, 2016; Guild, 2001).

At the same time, nomadic herders may be discriminated against by local communities who consider them to be a nuisance (Brané and Lundholm, 2007; Flynn, 2013; Joppke, 2010; Newman, Proctor, and Dudley, 2013; Sassen, 1997). This can lead to social exclusion and a failure to integrate within the local community (Webber, 2012; Welch, 2002; Wexler, 2007; Wilcox, 2009; Zúñiga and Hernández-León, 2005; Zwi and Mares, 2015). There have been reports of nomads that do not respect the national borders of the countries that they visit. Such patterns of migration can cause problems with maintaining a national migration policy (Brochmann and Hammar, 2020; Frederking, 2012; Kasimis, 2012; Oberman, 2016; Taylor, 2000). Hence, each year they can travel across two or even three countries without going through the normal immigration checks, not least because it would take an inordinate number of resources to do all these checks successfully (Guia, Koulish, and Mitsilegas, 2016; Guild, 2001; Guild and Niessen, 1996; Hailbronner, 2000; Hayter, 2000; Heisler, 2000).

Temporary movement for the purpose of certain activities such as travel, pilgrimages, tourism, or the work commute is also not regarded as migration in normal circumstances (Costello, 2012; Dauvergne, 2012; Den Heijer, 2010; Dudley et al., 2012; Dunn, 2001, 2010; Exdell, 2009; Fiske, 2016). This is because there is an absence of an intention to live and settle in the visited places; the implication being that this type of migration is unlikely to fundamentally change the host community (Cornelisse, 2010; Gilman, 2013; Kelson and DeLaet, 1999; Orfanos, 2019; Thym, 2008). At the same time, there is recognition of the importance of such travelers because they can stay for a significant period or may change their status over time. Moreover, such travelers may even contribute to the economy through their repeated visits (Joppke, 1999, 2010; Kasimis, 2012; Kelson and DeLaet, 1999; King, 2009; Lopez, 2005; Lorentzen, 2014; Mehan, 1997). The state must balance the need to control immigration and to bring in new people to replenish and invigorate the population in the area under its control (Orfanos, 2019; Ozdowski, 1985; Paz, 2016; Peberdy, 2001; Ramji-Nogales, 2007; Rubio-Marín, 2014; Ruhs, 2010).

The issuance of temporary movement visas can be a way to assess the capabilities of the person to contribute to their adopted home. It also opens the possibility of policy modifications after data comes in about the settlement process of migrants (Sanggaran, Haire, and Zion, 2016; Sassen, 1996, 1997; Shohamy and McNamara, 2009; Smith, 2014). Such visas can also be granted as an interim measure that acts as a regularization step for the migrants. This happens before full status can be confirmed after verifying the information that is being provided by the applicant (Jacobson, 1996; Johnson, 1996; Joppke, 1998, 1999, 2010; Kasimis, 2012; Kelson and DeLaet, 1999). In this way, the migration policy is seen to be humane and flexible in as far as it reflects the realities of the circumstances in which migrants find themselves. The next section introduces some formal typologies of migration.

3.3. TYPOLOGIES OF MIGRATION

Over time, several typologies of migration patterns and modalities have emerged. These have been explored and accepted in mainstream literature. The typologies are used to better describe the unique patterns of groups of migrants and the specific ways in which they travel (Miller, 2015, 2016; Molnar and Gill, 2018; Money, 1998; Morris, 2002, 2016; Motomura, 1999). Initially, there are two broad categories that had been traditionally acknowledged in existing literature (Thym, 2008; Webber, 2012; Welch, 2002; Wexler, 2007; Wilcox, 2009; Zúñiga and Hernández-León, 2005; Zwi and Mares, 2015). The first category is that of voluntary migration. Under this modality, the migrant opts (of their own free will in most cases) to change geographical location on a semi-permanent or permanent basis (Sassen, 1996, 1997; Shohamy and McNamara, 2009; Smith, 2014; Soysal, 2012; Spijkerboer and Van Walsum, 2007). Sometimes voluntary migration can focus on specific areas, such as the increasing presence of migrant workers in Shanghai in order to meet skill labor demand (see Figure 3.3 for an illustration of the gradual increments from 1993 to 2000).

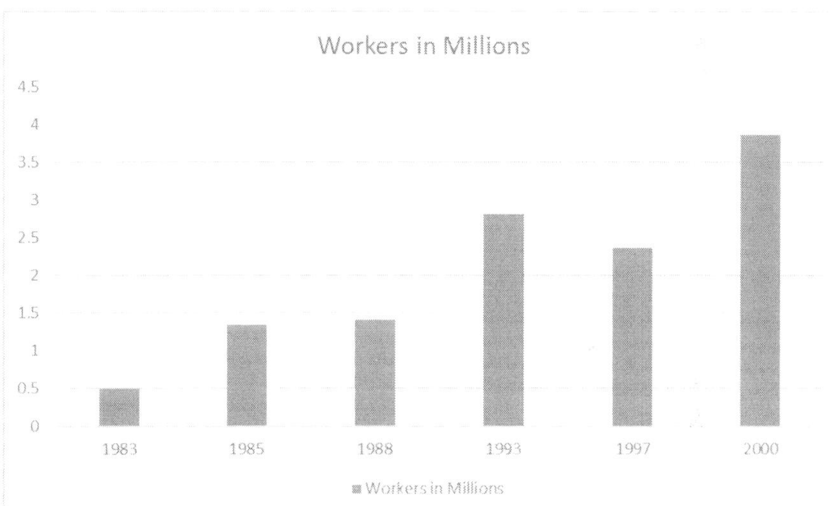

Figure 3.3: Migrant workers in Shanghai 1983 to 2000.

Source: Open Edition Journals.

The second broad category is that of forced immigration in which the person is forced by circumstances beyond their control to change their geographical location on a semi-permanent or permanent basis (Hayter, 2000; Heisler, 2000; Hernandez-Truyol and Johns, 1997; Hollifield, Martin, and Orrenius, 2014; Jacobson, 1996). In most cases, involuntary migrants are welcomed using a human rights approach. This contrasts with the approach that is used for voluntary migrants who are required to undergo a series of political, economic, and social limitation criterion before they can be allowed into the country (Costello, 2012; Dauvergne, 2012; Den Heijer, 2010; Dudley et al., 2012; Dunn, 2001, 2010; Exdell, 2009; Fiske, 2016). Nevertheless, there are international protections that are meant to prevent the abuse of the system. A case in point is how international law forbids the forced repatriation of involuntary migrants if it can be shown that they have a well-founded fear of persecution (Ryan and Mitsilegas, 2010; Saadi et al., 2020; Samers, 2004; Sampson, Mitchell, and Bowring, 2011; Sanggaran, Haire, and Zion, 2016). There are challenges in distinguishing voluntary and involuntary migration, a problem that leads to significant delays in making a final determination (Joppke, 1999, 2010; Kasimis, 2012; Kelson and DeLaet, 1999; King, 2009; Lopez, 2005; Lorentzen, 2014; Mehan, 1997). For example, some of the assessors point out the fact that although life may be harsh under the persecuting regime at home; the application has the option of moving to another place within the country or even masking their identity to avoid detection (Exdell, 2009; Fiske, 2016; Flynn, 2013; Frederking, 2012; Gilman, 2013; Guia, Koulish, and Mitsilegas, 2016; Guild, 2001).

For the most part, all these are huddles meant to stem the tide of voluntary migration to a few selection premium destinations in Europe and North America (Becerra, 2016; Brané and Lundholm, 2007; Brochmann and Hammar, 2020; Chavez, 2001; Chin, 1999; Cook, 2003). The rationale is that if the application process is sufficiently challenging, those that have an idea of exploiting it will be stopped before they can even try to come to the desirable destination (Dunn, 2010; Exdell, 2009; Fiske, 2016; Flynn, 2013; Frederking, 2012; Gilman, 2013; Guia, Koulish, and Mitsilegas, 2016). The reality is that the choice of destination or even migration modality can be very complex and there are many reasons that might still pull or pull people towards a particular destination. That is why all the restrictions that are increasingly being put in place have not sufficiently deterred people from migrating to Europe and North America (King, 2009; Lopez, 2005; Lorentzen, 2014; Mehan, 1997; Melis, 2001; Miller, 2015, 2016; Molnar and Gill, 2018).

The status of the immigrant can change along the way, and this complicates the classifications that are attached to them for purposes of implementing government policy. For example, there are certain bona fide refugees who come on tourists' visas and leave as soon as the situation at home is calmer (Lopez, 2005; Lorentzen, 2014; Mehan, 1997; Melis, 2001; Miller, 2015, 2016; Molnar and Gill, 2018; Money, 1998). Others are economic migrants that can secure asylum through the provision of fictitious stories of persecution (Den Heijer, 2010; Miller, 2015; Ruhs, 2010;

Welch, 2002; Zwi and Mares, 2015). Those that are making assessments are therefore faced with the daunting task of deciding which applicant to believe and which not to believe (Miller, 2015, 2016; Molnar and Gill, 2018; Money, 1998; Morris, 2002, 2016; Motomura, 1999; Nethery and Holman, 2016). As we shall see later in the book, this can turn into an immigration lottery in which the ultimate decision varies considerably depending on the assessor (and presumably, their prejudices).

The distinction between involuntary (such as fleeing political conflict or natural disaster) on one hand and voluntary migration (such as economic or labor migration) on the other is difficult to make (Kelson and DeLaet, 1999; King, 2009; Lopez, 2005; Lorentzen, 2014; Mehan, 1997; Melis, 2001; Miller, 2015, 2016). It is partially subjective in terms of perceiving and interpreting experiences of migration (Dauvergne, 2012; Hernandez-Truyol and Johns, 1997; Molnar and Gill, 2018; Zúñiga and Hernández-León, 2005). That creates problems when trying to develop standard markers for each category since there can be an obvious overlap (Hailbronner, 2000; Hayter, 2000; Heisler, 2000; Hernandez-Truyol and Johns, 1997; Hollifield, Martin, and Orrenius, 2014). One of the key issues is the fact that the motivators for migration are often correlated (Hollifield, Martin, and Orrenius, 2014; Jacobson, 1996; Johnson, 1996; Joppke, 1998, 1999, 2010; Kasimis, 2012). Despite this, there are specific trends that hold regardless of locations. For example, it is estimated that under 4% of the world population is a migrant and that figure has remained fairly constant since the 1970s (Taylor, 2000; Thym, 2008; Webber, 2012; Welch, 2002; Wexler, 2007; Wilcox, 2009; Zúñiga and Hernández-León, 2005). This is despite the constant anti-migrant rhetoric which suggests that many countries are being flooded with new and old migrants (Wexler, 2007; Wilcox, 2009; Zúñiga and Hernández-León, 2005; Zwi and Mares, 2015).

There is an aversion to those that migrate because they have chosen to. This is more so if that change of location is permanent. However, if they are only temporary visitors, then the likelihood is that they will be welcomed as tourists. Voluntary migration is based on the initiative and the free will of the person (Brané and Lundholm, 2007; Brochmann and Hammar, 2020; Chavez, 2001; Chin, 1999; Cook, 2003; Cornelisse, 2004). However, that decision is influenced by a combination of factors which may reduce the agency of the person in deciding whether to uproot their lives and move away or not (Taylor, 2000; Thym, 2008; Webber, 2012; Welch, 2002; Wexler, 2007; Wilcox, 2009; Zúñiga and Hernández-León, 2005; Zwi and Mares, 2015). These factors are complex across the economic, political, and social spheres (Baldwin-Edwards, 2006; Bangarth, 2003; Barak-Erez, 2008; Becerra, 2016; Brané and Lundholm, 2007).

The determinants of immigration can occur in the migrants` country of origin. Such factors are referred to as determinant factors or "push factors" (Saadi et al., 2020; Samers, 2004; Sampson, Mitchell, and Bowring, 2011; Sanggaran, Haire, and Zion, 2016; Sassen, 1996). Alternatively, the motivations for migration can occur in the country of destination. Such factors are known as attraction factors or "pull factors" (Heisler, 2000; Hernandez-Truyol and Johns, 1997; Hollifield, Martin, and Orrenius, 2014; Jacobson, 1996; Johnson, 1996). The problem with the current consensus on migration policy is the focus on pull factors and hence trying to make it very difficult to move to certain countries (Miller, 2015, 2016; Molnar and Gill, 2018; Money, 1998; Morris, 2002, 2016; Motomura, 1999). Meanwhile, the push factors are ignored despite the possibility that they can be incredibly powerful motivators for migrants (Newman, Proctor, and Dudley, 2013; Oberman, 2016; Orfanos, 2019; Ozdowski, 1985; Paz, 2016; Peberdy, 2001).

"Push-pull factors" are the reasons that push or attract people to a particular place during their migration journey or cycle (Welch, 2002; Wexler, 2007; Wilcox, 2009; Zúñiga and Hernández-León, 2005; Zwi and Mares, 2015). It is assumed that making certain places less attractive to immigrants will reduce the flow of immigration (Ruhs, 2010; Ryan and Mitsilegas, 2010; Saadi et al., 2020; Samers, 2004; Sampson, Mitchell, and Bowring, 2011). However, that is not always the case because there may be migrants that are determined to reach a particular destination (Heisler, 2000; Hernandez-Truyol and Johns, 1997; Hollifield, Martin, and Orrenius, 2014; Jacobson, 1996; Johnson, 1996). We have seen this in the form of migrants from Sub-Saharan Africa that are willing to risk death to get to Europe via the sea on illegal boat rides (Guild, 2001; Miller, 2016; Ryan and Mitsilegas, 2010; Wexler, 2007; Wilcox, 2009). In fact, the creation of the so-called "Fortress Europe" has ended up making it a premium destination for economic migrants who believe that they will be able to get job opportunities if they can land on specific shores (Ryan and Mitsilegas, 2010; Saadi et al., 2020; Samers, 2004; Sampson, Mitchell, and Bowring, 2011; Sanggaran, Haire, and Zion, 2016).

Those that make and implement policy may fail to recognize their own contribution to the migration crises that periodically arise in the most developed nations on earth. For example, the ultimate destination may be Western Europe because of easier communication and family ties (Lorentzen,

2014; Mehan, 1997; Melis, 2001; Miller, 2015, 2016; Molnar and Gill, 2018; Money, 1998; Morris, 2016). That means that even when people get to some parts of Europe, it could only be a stopgap until they reach their destination (Costello, 2012; Guia, Koulish, and Mitsilegas, 2016; Melis, 2001; Rubio-Marín, 2014; Webber, 2012). These patterns have created tensions within the union and partly led to the cessation of the United Kingdom (Costello, 2012; Dauvergne, 2012; Den Heijer, 2010; Dudley et al., 2012; Dunn, 2001, 2010; Exdell, 2009). Those countries that were colonial powers must contend with the reality that they are likely to receive more of migrants from the impoverished former colonies.

"Push" factors are the negative aspects of the country of origin which make it difficult or unsustainable for that person to remain in that country for an extended period (Chavez, 2001; Chin, 1999; Cook, 2003; Cornelisse, 2004, 2010; Costello, 2012; Dauvergne, 2012; Den Heijer, 2010). These push factors are often decisive in people's choice to emigrate. One reason for such decisiveness is the fact that they have a significant impact on the health and wellbeing of the person (Shohamy and McNamara, 2009; Smith, 2014; Soysal, 2012; Spijkerboer and Van Walsum, 2007; Taylor, 2000; Thym, 2008). Push factors are much more difficult to control from the perspective of the receiving country. They are unlike the "pull" factors which are the positive aspects of a different country that encourages people to emigrate in search of a better life (Melis, 2001; Miller, 2015, 2016; Molnar and Gill, 2018; Money, 1998; Morris, 2002, 2016; Motomura, 1999). Although the push-pull factors are apparently diametrically opposed, both are sides of the same coin and are thus treated in literature as being equally important (Bacon, 1996; Baldwin-Edwards, 2006; Bangarth, 2003; Barak-Erez, 2008; Becerra, 2016; Brané and Lundholm, 2007). However, from a policy perspective, receiving countries tend to focus on the pull factors that are well within their control such as creating a hostile asylum and immigration process (Bacon, 1996; Dudley et al., 2012; Hollifield, Martin, and Orrenius, 2014; Money, 1998; Saadi et al., 2020).

Although specific to forced migration, any other harmful factor can be considered a "push factor" or determinant or trigger factor for someone to change their geographical location on a permanent or semi-permanent basis (Joppke, 2010; Kasimis, 2012; Kelson and DeLaet, 1999; King, 2009; Lopez, 2005; Lorentzen, 2014; Mehan, 1997). There are known examples such as excessive pollution, a poor quality of life, hunger, drought, lack of jobs, and other natural disasters that shows no positive signs of improvement in the near future (Kasimis, 2012; Kelson and DeLaet, 1999; King, 2009;

Lopez, 2005; Lorentzen, 2014; Mehan, 1997; Melis, 2001). Ideally, the sending country should be able to deal with or mitigate these undesirable systems through a well-organized social support system (Hollifield, Martin, and Orrenius, 2014; Jacobson, 1996; Johnson, 1996; Joppke, 1998, 1999, 2010; Kasimis, 2012). However, in the developing world that are simply not enough resources to be able to deal with the multitude of serious social problems (Flynn, 2013; Frederking, 2012; Gilman, 2013; Guia, Koulish, and Mitsilegas, 2016; Guild, 2001; Guild and Niessen, 1996). Such conditions represent decisive reasons for voluntary migration and may even make the emigres desperate to escape their current existence (Acer and Goodman, 2009; Chavez, 2001; Guild and Niessen, 1996; King, 2009; Ozdowski, 1985; Shohamy and McNamara, 2009). That is why the developing world is facing a problem of an educated and perhaps potentially affluent segment population preferring to migrate to prevent financially unfavorable situations or even emotional and physical suffering if they were to remain in their home countries (Dunn, 2010; Exdell, 2009; Fiske, 2016; Flynn, 2013; Frederking, 2012; Gilman, 2013; Guia, Koulish, and Mitsilegas, 2016).

Those who successfully migrate will come back with stories of their success or may even have visible examples of their ability to send remittances (Saadi et al., 2020; Samers, 2004; Sampson, Mitchell, and Bowring, 2011; Sanggaran, Haire, and Zion, 2016). Such reports and evidence will then become a pull factor and encourage those that are still at home to seek new pastures (Saadi et al., 2020; Samers, 2004; Sampson, Mitchell, and Bowring, 2011; Sanggaran, Haire, and Zion, 2016; Sassen, 1996). Developing countries are not always attuned to the implications of having a significant part of their most dynamic populations moving abroad (Becerra, 2016; Fiske, 2016; Joppke, 1999; Nethery and Holman, 2016; Sassen, 1996). These migrants represent resourceful and sometimes well-educated people that would otherwise have contributed to the development of their homelands (Paz, 2016; Peberdy, 2001; Ramji-Nogales, 2007; Rubio-Marín, 2014; Ruhs, 2010; Ryan and Mitsilegas, 2010; Saadi et al., 2020). At the international level, there is social injustice which means that the prospects of developing countries attaining full industrialization within the next 50 years is very dim (Nethery and Holman, 2016; Newman, Proctor, and Dudley, 2013; Oberman, 2016; Orfanos, 2019; Ozdowski, 1985). Indeed, issues such as unfair trade ensure that these developing countries are trapped in a cycle of poverty (Spijkerboer and Van Walsum, 2007; Taylor, 2000; Thym, 2008; Webber, 2012; Welch, 2002; Wexler, 2007; Wilcox, 2009). Meanwhile, the developed countries make valiant efforts to stop the flow of people looking for greener pastures, so to speak (Acer and Goodman, 2009; Ackerman and Furman, 2014; Adelman, 2002; Aynsley-Green et al., 2012; Bacon, 1996).

In international law, there is special consideration for those that migrate because they have been forced to do so (Den Heijer, 2010; Dudley et al., 2012; Dunn, 2001, 2010; Exdell, 2009; Fiske, 2016; Flynn, 2013; Frederking, 2012). The rationale is that these people are traveling because of circumstances beyond their control (Adelman, 2002; Cook, 2003; Hayter, 2000; Lorentzen, 2014; Peberdy, 2001; Soysal, 2012). That means that there is a moral and practical imperative to give them sanctuary (Cook, 2003; Cornelisse, 2004, 2010; Costello, 2012; Dauvergne, 2012; Den Heijer, 2010; Dudley et al., 2012). The challenge then becomes distinguishing economic migrants who travel of their own volition from those that are forced to do so (Bacon, 1996; Dudley et al., 2012; Hollifield, Martin, and Orrenius, 2014; Money, 1998; Saadi et al., 2020). In any case, the push factors can in of themselves be somewhat ambiguous (Hayter, 2000; Heisler, 2000; Hernandez-Truyol and Johns, 1997; Hollifield, Martin, and Orrenius, 2014; Jacobson, 1996). For example, someone may have to migrate because of biting poverty (Adelman, 2002; Cook, 2003; Hayter, 2000; Lorentzen, 2014; Peberdy, 2001; Soysal, 2012). This is not listed as an admissible reason under the asylum rules. However, it is definitely a push factor that inspires many people to move away even if they would otherwise stay at home (Aynsley-Green et al., 2012; Cornelisse, 2004; Heisler, 2000; Mehan, 1997; Ramji-Nogales, 2007; Spijkerboer and Van Walsum, 2007). Unfortunately, immigration controls do not pay enough attention to these subtleties and therefore end up painting a very broad brush (Melis, 2001; Miller, 2015, 2016; Molnar and Gill, 2018; Money, 1998; Morris, 2002, 2016; Motomura, 1999). That renders the overall immigration control framework rather ineffective (Dudley et al., 2012; Dunn, 2001, 2010; Exdell, 2009; Fiske, 2016; Flynn, 2013; Frederking, 2012; Gilman, 2013).

There exist contested definitions of forced migration which have policy implications in terms of the reception that is given to various categories of travelers when they arrive on the borders of the receiving country (Wexler, 2007; Wilcox, 2009; Zúñiga and Hernández-León, 2005; Zwi and Mares, 2015). As seen in the example of poverty above, many countries consider this to be the exclusive responsibility of the individual and their home country even if there are international efforts to reduce poverty generally (Baldwin-Edwards, 2006; Bangarth, 2003; Barak-Erez, 2008; Becerra, 2016; Brané and Lundholm, 2007; Brochmann and Hammar, 2020). It is therefore very hard to sustain a claim for sanctuary based on poverty alone (Ozdowski,

1985; Paz, 2016; Peberdy, 2001; Ramji-Nogales, 2007; Rubio-Marín, 2014; Ruhs, 2010; Ryan and Mitsilegas, 2010). The disputes about what forced migration really is have seeped into academia and research (Shohamy and McNamara, 2009; Smith, 2014; Soysal, 2012; Spijkerboer and Van Walsum, 2007; Taylor, 2000; Thym, 2008). For instance, qualitative studies focus on the unique experiences of migration rather than taking on a reductivist approach that attempts to generalize about migrants (Den Heijer, 2010; Dudley et al., 2012; Dunn, 2001, 2010; Exdell, 2009; Fiske, 2016; Flynn, 2013; Frederking, 2012). In contrast, quantitative studies attempt to make inferences about general immigration patterns based on sample behavior from selected and representative migrants (Sassen, 1996, 1997; Shohamy and McNamara, 2009; Smith, 2014; Soysal, 2012; Spijkerboer and Van Walsum, 2007). Invariably, these assumptions are not fully supported by empirical evidence (Nethery and Holman, 2016; Newman, Proctor, and Dudley, 2013; Oberman, 2016; Orfanos, 2019; Ozdowski, 1985). The next section examines the theoretical basis for migration.

3.4. THEORETICAL BASIS FOR MIGRATION

Several contemporary labor migration theories have emerged to describe, explain, and predict the movement of people from one place to another (King, 2009; Lopez, 2005; Lorentzen, 2014; Mehan, 1997; Melis, 2001; Miller, 2015, 2016; Molnar and Gill, 2018). Numerous causes impel migrants to move to another country, despite the relative security of living in one's own community with familiar people (Bangarth, 2003; Dunn, 2010; Johnson, 1996; Morris, 2002; Sampson, Mitchell, and Bowring, 2011). For instance, globalization has increased the demand for workers to sustain national economies. This means that migrants are needed for specific sectors in various parts of the world (Cornelisse, 2010; Costello, 2012; Dauvergne, 2012; Den Heijer, 2010; Dudley et al., 2012; Dunn, 2001, 2010). There are important economic imperatives that support the use of migrant labor, although these are often ignored in popular debates about immigration (Den Heijer, 2010; Miller, 2015; Ruhs, 2010; Welch, 2002; Zwi and Mares, 2015). As the case of Chinese migrant workers shows (see Figure 3.4), economic migrants face significant vulnerabilities even if they may have decided to voluntarily change location.

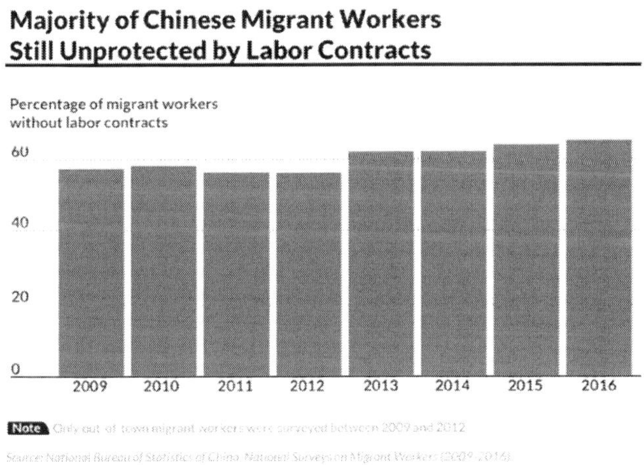

Figure 3.4: Low protection for Chinese migrant workers 2009 to 2016.

Source: Sixth Tone (Liu Chang).

There exists a category of economic migrants who have been the subject of harsh and restrictive enforcement (Guild and Niessen, 1996; Hailbronner, 2000; Hayter, 2000; Heisler, 2000; Hernandez-Truyol and Johns, 1997). These migrants are generally from impoverished developing countries with poor or nonexistent social support systems (Rubio-Marín, 2014; Ruhs, 2010; Ryan and Mitsilegas, 2010; Saadi et al., 2020; Samers, 2004; Sampson, Mitchell, and Bowring, 2011). Such people are ambitious and dynamic to the extent that they can perceive immigration as a way out of their unsatisfactory present circumstances (Dunn, 2001, 2010; Exdell, 2009; Fiske, 2016; Flynn, 2013; Frederking, 2012; Gilman, 2013; Guia, Koulish, and Mitsilegas, 2016). Such a person migrates to obtain sufficient income for survival and also to better themselves for the future (Becerra, 2016; Fiske, 2016; Joppke, 1999; Nethery and Holman, 2016; Sassen, 1996). These migrants often send some of their income home to family members in the form of economic remittances once they are sufficiently settled and obtained gainful employment (Ackerman and Furman, 2014; Adelman, 2002; Aynsley-Green et al., 2012; Bacon, 1996; Baldwin-Edwards, 2006).

Economic migrants are important to both the sending and receiving country because they are conduits for economic remittances (Morris, 2002; Motomura, 1999; Nethery and Holman, 2016; Newman, Proctor, and Dudley, 2013; Oberman, 2016). Indeed, this is a category of migrants which has become an economic staple in several developing countries which rely on them to shore up a failing social security network (Johnson,

1996; Joppke, 1998, 1999, 2010; Kasimis, 2012; Kelson and DeLaet, 1999; King, 2009; Lopez, 2005). So much so, that some governments unwisely proposed taxing remittances and re-orienting them towards development activities (Guild, 2001; Guild and Niessen, 1996; Hailbronner, 2000; Hayter, 2000; Heisler, 2000; Hernandez-Truyol and Johns, 1997). Many people in receiving countries worry that economic migrants will take away the little jobs that are available and ought to be otherwise ring-fenced to local workers (Guild and Niessen, 1996; Hailbronner, 2000; Hayter, 2000; Heisler, 2000; Hernandez-Truyol and Johns, 1997). Over time, economic migrants might secure permanent residence and therefore engage in a political process that will ultimately overturn the old order (Ackerman and Furman, 2014; Chin, 1999; Hailbronner, 2000; Lopez, 2005; Paz, 2016; Smith, 2014). It is for this reason, that a lot of anti-migrant rhetoric tends to focus on economic migrants even though they are necessary for the smooth running of the most industrialized economies (Sassen, 1997; Shohamy and McNamara, 2009; Smith, 2014; Soysal, 2012; Spijkerboer and Van Walsum, 2007).

People may also move or are forced to move because of conflict. Typically, this happens in a situation involving incredible human suffering (Hollifield, Martin, and Orrenius, 2014; Jacobson, 1996; Johnson, 1996; Joppke, 1998, 1999, 2010). The move to another location may be permanent. However, it can also be temporary with the intention of returning once the threat of violence and instability has subsided to an acceptable level (Barak-Erez, 2008; Exdell, 2009; Joppke, 1998; Motomura, 1999; Sanggaran, Haire, and Zion, 2016). Others may decide to change location because they are victims of human rights violations by their own governments or fellow citizens (Taylor, 2000; Thym, 2008; Webber, 2012; Welch, 2002; Wexler, 2007; Wilcox, 2009; Zúñiga and Hernández-León, 2005). This is particularly true of countries with a poor record in terms of maintaining personal freedom from undue state interference (Sassen, 1996, 1997; Shohamy and McNamara, 2009; Smith, 2014; Soysal, 2012; Spijkerboer and Van Walsum, 2007). There have been instances of rogue governments that continue to pursue the people that have fled persecution with a view to threatening, harassing, or even assassinating them (Paz, 2016; Peberdy, 2001; Ramji-Nogales, 2007; Rubio-Marín, 2014; Ruhs, 2010; Ryan and Mitsilegas, 2010).

The threat of violence is not always restricted to state actors (Brané and Lundholm, 2007; Flynn, 2013; Joppke, 2010; Newman, Proctor, and Dudley, 2013; Sassen, 1997). There are individuals that face particularly harmful forms of domestic and gender-based violence that can only be mitigated by moving to a safer environment (Aynsley-Green et al., 2012; Cornelisse,

2004; Heisler, 2000; Mehan, 1997; Ramji-Nogales, 2007; Spijkerboer and Van Walsum, 2007). The decision to move is part of a survival instinct in which the person is attempting to preserve life at any cost. Such a self-preservation instinct may persist even if it means breaking the immigration rules of another country (Nethery and Holman, 2016; Newman, Proctor, and Dudley, 2013; Oberman, 2016; Orfanos, 2019; Ozdowski, 1985). Such changes in location are made under emergency situations and the people involved may later regularize their stay through an asylum claim (Bangarth, 2003; Barak-Erez, 2008; Becerra, 2016; Brané and Lundholm, 2007; Brochmann and Hammar, 2020; Chavez, 2001). Over 50 million people change their location for this reason in any given year. An anthropological examination of this type of migration may reflect the relative instability that exists in certain parts of the world (Peberdy, 2001; Ramji-Nogales, 2007; Rubio-Marín, 2014; Ruhs, 2010; Ryan and Mitsilegas, 2010; Saadi et al., 2020; Samers, 2004). A case in point is where the proxy imperial wars of the West within the Middle East led to an influx of refugees who wanted to escape the unbearable living conditions in that part of the world (Sanggaran, Haire, and Zion, 2016; Sassen, 1996, 1997; Shohamy and McNamara, 2009; Smith, 2014).

It is a natural human instinct to find better opportunities and to move away from places that represent a danger to that person or their communities (Flynn, 2013; Frederking, 2012; Gilman, 2013; Guia, Koulish, and Mitsilegas, 2016; Guild, 2001; Guild and Niessen, 1996). The countries that seem to offer better opportunities in terms of political rights, economic empowerment, and social progress are then turned into premium destinations for emigres (Ackerman and Furman, 2014; Chin, 1999; Hailbronner, 2000; Lopez, 2005; Paz, 2016; Smith, 2014). The problem is that the more popular areas are dealing with an increasing number of migrants and yet they have not recalibrated their society to take on these new entrants (Acer and Goodman, 2009; Ackerman and Furman, 2014; Adelman, 2002; Aynsley-Green et al., 2012; Bacon, 1996). The strategy of trying to discourage people from coming has not worked, not least because many of the potential immigrants are living in conditions that are so much worse than the life that they anticipate they will find in their new location (Mehan, 1997; Melis, 2001; Miller, 2015, 2016; Molnar and Gill, 2018; Money, 1998; Morris, 2002, 2016).

The search for better opportunities does not have to be international in nature. Instead, it can be local or national (Acer and Goodman, 2009; Ackerman and Furman, 2014; Adelman, 2002; Aynsley-Green et al.,

2012; Bacon, 1996). That is why there is renewed interest in the politics, economics, and sociology if internal migration (Orfanos, 2019; Ozdowski, 1985; Paz, 2016; Peberdy, 2001; Ramji-Nogales, 2007; Rubio-Marín, 2014; Ruhs, 2010). This type of movement is usually from rural to urban areas. Such internal migrations may even reflect class divisions (Cornelisse, 2010; Gilman, 2013; Kelson and DeLaet, 1999; Orfanos, 2019; Thym, 2008). For example, in countries where certain tribes or communities are privileged; there is a high probability that underprivileged communities will want to shift towards those communities that are well-off (Miller, 2016; Molnar and Gill, 2018; Money, 1998; Morris, 2002, 2016; Motomura, 1999; Nethery and Holman, 2016). In fact, this type of movement may not be rooted in fact, but rather because of speculation and supposition about privileges accorded to certain members of the society (Cornelisse, 2010; Gilman, 2013; Kelson and DeLaet, 1999; Orfanos, 2019; Thym, 2008). Given the lack of internal borders, this type of migration is often under-reported and any resistance to it never rises to a national concern (Lopez, 2005; Lorentzen, 2014; Mehan, 1997; Melis, 2001; Miller, 2015, 2016; Molnar and Gill, 2018; Money, 1998). The only exception is China which has the power to determine the locations of residences according to the stipulations set by the government (Adelman, 2002; Aynsley-Green et al., 2012; Bacon, 1996; Baldwin-Edwards, 2006; Bangarth, 2003; Barak-Erez, 2008).

Sociology-cultural as well as ego-historical factors also play a major role in migration patterns and categorizations (Brané and Lundholm, 2007; Brochmann and Hammar, 2020; Chavez, 2001; Chin, 1999; Cook, 2003; Cornelisse, 2004). In North Africa, for example, emigrating to Europe counts as a sign of social prestige within the local community that is left behind (Bangarth, 2003; Dunn, 2010; Johnson, 1996; Morris, 2002; Sampson, Mitchell, and Bowring, 2011). Moreover, many countries that were former colonies aspire to be closely associated with the colonial master as a sign of prestige. This means that people with relatives who live legally in the (former) colonial metropole are particularly privileged in their home communities (Paz, 2016; Peberdy, 2001; Ramji-Nogales, 2007; Rubio-Marín, 2014; Ruhs, 2010; Ryan and Mitsilegas, 2010). These are people who often provide important help for immigrants arriving in that metropole and will therefore have practical benefits for the community at large.

The instrumentality of connections cannot be ignored when discussing the motivations to target destinations. This is also related to a language barrier, where migrants tend to select those areas where the lingua-franca is similar or identical to their own (Aynsley-Green et al., 2012; Cornelisse,

2004; Heisler, 2000; Mehan, 1997; Ramji-Nogales, 2007; Spijkerboer and Van Walsum, 2007). The irony is that the countries that are complaining about immigration are the very ones that spent a good deal of their colonial hegemony towards ensuring that the people who were subjugated by their imperial government learnt the language of the imperialists. This mainly includes English and French, but to a lesser extent may include Spanish, Portuguese, and Italian languages. Immigrants from former colonies may also act as a facilitator whereby they are already conversant with the main language of the colonial masters (Flynn, 2013; Frederking, 2012; Gilman, 2013; Guia, Koulish, and Mitsilegas, 2016; Guild, 2001; Guild and Niessen, 1996). In contrast, countries like the Czech Republic, which have never had colonies will have low migration levels because very few people speak the national language (Adelman, 2002; Cook, 2003; Hayter, 2000; Lorentzen, 2014; Peberdy, 2001; Soysal, 2012).

The presence of other community members in the host country cannot be ignored when selecting an ultimate destination (Wexler, 2007; Wilcox, 2009; Zúñiga and Hernández-León, 2005; Zwi and Mares, 2015). All other factors being constant, people are more likely than not to choose a destination where they have relatives, friends, and community associates (Lopez, 2005; Lorentzen, 2014; Mehan, 1997; Melis, 2001; Miller, 2015, 2016; Molnar and Gill, 2018; Money, 1998). These social capital networks are important for establishing oneself in a new territory where the indigenous community may be either unhelpful or outwardly hostile (Welch, 2002; Wexler, 2007; Wilcox, 2009; Zúñiga and Hernández-León, 2005; Zwi and Mares, 2015). Relatives may help with job research and with accommodation as well as other practical matters that are of the essence for a new migrant (Hailbronner, 2000; Hayter, 2000; Heisler, 2000; Hernandez-Truyol and Johns, 1997; Hollifield, Martin, and Orrenius, 2014). The geographical proximity of Africa to Europe as well as the social ties between Northern and Southern Mediterranean contribute to the specific migration patterns that exist between them (Saadi et al., 2020; Samers, 2004; Sampson, Mitchell, and Bowring, 2011; Sanggaran, Haire, and Zion, 2016). This is one of the reasons why some European nations have attempted to create physical barriers and technological barriers against migrants from Sub-Saharan Africa in order to stem the tide of increasing numbers (Dunn, 2010; Exdell, 2009; Fiske, 2016; Flynn, 2013; Frederking, 2012; Gilman, 2013; Guia, Koulish, and Mitsilegas, 2016).

The question whether a person takes the decision to move to another country depends on a number of actors. One of the critical factors is the relative skill premia of the source and host countries (Money, 1998; Morris,

2002, 2016; Motomura, 1999; Nethery and Holman, 2016; Newman, Proctor, and Dudley, 2013). A case in point is the existence of positive selection in which the host country shows a higher skill premium than the source country (Acer and Goodman, 2009; Chavez, 2001; Guild and Niessen, 1996; King, 2009; Ozdowski, 1985; Shohamy and McNamara, 2009). Negative selection describes a situation when the source country displays a lower skill premium than the host country (Baldwin-Edwards, 2006; Bangarth, 2003; Barak-Erez, 2008; Becerra, 2016; Brané and Lundholm, 2007). The relative skill premia are related to the level of selectivity associated with particular types of migrants on the job (and other similar) markets (Taylor, 2000; Thym, 2008; Webber, 2012; Welch, 2002; Wexler, 2007; Wilcox, 2009; Zúñiga and Hernández-León, 2005). Age heaping techniques may be used to measure the relative skill premia of a country (Dauvergne, 2012; Hernandez-Truyol and Johns, 1997; Molnar and Gill, 2018; Zúñiga and Hernández-León, 2005).

A number of theories attempt to explain the international flow of capital and people from one country to another (Hollifield, Martin, and Orrenius, 2014; Jacobson, 1996; Johnson, 1996; Joppke, 1998, 1999, 2010). These then comprise the vast majority of contemporary research contributions in the field of migration (Orfanos, 2019; Ozdowski, 1985; Paz, 2016; Peberdy, 2001; Ramji-Nogales, 2007; Rubio-Marín, 2014; Ruhs, 2010). For example, recent academic output on migration comprises mainly journal articles that try to explain how and why people move from one place to another (Hollifield, Martin, and Orrenius, 2014; Jacobson, 1996; Johnson, 1996; Joppke, 1998, 1999, 2010; Kasimis, 2012). However, the long-term trend shows a gradual increase in academic publishing on migration generally (Barak-Erez, 2008; Becerra, 2016; Brané and Lundholm, 2007; Brochmann and Hammar, 2020; Chavez, 2001; Chin, 1999). Some argue that this due to both the general expansion of academic literature production, and the increased prominence of migration research (Spijkerboer and Van Walsum, 2007; Taylor, 2000; Thym, 2008; Webber, 2012; Welch, 2002; Wexler, 2007; Wilcox, 2009). Migration research now takes into account new relevant developments such as information and communication technologies (Acer and Goodman, 2009; Ackerman and Furman, 2014; Adelman, 2002; Aynsley-Green et al., 2012; Bacon, 1996).

Neoclassical economic theory has provided some explanations for migration and its patterns. This theory of migration states that the main reason for labor migration is wage difference between two geographic locations, which is often related to other inequalities (Wexler, 2007; Wilcox,

2009; Zúñiga and Hernández-León, 2005; Zwi and Mares, 2015). These wage differences are usually linked to geographic labor demand and supply patterns within both nations (Saadi et al., 2020; Samers, 2004; Sampson, Mitchell, and Bowring, 2011; Sanggaran, Haire, and Zion, 2016). It can be said that areas with a shortage of labor despite excess of capital have a high relative wage while areas with a high labor supply despite a dearth of capital have a low relative wage (Webber, 2012; Welch, 2002; Wexler, 2007; Wilcox, 2009; Zúñiga and Hernández-León, 2005; Zwi and Mares, 2015). Labor tends to flow from low-wage areas to high-wage areas, and therefore reflect the inequalities that exist between and among regions (Morris, 2002, 2016; Motomura, 1999; Nethery and Holman, 2016; Newman, Proctor, and Dudley, 2013; Oberman, 2016). This flow of labor comes with important changes in the labor market as well as social fabric. The effect can be felt in both the sending and receiving country (Acer and Goodman, 2009; Ackerman and Furman, 2014; Adelman, 2002; Aynsley-Green et al., 2012; Bacon, 1996). Neoclassical economic theory is best used to describe transnational migration involve one or more nations (Cornelisse, 2010; Costello, 2012; Dauvergne, 2012; Den Heijer, 2010; Dudley et al., 2012; Dunn, 2001, 2010). This is because it is not confined by international immigration laws and similar governmental regulations (Smith, 2014; Soysal, 2012; Spijkerboer and Van Walsum, 2007; Taylor, 2000; Thym, 2008; Webber, 2012; Welch, 2002).

Another explanation comes from the dual labor market theory. This construct postulates that migration is mainly caused by pull factors in more developed countries (Molnar and Gill, 2018; Money, 1998; Morris, 2002, 2016; Motomura, 1999; Nethery and Holman, 2016). There is an assumption that the labor markets in these developed countries consist of two segments. The first segment is known as the primary market and necessarily requires highly skilled labor (Dunn, 2001, 2010; Exdell, 2009; Fiske, 2016; Flynn, 2013; Frederking, 2012; Gilman, 2013; Guia, Koulish, and Mitsilegas, 2016). Then there is the secondary market which is very labor-intensive and hence requiring low-skilled workers (Joppke, 1999, 2010; Kasimis, 2012; Kelson and DeLaet, 1999; King, 2009; Lopez, 2005; Lorentzen, 2014; Mehan, 1997). This theory assumes that migration from less developed countries into more developed countries is a result of a pull created by a need for labor in the developed countries in their secondary market (Becerra, 2016; Brané and Lundholm, 2007; Brochmann and Hammar, 2020; Chavez, 2001; Chin, 1999; Cook, 2003). Migrant workers are needed to fill the lowest rung of the labor market because the native laborers do not want to do these jobs as they present a lack of mobility upwards into the privileged echelons of society (Miller, 2016; Molnar and Gill, 2018; Money, 1998; Morris, 2002, 2016; Motomura, 1999; Nethery and Holman, 2016). This creates a need for migrant workers. Furthermore, the initial dearth in available labor pushes wages up, making migration even more enticing (Soysal, 2012; Spijkerboer and Van Walsum, 2007; Taylor, 2000; Thym, 2008; Webber, 2012; Welch, 2002; Wexler, 2007).

New economics of labor migration have also been used to explain migration patterns and motivations (Chavez, 2001; Chin, 1999; Cook, 2003; Cornelisse, 2004, 2010; Costello, 2012; Dauvergne, 2012; Den Heijer, 2010). This theory postulates that migration flows and patterns go beyond the plight of individual workers and their economic incentives (Jacobson, 1996; Johnson, 1996; Joppke, 1998, 1999, 2010; Kasimis, 2012; Kelson and DeLaet, 1999). Instead, this theoretical construct calls for an explanation of wider social entities which can be powerful motivators. One such social entity is the household, its conceptualization, and the way it is arranged to nurture individuals and communities (Bacon, 1996; Dudley et al., 2012; Hollifield, Martin, and Orrenius, 2014; Money, 1998; Saadi et al., 2020). Migration can be viewed as a result of risk aversion on the part of a household that has insufficient income, and hence unable to provide the kind of support that one might expect (Money, 1998; Morris, 2002, 2016; Motomura, 1999; Nethery and Holman, 2016; Newman, Proctor, and Dudley, 2013). The household, in this case, is in need of extra capital to carry out its function of supporting members. That cash and capital in-flow can be achieved through remittances sent back by family members who participate in migrant labor abroad (Ruhs, 2010; Ryan and Mitsilegas, 2010; Saadi et al., 2020; Samers, 2004; Sampson, Mitchell, and Bowring, 2011). These remittances can also have a broader effect on the economy as emigrants bring in capital which can be used for developmental purposes (Miller, 2015, 2016; Molnar and Gill, 2018; Money, 1998; Morris, 2002, 2016; Motomura, 1999).

The role of geographic specificity of occupations cannot be ignored as a factor in migration patterns. This is because people gravitate to certain localities in order to take advantage of jobs that can only be found in that locality (Guild and Niessen, 1996; Hailbronner, 2000; Hayter, 2000; Heisler, 2000; Hernandez-Truyol and Johns, 1997). We have already seen some level of temporary migration in which people move to an area (such as the oil rigs) in order to take advantage of job opportunities that they can only find that at that point in time (Taylor, 2000; Thym, 2008; Webber, 2012; Welch, 2002; Wexler, 2007; Wilcox, 2009; Zúñiga and Hernández-León, 2005; Zwi and Mares, 2015). Recent research has examined a decline in U.S. interstate migration from 1991 to 2011. One of the possible explanations is that the reduced interstate migration is due to a decline in the geographic specificity of occupations (Baldwin-Edwards, 2006; Bangarth, 2003; Barak-Erez, 2008; Becerra, 2016; Brané and Lundholm, 2007; Brochmann and Hammar, 2020). Others argue that an increase in workers' ability to learn about other locations before moving there is important in determining migration preferences and routes (Lorentzen, 2014; Mehan, 1997; Melis, 2001; Miller, 2015, 2016; Molnar and Gill, 2018; Money, 1998; Morris, 2016). Access to information technology as well as inexpensive travel allows for greater geographical mobility of labor in the modern age (Bacon, 1996; Baldwin-Edwards, 2006; Bangarth, 2003; Barak-Erez, 2008; Becerra, 2016; Brané and Lundholm, 2007). Other researchers find that the location-specific nature of housing is more important than moving costs in determining labor reallocation (Miller, 2016; Molnar and Gill, 2018; Money, 1998; Morris, 2002, 2016; Motomura, 1999; Nethery and Holman, 2016). There are many people that will change location in order to access cheaper and more appropriate housing for their needs.

The relative deprivation theory is another important explanatory model for migration. It postulates that an awareness of the income difference between neighbors or other households in the migrant-sending community is an important factor in migration (Ramji-Nogales, 2007; Rubio-Marín, 2014; Ruhs, 2010; Ryan and Mitsilegas, 2010; Saadi et al., 2020; Samers, 2004). The incentive to migrate is a lot higher in areas that have a high level of economic inequality (Kasimis, 2012; Kelson and DeLaet, 1999; King, 2009; Lopez, 2005; Lorentzen, 2014; Mehan, 1997; Melis, 2001). In the short run, remittances may increase inequality. However, in the long run, remittances from emigrants may actually decrease inequality (Saadi et al., 2020; Samers, 2004; Sampson, Mitchell, and Bowring, 2011; Sanggaran, Haire, and Zion, 2016; Sassen, 1996). There are two stages of migration for a worker. The first stage arises when the worker invests in human capital formation for purposes of facilitating their move (Ruhs, 2010; Ryan and Mitsilegas, 2010; Saadi et al., 2020; Samers, 2004; Sampson, Mitchell, and Bowring, 2011). The second phase is when the migrant worker tries to capitalize on their investments in order to attract as much cash as possible from the market (King, 2009; Lopez, 2005; Lorentzen, 2014; Mehan, 1997; Melis, 2001; Miller, 2015, 2016; Molnar and Gill, 2018). In this way, successful migrants may use their new capital to provide for better schooling for their children and better homes for their families (Adelman, 2002; Aynsley-Green et al., 2012;

Bacon, 1996; Baldwin-Edwards, 2006; Bangarth, 2003; Barak-Erez, 2008). Successful high-skilled emigrants may serve as an example for neighbors and potential migrants who hope to achieve that level of success (Costello, 2012; Dauvergne, 2012; Den Heijer, 2010; Dudley et al., 2012; Dunn, 2001, 2010; Exdell, 2009; Fiske, 2016). That is why many immigrants provide inspiration for others to similarly emigrate in order to enjoy the luxuries and financial security that comes with such a choice.

The world-systems theory looks at migration from a global perspective (Brochmann and Hammar, 2020; Frederking, 2012; Kasimis, 2012; Oberman, 2016; Taylor, 2000). It explains that interaction between different societies can be an important factor in social change within societies which eventually leads to the movement of people. A case in point is trade where one country tends to cause economic decline in another, a claim is sometimes used to justify protectionism (Guild and Niessen, 1996; Hailbronner, 2000; Hayter, 2000; Heisler, 2000; Hernandez-Truyol and Johns, 1997). The disadvantages that are experienced in one country as a result of an unequal trade relationship may create incentive to migrate to a country with a more vibrant economy (Rubio-Marín, 2014; Ruhs, 2010; Ryan and Mitsilegas, 2010; Saadi et al., 2020; Samers, 2004; Sampson, Mitchell, and Bowring, 2011).

The post-colonial settlement is an example of how unequal trading conditions can keep countries in perpetual bondage, even if they seem to be independent. It can be argued that even after decolonization, the economic dependence of former colonies still remains on mother countries or former colonial masters (Aynsley-Green et al., 2012; Cornelisse, 2004; Heisler, 2000; Mehan, 1997; Ramji-Nogales, 2007; Spijkerboer and Van Walsum, 2007). This view of international trade is controversial. For example, some argue that free trade can actually reduce migration between developing and developed countries (Den Heijer, 2010; Dudley et al., 2012; Dunn, 2001, 2010; Exdell, 2009; Fiske, 2016; Flynn, 2013; Frederking, 2012). It can be argued that the developed countries import labor-intensive goods in order to take advantage of the relatively low wages in developing countries (Hernandez-Truyol and Johns, 1997; Hollifield, Martin, and Orrenius, 2014; Jacobson, 1996; Johnson, 1996; Joppke, 1998). This causes an increase in the employment of unskilled workers in the less developed countries. Moreover, it also helps in decreasing the outflow of migrant workers (Taylor, 2000; Thym, 2008; Webber, 2012; Welch, 2002; Wexler, 2007; Wilcox, 2009; Zúñiga and Hernández-León, 2005; Zwi and Mares, 2015). However, such an approach is not associated with human capital development and leads to a stagnation of worker rights over time. Those that favor free trade in its most liberal forms have argued that the export of capital-intensive goods from rich countries to poor countries equalizes income and employment conditions. In doing so doing, this type of migration can slow migration over the long run (Ozdowski, 1985; Paz, 2016; Peberdy, 2001; Ramji-Nogales, 2007; Rubio-Marín, 2014; Ruhs, 2010; Ryan and Mitsilegas, 2010). In either direction, this theory can be used to explain migration between countries that are geographically far apart. This is because these needs and expectations among potential migrants motivate them to break all geographical barriers in order to land in their desired country of destination (Sanggaran, Haire, and Zion, 2016; Sassen, 1996, 1997; Shohamy and McNamara, 2009; Smith, 2014). This chapter will close with a review of the social-scientific views of migration.

3.5. SOCIAL-SCIENTIFIC PERSPECTIVES ON HUMAN MIGRATION

One of the philosophical contributions to the immigration debate is that of the social-scientific perspective (Ackerman and Furman, 2014; Chin, 1999; Hailbronner, 2000; Lopez, 2005; Paz, 2016; Smith, 2014). More broadly, this is sometimes understood as a sociology of immigration which seeks to develop a number understanding of the motivations and experiences of migration (Miller, 2015, 2016; Molnar and Gill, 2018; Money, 1998; Morris, 2002, 2016; Motomura, 1999; Nethery and Holman, 2016). To that end, a number of social scientists have examined immigration from a sociological perspective (Hollifield, Martin, and Orrenius, 2014; Jacobson, 1996; Johnson, 1996; Joppke, 1998, 1999, 2010; Kasimis, 2012). These scholars are noted for paying particular attention to how immigration affects, and is affected by, matters of race and ethnicity (Brochmann and Hammar, 2020; Chavez, 2001; Chin, 1999; Cook, 2003; Cornelisse, 2004, 2010). Another point of interest relates to the ways in which migration is impacted by social structure and also creates a new social structure (Rubio-Marín, 2014; Ruhs, 2010; Ryan and Mitsilegas, 2010; Saadi et al., 2020; Samers, 2004; Sampson, Mitchell, and Bowring, 2011).

There is no single unified theory of migration (Miller, 2015, 2016; Molnar and Gill, 2018; Money, 1998; Morris, 2002, 2016; Motomura, 1999). Rather, over time various perspectives have emerged (Sassen, 1996, 1997; Shohamy and McNamara, 2009; Smith, 2014; Soysal, 2012; Spijkerboer and Van Walsum, 2007). Each of these perspectives plays a role in adding to our understanding of migration. Many of these theories predict and describe particular aspects of the entirety of migration as a concept rather than providing a holistic representation that is comprehensive (Frederking, 2012; Gilman, 2013; Guia, Koulish, and Mitsilegas, 2016; Guild, 2001; Guild and Niessen, 1996; Hailbronner, 2000). That implies that migration can be best understood from an eclectic point of view that is not afraid to borrow knowledge from various disciplines (Guild, 2001; Miller, 2016; Ryan and Mitsilegas, 2010; Wexler, 2007; Wilcox, 2009). Figure 3.5 summarizes the theoretical foundation of migration in existing literature.

Theory	Subject of Analysis	Level of Analysis	Pet Variable(s)	Critique
Neoclassical theory of migration	*Determinants of migration*	Macro Micro	• Wage and income differentials • Probability of employment	• Mechanically reduces migration determinants-exclusion of politics and policies. • Assumes linearity-unable to explain differential migration, why people do not move, or why migration ceases before wage differentials equalize. • Ignores market imperfections. • Homogenization of migrants and societies. • Static perspective.
Human capital theory of migration		Micro	• Wages, economic benefits affected by individual characteristics	• Overly optimistic (functionalist) view-migration is not always a voluntary process to maximize gains.
New economics theory of migration		Micro Mezzo	• Wages and income distribution (relative deprivation) • Institutional failures-credit market, labor market deficiencies	• Critique of the neoclassical theory rather than a theory in its own right. • Sending side bias. • Limited applicability-difficult to isolate the effect of market imperfections and risk in migration decisions from other income and employment variables.
World system theory (historical-structural approaches)		Macro: global and international processes	Structural changes induced by the flow of capital	• Only applicable at the global level. • Explanation formulated *ex ante*, cannot be empirically tested.

Dual labor market theory		Macro: Nation-state Mezzo	• Labor demand • Bifurcation of labor markets • FDI • State immigration policies and recruitment efforts	• Receiving state bias-excludes push factors, formal recruitment practices overemphasized. • Unable to account for differential immigration rates in different advanced economies with similar economic structures. • Distinction between primary and secondary sector is usually arbitrary, which leads to instability in empirical estimates.
Network theory	Perpetuation of migration and/or directionality of flows	Mezzo	• Networks, diaspora	• Conceptual framework rather than a theory. • Networks can be exclusionary and undermine (not facilitate) migration.
Migration systems theory		Macro	• Developmental space	• Purely descriptive. Unable to account for decline of migration systems overtime.
Transnational migration		Transnational level	• Transnational social spaces	• Novelty of the concepts has been questioned. • Research within this paradigm usually selects on dependent variable.

Figure 3.5: Theoretical foundation of migration.

Source: Bada, Migracyjnych via Semantic Scholar.

Existing literature to this end has emerged in three main sociological perspectives, which are classical paradigms of sociology (Dudley et al., 2012; Dunn, 2001, 2010; Exdell, 2009; Fiske, 2016; Flynn, 2013; Frederking, 2012; Gilman, 2013). The first is symbolic interactionism which aims to understand migration through an examination of the face-to-face interactions that are involved on a micro-level (Bangarth, 2003; Dunn, 2010; Johnson, 1996; Morris, 2002; Sampson, Mitchell, and Bowring, 2011). The second perspective is that of the social conflict theory which examines migration through the prism of competition for power and resources (Aynsley-Green et al., 2012; Bacon, 1996; Baldwin-Edwards, 2006; Bangarth, 2003; Barak-Erez, 2008; Becerra, 2016). The third perspective is that of structural functionalism, which is based on the ideas of Émile Durkheim (Newman, Proctor, and Dudley, 2013; Oberman, 2016; Orfanos, 2019; Ozdowski, 1985; Paz, 2016; Peberdy, 2001). This third perspective examines the role of migration in fulfilling certain functions within each society (Baldwin-Edwards, 2006; Bangarth, 2003; Barak-Erez, 2008; Becerra, 2016; Brané and Lundholm, 2007). Examples of those functions include the decrease of despair and aimlessness and the consolidation of social networks (Cornelisse, 2010; Costello, 2012; Dauvergne, 2012; Den Heijer, 2010; Dudley et al., 2012; Dunn, 2001, 2010).

In recent times, attention has shifted away from countries of destination (Sampson, Mitchell, and Bowring, 2011; Sanggaran, Haire, and Zion, 2016; Sassen, 1996, 1997; Shohamy and McNamara, 2009). Instead, sociologists have attempted to understand how transnationalism occurs and its impact on migration patterns generally (Molnar and Gill, 2018; Money, 1998; Morris, 2002, 2016; Motomura, 1999; Nethery and Holman, 2016). Such an approach allows us to understand the interplay between migrants, their countries of destination, and their countries of origins in a holistic way (Oberman, 2016; Orfanos, 2019; Ozdowski, 1985; Paz, 2016; Peberdy, 2001; Ramji-Nogales, 2007; Rubio-Marín, 2014). In this framework, research surrounding the notion of social remittances has led to a stronger conceptualization of how migrants affect socio-political processes in their countries of origin (Mehan, 1997; Melis, 2001; Miller, 2015, 2016; Molnar and Gill, 2018; Money, 1998; Morris, 2002, 2016). Much of the research work involved also takes place in the field of integration of migrants into destination societies. There is specific reference to the reception that migrants receive and the motivations for such a reception (Morris, 2002; Motomura, 1999; Nethery and Holman, 2016; Newman, Proctor, and Dudley, 2013; Oberman, 2016).

Political scientists have put forth a number of theoretical frameworks relating to migration (Den Heijer, 2010; Miller, 2015; Ruhs, 2010; Welch, 2002; Zwi and Mares, 2015). These frameworks are notable for offering different perspectives on processes of citizenship, security, and international relations in as far as they affect the experiences of migrants (Acer and Goodman, 2009; Chavez, 2001; Guild and Niessen, 1996; King, 2009; Ozdowski, 1985; Shohamy and McNamara, 2009). The political importance of diasporas has also become a growing field of interest (Paz, 2016; Peberdy, 2001; Ramji-Nogales, 2007; Rubio-Marín, 2014; Ruhs, 2010; Ryan and Mitsilegas, 2010; Saadi et al., 2020). For example, scholars have examined questions of diaspora activism and its impact on both their home countries and their countries of destination (Costello, 2012; Dauvergne, 2012; Den Heijer, 2010; Dudley et al., 2012; Dunn, 2001, 2010; Exdell, 2009). In particular, there is interest in how state-diaspora relations emerge and how they impact on the treatment of future immigration and other immigrants (Sassen, 1996, 1997; Shohamy and McNamara, 2009; Smith, 2014; Soysal, 2012; Spijkerboer and Van Walsum, 2007). A case in point is the political role played by out-of-country voting processes which are dominated by emigrants who may have been exposed to an entirely different political system (Guild, 2001; Guild and Niessen, 1996; Hailbronner, 2000; Hayter, 2000; Heisler, 2000; Hernandez-Truyol and Johns, 1997). Other researchers have focused on the soft power strategies adopted by different countries to control and manage immigration and whether those strategies are effective (Baldwin-Edwards, 2006; Bangarth, 2003; Barak-Erez, 2008; Becerra, 2016; Brané and Lundholm, 2007; Brochmann and Hammar, 2020).

In this field, the majority of work has focused on immigration politics and their impact on discourses on migration generally (Costello, 2012; Dauvergne, 2012; Den Heijer, 2010; Dudley et al., 2012; Dunn, 2001, 2010; Exdell, 2009; Fiske, 2016). That necessarily entails viewing migration from the perspective of the country of destination, as opposed to the country of origin (Kasimis, 2012; Kelson and DeLaet, 1999; King, 2009; Lopez, 2005; Lorentzen, 2014; Mehan, 1997; Melis, 2001; Miller, 2015). Others argue that the country of origin has much to lose and gain from migration, even more than the country of destination in some respects (Guild and Niessen, 1996; Hailbronner, 2000; Hayter, 2000; Heisler, 2000; Hernandez-Truyol and Johns, 1997). With regard to emigration processes, political scientists have expanded on Albert Hirschman's framework on "“voice” vs. “exit” to discuss how emigration affects the politics within countries of origin (Guild, 2001; Guild and Niessen, 1996; Hailbronner, 2000; Hayter, 2000; Heisler, 2000; Hernandez-Truyol and Johns, 1997). This is particularly important at a time when many developed countries are concerned about the long-term impact of immigrants on their populations and politics generally (Soysal, 2012; Spijkerboer and Van Walsum, 2007; Taylor, 2000; Thym, 2008; Webber, 2012; Welch, 2002; Wexler, 2007). A case in point is the oft-repeated fear among rightwing elements that the Democratic Party in the USA is importing Mexican migrants in order to gain a permanent political majority.

The analysis of immigration is not merely descriptive, but actually challenges some harmful tropes and assumptions (Shohamy and McNamara, 2009; Smith, 2014; Soysal, 2012; Spijkerboer and Van Walsum, 2007; Taylor, 2000; Thym, 2008). For example, certain laws of social science have been proposed to describe human migration (Nethery and Holman, 2016; Newman, Proctor, and Dudley, 2013; Oberman, 2016; Orfanos, 2019; Ozdowski, 1985). A case in point is the argument that every migration flow generates a return or counter migration. The implication is that migrants are not threatening to take over the country of destination, contrary to what many anti-migrant voices state (Johnson, 1996; Joppke, 1998, 1999, 2010; Kasimis, 2012; Kelson and DeLaet, 1999; King, 2009; Lopez, 2005). Moreover, it is argued that the majority of migrants move a short distance and live within their region. The implication is that the crisis of international immigration has been over-stated (Melis, 2001; Miller, 2015, 2016; Molnar and Gill, 2018; Money, 1998; Morris, 2002, 2016; Motomura, 1999). The dire predictions of an immigration deluge from poor countries into far-flung industrialized countries is over-blown (Cook, 2003; Cornelisse, 2004, 2010; Costello, 2012; Dauvergne, 2012; Den Heijer, 2010; Dudley et al., 2012). In many debates, this apparent misunderstanding of migration in general is suppressed in favor of much more inflammatory interpretations of migration patterns (Brané and Lundholm, 2007; Flynn, 2013; Joppke, 2010; Newman, Proctor, and Dudley, 2013; Sassen, 1997). In many cases, the incendiary narratives of indignant local people who wish to control migration are promoted as legitimate aspects of public discourse and even public policy (Dunn, 2010; Exdell, 2009; Fiske, 2016; Flynn, 2013; Frederking, 2012; Gilman, 2013; Guia, Koulish, and Mitsilegas, 2016). Consequently, a lot of policy reform focuses on tightening the rules and preventing even more immigrants from coming in (Acer and Goodman, 2009; Ackerman and Furman, 2014; Adelman, 2002; Aynsley-Green et al., 2012; Bacon, 1996).

It is suggested that migrants who move longer distances tend to choose more urban destinations, including the biggest cities in a country (Spijkerboer and Van Walsum, 2007; Taylor, 2000; Thym, 2008; Webber, 2012; Welch, 2002; Wexler, 2007; Wilcox, 2009). That belies the notion that rural communities in the country of destination face their way of life being destroyed by the influx of foreigners through lax immigration (Fiske, 2016; Flynn, 2013; Frederking, 2012; Gilman, 2013; Guia, Koulish, and Mitsilegas, 2016; Guild, 2001; Guild and Niessen, 1996). Some researchers argue that urban residents are often less migratory than inhabitants of rural areas (Ackerman and Furman, 2014; Adelman, 2002; Aynsley-Green et al., 2012; Bacon, 1996; Baldwin-Edwards, 2006). This means that it is actually the rural residents that come to town in search of work and other opportunities, rather than urban people moving to the villages to disrupt live there (Jacobson, 1996; Johnson, 1996; Joppke, 1998, 1999, 2010; Kasimis, 2012; Kelson and DeLaet, 1999). In doing this work, researchers inadvertently question the widely held negative stereotypes concerning the nature and effects of human migration (Hailbronner, 2000; Hayter, 2000; Heisler, 2000; Hernandez-Truyol and Johns, 1997; Hollifield, Martin, and Orrenius, 2014).

Other sociological assumptions and theories are used in the actual policy formulation and implementation regarding immigration generally (Aynsley-Green et al., 2012; Bacon, 1996; Baldwin-Edwards, 2006; Bangarth, 2003; Barak-Erez, 2008; Becerra, 2016). For example, it is assumed that families are less likely to make international moves than young adults (Kelson and DeLaet, 1999; King, 2009; Lopez, 2005; Lorentzen, 2014; Mehan, 1997; Melis, 2001; Miller, 2015, 2016). That is why people with families that request tourist visas are more likely to be allowed entry when compared to young people without family ties (Samers, 2004; Sampson, Mitchell, and Bowring, 2011; Sanggaran, Haire, and Zion, 2016; Sassen, 1996, 1997). The assumption that most migrants are adults determines how children are treated, a case in point being the plight of unaccompanied children and the problem of separating families during immigration enforcement (Oberman, 2016; Orfanos, 2019; Ozdowski, 1985; Paz, 2016; Peberdy, 2001; Ramji-Nogales, 2007; Rubio-Marín, 2014). Those who look to stem the tide of immigration are using a gradual approach based on the assumption that migration occurs in a stage-by-stage process rather than through a single event (Adelman, 2002; Cook, 2003; Hayter, 2000; Lorentzen, 2014; Peberdy, 2001; Soysal, 2012) (Taylor, 2000; Thym, 2008; Webber, 2012; Welch, 2002; Wexler, 2007; Wilcox, 2009; Zúñiga and Hernández-León, 2005). Indeed, that is why some nations have developed stop-gap prevention, which insists that migrants who wish to claim refugee status must apply for asylum in the first safe country (Thym, 2008; Webber, 2012; Welch, 2002; Wexler, 2007; Wilcox, 2009; Zúñiga and Hernández-León, 2005; Zwi and Mares, 2015).

CHAPTER 3 SUMMARY

This chapter has attempted to link the nature of migration and its consequences with regard to human beings. As the chapter demonstrates, this link is not always rooted in fact and can be abused by those with a self-interest in order to demonize migration generally. The first section showed that the conceptualization of migration tends to focus on the problematic aspects of this phenomenon. Hence, any study of some of the positive aspects of immigration is largely ignored. In the second section, we saw that immigration is patterned. Those patterns are not just important for conceptualizing migrations, but also understanding how the patterns affect the policy formulation process.

The third section summarized some typologies of migration, noting that many of these were subjectively and situationally defined. These categorizations of migrations are a standing point rather than being an endpoint. Hence, it should be recognized that the experiences of migration can be highly individualized. The penultimate section of this chapter attempted to establish a theoretical foundation of migration. This chapter has shown that theories of migration are never comprehensive. Rather an eclectic approach is utilized in order to borrow from as many disciplines as possible. The chapter then concludes by exploring some social-scientific perspectives on human immigration, noting the important role that sociology plays in helping us understand the nature and effects of human migration. This theme continues in the next chapter, we consider community responses to human migration.

CHAPTER 3

COMMUNITIES LIVING AND EXPERIENCING MIGRATION

CONTENTS

This chapter explores the ways in which communities respond to and engage with migration as well as its consequences. The first section in the chapter will focus on how diasporas are formed and their impact on both the home and destination countries. This theme is further explored in the second section that focuses on the categorization of diasporas. In the third section, we consider the specific circumstances of environmental migrants who are responding to the effects of climate change. The penultimate section of this chapter focuses on existential migration patterns and their implication for the entirety of the immigration debate. The chapter will then close with an examination of the role and experiences of global nomads as well as third culture children.

4.1. FORMATION OF DIASPORAS

Recently, there has been interest in the formation and impact of diasporas (Sanggaran, Haire, and Zion, 2016; Sassen, 1996, 1997; Shohamy and McNamara, 2009; Smith, 2014). This is especially true of second-generation and first-generation migrants who have now acquired full citizenship. Some are seeking to revisit their roots and re-establish their identities (Sassen, 1997; Shohamy and McNamara, 2009; Smith, 2014; Soysal, 2012; Spijkerboer and Van Walsum, 2007). Such revisits are meant to recapture old social capital networks and also to gain strength from a level of confidence in the past (Flynn, 2013; Frederking, 2012; Gilman, 2013; Guia, Koulish, and Mitsilegas, 2016; Guild, 2001; Guild and Niessen, 1996). It makes sense for diasporas to emerge as newly created citizens and legal residents begin to grapple with issues of religious intolerance, permissiveness, racism, xenophobia, and discrimination in their new locations (Saadi et al., 2020; Samers, 2004; Sampson, Mitchell, and Bowring, 2011; Sanggaran, Haire, and Zion, 2016; Sassen, 1996). A diaspora is defined as a scattered population whose origin lies in a separate geographic locale from where members are currently located (Cook, 2003; Cornelisse, 2004, 2010; Costello, 2012; Dauvergne, 2012; Den Heijer, 2010; Dudley et al., 2012). Historically, the word diaspora was used to refer to the mass dispersion of a population from its indigenous territories. One of the famous examples of this phenomena were Jews who routinely left their homelands voluntarily and involuntarily throughout their history (Kasimis, 2012; Kelson and DeLaet, 1999; King, 2009; Lopez, 2005; Lorentzen, 2014; Mehan, 1997; Melis, 2001; Miller, 2015). The term "diaspora" was originally used to describe the forced displacement of certain peoples, then later expanded to all people in that situation (Bangarth, 2003;

Barak-Erez, 2008; Becerra, 2016; Brané and Lundholm, 2007; Brochmann and Hammar, 2020; Chavez, 2001). Hence, "diasporas" is now generally used to describe those who identify with a "homeland," but live outside of it (Kasimis, 2012; Kelson and DeLaet, 1999; King, 2009; Lopez, 2005; Lorentzen, 2014; Mehan, 1997; Melis, 2001). Some notable diasporas include the African diaspora which primarily includes the descendants of the Africans who were transported to the Americas during the Transatlantic slave trade (Dauvergne, 2012; Den Heijer, 2010; Dudley et al., 2012; Dunn, 2001, 2010; Exdell, 2009; Fiske, 2016; Flynn, 2013). Then there is the Assyrian Diaspora which originated during and after the Arab conquest of Iraq, Turkey, Syria, and Iran (Barak-Erez, 2008; Exdell, 2009; Joppke, 1998; Motomura, 1999; Sanggaran, Haire, and Zion, 2016). That particular diaspora continued in the aftermath of the Assyrian Genocide (King, 2009; Lopez, 2005; Lorentzen, 2014; Mehan, 1997; Melis, 2001; Miller, 2015, 2016; Molnar and Gill, 2018). The southern Chinese and Indians have also created diasporas comprising of people who left their homelands during the 19th to 20th century (Kelson and DeLaet, 1999; King, 2009; Lopez, 2005; Lorentzen, 2014; Mehan, 1997; Melis, 2001; Miller, 2015, 2016). Figure 4.1 highlights some of the key features of a diaspora.

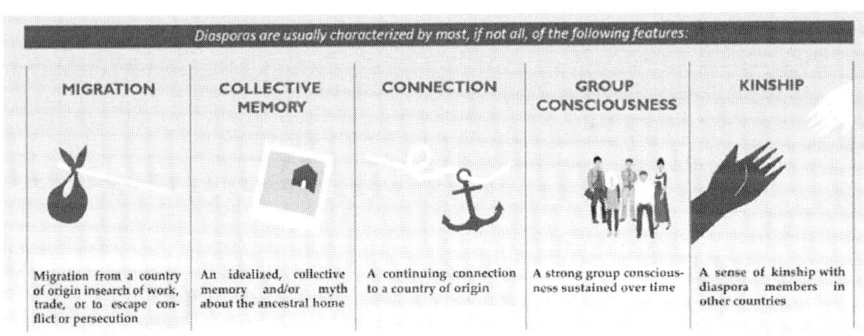

Figure 4.1: Key characteristics of a diaspora.

Source: IOM via Immigration Data Portal.

In Europe, the Irish comprise people who left Ireland during and after the Great Famine (Frederking, 2012; Gilman, 2013; Guia, Koulish, and Mitsilegas, 2016; Guild, 2001; Guild and Niessen, 1996; Hailbronner, 2000). Another important diaspora is that of the Romani from India who face specific forms of discrimination in their new locations (Gilman, 2013; Guia, Koulish, and Mitsilegas, 2016; Guild, 2001; Guild and Niessen, 1996;

Hailbronner, 2000; Hayter, 2000). The Italian diaspora and the Mexican diaspora have emerged in the USA and become an important political force (Ackerman and Furman, 2014; Adelman, 2002; Aynsley-Green et al., 2012; Bacon, 1996; Baldwin-Edwards, 2006). A diaspora arose out of the exile and deportation of Circassians (Exdell, 2009; Fiske, 2016; Flynn, 2013; Frederking, 2012; Gilman, 2013; Guia, Koulish, and Mitsilegas, 2016; Guild, 2001). The Palestinian diaspora arose following the flight or expulsion of Arabs from Palestine. This particular diaspora has continued to be a strong advocate for the independence of the Palestinian state and for the so-called two-state solution with Israel (Welch, 2002; Wexler, 2007; Wilcox, 2009; Zúñiga and Hernández-León, 2005; Zwi and Mares, 2015). The Armenian diaspora emerged following the Armenian Genocide, which up today remains a controversial issue for Turkey that refuses to accept responsibility for it (Hayter, 2000; Heisler, 2000; Hernandez-Truyol and Johns, 1997; Hollifield, Martin, and Orrenius, 2014; Jacobson, 1996).

Conflict (political, economic, and social) might lead to the significant and widespread dispersal of a community that then becomes a diaspora (Chin, 1999; Cook, 2003; Cornelisse, 2004, 2010; Costello, 2012; Dauvergne, 2012; Den Heijer, 2010; Dudley et al., 2012). A case in point is the Lebanese diaspora which emerged due to the Lebanese Civil War, with many Lebanese moving to European countries like Germany (Bacon, 1996; Dudley et al., 2012; Hollifield, Martin, and Orrenius, 2014; Money, 1998; Saadi et al., 2020). Recently, scholars have distinguished between different kinds of diaspora (Brané and Lundholm, 2007; Brochmann and Hammar, 2020; Chavez, 2001; Chin, 1999; Cook, 2003; Cornelisse, 2004). One of the defining characteristics that distinguish one diaspora from another is based on its causes. Examples of such causes include trade, colonialism, and even labor migrations (Guild and Niessen, 1996; Hailbronner, 2000; Hayter, 2000; Heisler, 2000; Hernandez-Truyol and Johns, 1997). Another criterion for distinguishing diasporas is by looking at the kind of social coherence within the diaspora community and its ties to the ancestral lands (Becerra, 2016; Brané and Lundholm, 2007; Brochmann and Hammar, 2020; Chavez, 2001; Chin, 1999; Cook, 2003). Some diaspora communities maintain strong political ties with their homeland, while others quickly disperse into different units (Becerra, 2016; Fiske, 2016; Joppke, 1999; Nethery and Holman, 2016; Sassen, 1996).

Other qualities that may be typical of many diasporas are thoughts of return and the extent to which these are embedded in the psyche of the diaspora (Brochmann and Hammar, 2020; Chavez, 2001; Chin, 1999; Cook,

2003; Cornelisse, 2004, 2010; Costello, 2012). It may also be distinguished by the fact that there is a strong or weak desire for keeping ties with the country of origin (Brané and Lundholm, 2007; Flynn, 2013; Joppke, 2010; Newman, Proctor, and Dudley, 2013; Sassen, 1997). Some diasporas are distinguished by their relationships with other communities in the diaspora, a case in point is where a number of diasporas unite to improve their political voice (Mehan, 1997; Melis, 2001; Miller, 2015, 2016; Molnar and Gill, 2018; Money, 1998; Morris, 2002, 2016). Then, recently that has been concerned about specific diasporas that are associated with a distinct lack of full integration into the host countries and hence causing concern about the entire premise of a liberal immigration policy (Dudley et al., 2012; Dunn, 2001, 2010; Exdell, 2009; Fiske, 2016; Flynn, 2013; Frederking, 2012; Gilman, 2013). Diasporas often maintain ties to the country of their historical affiliation and influence the policies of the country where they are located (Joppke, 1998, 1999, 2010; Kasimis, 2012; Kelson and DeLaet, 1999; King, 2009; Lopez, 2005; Lorentzen, 2014).

Countries like the USA are based on immigrant communities, and that has made their diasporas very powerful (Ramji-Nogales, 2007; Rubio-Marín, 2014; Ruhs, 2010; Ryan and Mitsilegas, 2010; Saadi et al., 2020; Samers, 2004). For example, by 2019, there is a strong Indian diaspora of 17.5 million people. This is followed by 11.8 million Mexican diaspora and 10.7 million of the Chinese diaspora. The host countries may become concerned about the influence of these diasporas, particularly if they are concentrated in specific areas where they dominate (Motomura, 1999; Nethery and Holman, 2016; Newman, Proctor, and Dudley, 2013; Oberman, 2016; Orfanos, 2019). Other voices demand full allegiance from members of the diaspora, regardless of the negative experiences that members of the diaspora may have had in the host country (Fiske, 2016; Flynn, 2013; Frederking, 2012; Gilman, 2013; Guia, Koulish, and Mitsilegas, 2016; Guild, 2001; Guild and Niessen, 1996). A case in point is how anti-migrant movements in the USA fully anticipate that the Mexican diaspora must disavow other Mexican immigrants that have recently arrived, particularly if they have entered illegally. It is for this reason that some countries diaspora as an existential threat that must be controlled through limiting immigration (Hollifield, Martin, and Orrenius, 2014; Jacobson, 1996; Johnson, 1996; Joppke, 1998, 1999, 2010). In the next section, we further explore specific categories of diaspora.

4.2. CATEGORIES OF DIASPORAS

There are several categories of diaspora (Hernandez-Truyol and Johns, 1997; Hollifield, Martin, and Orrenius, 2014; Jacobson, 1996; Johnson, 1996; Joppke, 1998). Each of these categorizations has its own histories and characteristics (Nethery and Holman, 2016; Newman, Proctor, and Dudley, 2013; Oberman, 2016; Orfanos, 2019; Ozdowski, 1985). A case in point is the African diaspora or the collection of various African diasporas. One of the largest diasporas of modern times is that of sub-Saharan Africans (Heisler, 2000; Hernandez-Truyol and Johns, 1997; Hollifield, Martin, and Orrenius, 2014; Jacobson, 1996; Johnson, 1996). This particularly diaspora dates back several centuries and has a special historical importance given its linkages with slavery (Peberdy, 2001; Ramji-Nogales, 2007; Rubio-Marín, 2014; Ruhs, 2010; Ryan and Mitsilegas, 2010; Saadi et al., 2020; Samers, 2004). Figure 4.2 is a representation of the history and state of the African diaspora.

Figure 4.2: Origins and state of African diaspora.

Source: Kuala.

During the Atlantic slave trade, over 11 million people from West Africa who managed to survive their arduous transportation to the Americas, arrived there as slaves (Guild, 2001; Miller, 2016; Ryan and Mitsilegas, 2010; Wexler, 2007; Wilcox, 2009). This population and their descendants were major influences on the culture of British, Portuguese, French, and Spanish New World colonies (Acer and Goodman, 2009; Ackerman and Furman, 2014; Adelman, 2002; Aynsley-Green et al., 2012; Bacon, 1996). It is important to remember that there was already transnational travel prior to the trans-Atlantic slave trade. This travel comprised mainly millions of Africans who were merchants, seamen, and slaves in different parts of Europe and Asia (Miller, 2015, 2016; Molnar and Gill, 2018; Money, 1998; Morris, 2002, 2016; Motomura, 1999; Nethery and Holman, 2016). From the 8th through the 19th century, an Arab-controlled slave trade dispersed millions of Africans to Asia and the islands of the Indian Ocean (Dauvergne, 2012; Hernandez-Truyol and Johns, 1997; Molnar and Gill, 2018; Zúñiga and Hernández-León, 2005). There are significant restrictions on new African migrants and those that are already settled in the West have to deal with significant discrimination (Peberdy, 2001; Ramji-Nogales, 2007; Rubio-Marín, 2014; Ruhs, 2010; Ryan and Mitsilegas, 2010; Saadi et al., 2020; Samers, 2004). Indeed, it has been argued that immigration policy specifically regulates the movement of African people while opening up frontiers for Europeans and other Caucasian communities (Sassen, 1997; Shohamy and McNamara, 2009; Smith, 2014; Soysal, 2012; Spijkerboer and Van Walsum, 2007).

Another important diaspora is that of Indian communities which remains the largest diaspora in the world today (Webber, 2012; Welch, 2002; Wexler, 2007; Wilcox, 2009; Zúñiga and Hernández-León, 2005; Zwi and Mares, 2015). The overseas Indian community, estimated at over 17 million, is spread across many regions in the world (China, 1999; Cook, 2003; Cornelisse, 2004, 2010; Costello, 2012; Dauvergne, 2012; Den Heijer, 2010; Dudley et al., 2012). Indians in the diaspora constitute a diverse, heterogeneous, and eclectic global community representing different regions, languages, cultures, and faiths (Gilman, 2013; Guia, Koulish, and Mitsilegas, 2016; Guild, 2001; Guild and Niessen, 1996; Hailbronner, 2000; Hayter, 2000). The earliest known Asian diaspora of note is the Jewish diaspora.

China has a well-established diaspora based on its trade and cultural links across the globe (Orfanos, 2019; Ozdowski, 1985; Paz, 2016; Peberdy, 2001; Ramji-Nogales, 2007; Rubio-Marín, 2014; Ruhs, 2010). At one point, the Chinese had to ask for permission to emigrate, but that has changed over time (Chavez, 2001; Chin, 1999; Cook, 2003; Cornelisse, 2004, 2010; Costello, 2012; Dauvergne, 2012; Den Heijer, 2010). Indeed, there was a time when immigration authorities in the Western world were struggling to get cooperation from the Chinese government when attempting to return citizens that had entered illegally (Dauvergne, 2012; Den Heijer, 2010; Dudley et al., 2012; Dunn, 2001, 2010; Exdell, 2009; Fiske, 2016; Flynn, 2013). Chinese emigration first occurred thousands of years ago (Den Heijer, 2010; Dudley et al., 2012; Dunn, 2001, 2010; Exdell, 2009; Fiske, 2016; Flynn, 2013; Frederking, 2012). The mass emigration that occurred from the

19th century to 1949 (Exdell, 2009; Fiske, 2016; Flynn, 2013; Frederking, 2012; Gilman, 2013; Guia, Koulish, and Mitsilegas, 2016; Guild, 2001). This type of emigration was caused mainly by wars and starvation in mainland China, as well as political corruption (Sassen, 1996, 1997; Shohamy and McNamara, 2009; Smith, 2014; Soysal, 2012; Spijkerboer and Van Walsum, 2007).

Recently, there has been an interest in internal and more recent diasporas which in many ways are more relevant to the modern context (Thym, 2008; Webber, 2012; Welch, 2002; Wexler, 2007; Wilcox, 2009; Zúñiga and Hernández-León, 2005; Zwi and Mares, 2015). For example, over 4 million people moved outside their home states in 2010. Some experts have noted the development of distinct "Detroit diaspora" communities in Seattle and in Washington (DC) (Barak-Erez, 2008; Becerra, 2016; Brané and Lundholm, 2007; Brochmann and Hammar, 2020; Chavez, 2001; Chin, 1999). Moreover, layoffs in the auto industry also led to substantial blue-collar migration from Michigan to Wyoming around 2005. These are communities that do not necessarily change countries but move internally and have significant impacts on the communities that they leave and the ones that they move to (Samers, 2004; Sampson, Mitchell, and Bowring, 2011; Sanggaran, Haire, and Zion, 2016; Sassen, 1996, 1997). The challenge then becomes controlling such migrations and whether such controls are even desirable in a dynamic democracy where citizens have a right to move within the borders of that country (Melis, 2001; Miller, 2015, 2016; Molnar and Gill, 2018; Money, 1998; Morris, 2002, 2016; Motomura, 1999).

Similar patterns are seen in China, where the impetus to find work has meant that it is desirable to change location (Fiske, 2016; Flynn, 2013; Frederking, 2012; Gilman, 2013; Guia, Koulish, and Mitsilegas, 2016; Guild, 2001). So much so, that the government has started placing movement controls which are very similar to immigration controls at the borders (Morris, 2002, 2016; Motomura, 1999; Nethery and Holman, 2016; Newman, Proctor, and Dudley, 2013; Oberman, 2016). We know that millions of migrant workers have sought greater opportunity in the country's booming coastal metropolises of China (Hayter, 2000; Heisler, 2000; Hernandez-Truyol and Johns, 1997; Hollifield, Martin, and Orrenius, 2014; Jacobson, 1996). One of the negative impacts of these trends is a slowing down of development in the interior, an area that was already under-developed (Costello, 2012; Guia, Koulish, and Mitsilegas, 2016; Melis, 2001; Rubio-Marín, 2014; Webber, 2012). Migrant social structures in Chinese megacities are often based on place of origin, such as a shared hometown or province (Sampson, Mitchell, and Bowring, 2011; Sanggaran, Haire, and Zion, 2016; Sassen, 1996, 1997; Shohamy and McNamara, 2009). Hence, recruiters and foremen commonly select entire work crews from the same village (Brochmann and Hammar, 2020; Chavez, 2001; Chin, 1999; Cook, 2003; Cornelisse, 2004, 2010; Costello, 2012). These incidents and patterns demonstrate the power of internal immigration and the formation of new diasporas that are not international in nature (Baldwin-Edwards, 2006; Dunn, 2001; Jacobson, 1996; Morris, 2016; Samers, 2004). The next section examines the role and experiences of environmental migrants in responding to climate change.

4.3. ENVIRONMENTAL MIGRANTS AND CLIMATE CHANGE

Recently, there has been interest in the impact of climate change in terms of creating new migrations (Motomura, 1999; Nethery and Holman, 2016; Newman, Proctor, and Dudley, 2013; Oberman, 2016; Orfanos, 2019). Environmental migrants are people who are forced to leave their home region due to sudden or long-term changes to their local environment (Nethery and Holman, 2016; Newman, Proctor, and Dudley, 2013; Oberman, 2016; Orfanos, 2019; Ozdowski, 1985). These changes compromise their well-being or alternatively render their livelihood less secure (Shohamy and McNamara, 2009; Smith, 2014; Soysal, 2012; Spijkerboer and Van Walsum, 2007; Taylor, 2000; Thym, 2008). Some of the key events that might inspire such movements include increased drought, desertification, sea-level rise, and disruption of seasonal weather patterns (Barak-Erez, 2008; Exdell, 2009; Joppke, 1998; Motomura, 1999; Sanggaran, Haire, and Zion, 2016). In Figure 4.3, policy makers in Europe predict a positive relationship between increases in temperature and asylum applications.

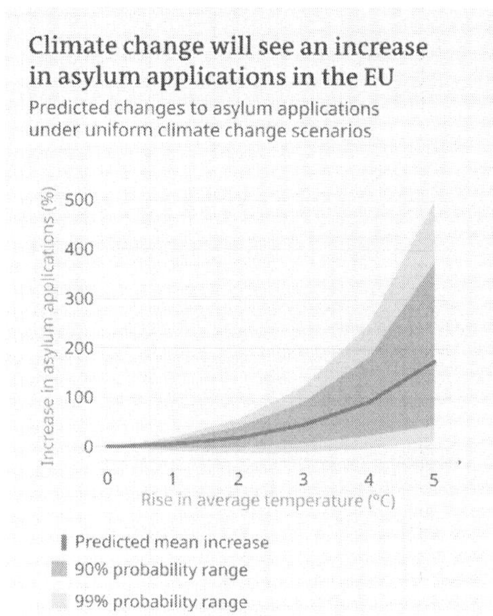

Figure 4.3: Climate change and asylum applications in Europe.

Source: Anouch Missirian and Wolfram (2017) via DW.

Climate refugees may flee or migrate to another country, or they may migrate internally within their own country (Joppke, 1998, 1999, 2010; Kasimis, 2012; Kelson and DeLaet, 1999; King, 2009; Lopez, 2005; Lorentzen, 2014). Though there is no uniform and clear-cut definition of environmental migration (Ryan and Mitsilegas, 2010; Saadi et al., 2020; Samers, 2004; Sampson, Mitchell, and Bowring, 2011; Sanggaran, Haire, and Zion, 2016). However, the idea is gaining growing attention as policy-makers and environmental and social scientists (Paz, 2016; Peberdy, 2001; Ramji-Nogales, 2007; Rubio-Marín, 2014; Ruhs, 2010; Ryan and Mitsilegas, 2010). Such attentions attempt to conceptualize the potential societal effects of climate change and environmental degradation (Ozdowski, 1985; Paz, 2016; Peberdy, 2001; Ramji-Nogales, 2007; Rubio-Marín, 2014; Ruhs, 2010; Ryan and Mitsilegas, 2010).

Climate refugees do not really fit into any of the legal definitions of a refugee under traditional international law (Johnson, 1996; Joppke, 1998, 1999, 2010; Kasimis, 2012; Kelson and DeLaet, 1999; King, 2009; Lopez, 2005). Indeed, some researchers have questioned the very concept of climate refugees. They argue that it is lacking any scientific basis and is therefore open to misrepresentation (Ackerman and Furman, 2014; Chin,

1999; Hailbronner, 2000; Lopez, 2005; Paz, 2016; Smith, 2014). Others refer to it as the 'fabrication of a migration threat' as part of attempts to obscure the political causes of most displacement, not least because they are much more difficult to confront (Cornelisse, 2010; Gilman, 2013; Kelson and DeLaet, 1999; Orfanos, 2019; Thym, 2008). Such obfuscation can be ultimately damaging to the entire immigration system and mean that deserving applicants are not given the attention that they need and deserve (Cornelisse, 2004, 2010; Costello, 2012; Dauvergne, 2012; Den Heijer, 2010; Dudley et al., 2012; Dunn, 2001). Nevertheless, there is interest in the plight of people that change location due to climate change and its effects (Paz, 2016; Peberdy, 2001; Ramji-Nogales, 2007; Rubio-Marín, 2014; Ruhs, 2010; Ryan and Mitsilegas, 2010; Saadi et al., 2020).

The vast majority of people fleeing environmental distress migrate over short distances. These changes in location tend to last for a relatively short period of time and people will tend to return to their homeland once the climate change effects have subsided (Brochmann and Hammar, 2020; Chavez, 2001; Chin, 1999; Cook, 2003; Cornelisse, 2004, 2010). Moreover, the refugees are likely to have been persecuted by the government or citizens. Instead, the threat to them is directly linked to the environment. Because such migrants do not face generalized violence or events seriously disturbing public order, they are often ignored from a public policy perspective (Baldwin-Edwards, 2006; Dunn, 2001; Jacobson, 1996; Morris, 2016; Samers, 2004). There is nevertheless a recognition of the changes that are happening in migration and their motivation (Joppke, 2010; Kasimis, 2012; Kelson and DeLaet, 1999; King, 2009; Lopez, 2005; Lorentzen, 2014; Mehan, 1997).

International law is gradually coming to terms with the reality of climate refugees. For example, the definition of who is a refugee was expanded since its first international and legally binding definition in 1951 (Fiske, 2016; Flynn, 2013; Frederking, 2012; Gilman, 2013; Guia, Koulish, and Mitsilegas, 2016; Guild, 2001). These changes notwithstanding, people who are forced to flee due to environmental change are still not offered the same legal protection as refugees (Sassen, 1996, 1997; Shohamy and McNamara, 2009; Smith, 2014; Soysal, 2012; Spijkerboer and Van Walsum, 2007). That means that those who are in this situation are not given the protections that would be due them if they were clearly included in international law (Exdell, 2009; Fiske, 2016; Flynn, 2013; Frederking, 2012; Gilman, 2013; Guia, Koulish, and Mitsilegas, 2016; Guild, 2001).

The typologies of environmental migrants are still being developed and will likely be contested in the future, as more up to date knowledge emerges (Chin, 1999; Cook, 2003; Cornelisse, 2004, 2010; Costello, 2012; Dauvergne, 2012; Den Heijer, 2010; Dudley et al., 2012). At the moment, the International Organization for Migration proposes three types of environmental migrants (Webber, 2012; Welch, 2002; Wexler, 2007; Wilcox, 2009; Zúñiga and Hernández-León, 2005; Zwi and Mares, 2015). The first category is that of environmental emergency migrants (Sassen, 1997; Shohamy and McNamara, 2009; Smith, 2014; Soysal, 2012; Spijkerboer and Van Walsum, 2007). This group comprises people who flee temporarily due to an environmental disaster or sudden environmental event (Peberdy, 2001; Ramji-Nogales, 2007; Rubio-Marín, 2014; Ruhs, 2010; Ryan and Mitsilegas, 2010; Saadi et al., 2020; Samers, 2004). Some of the triggering events include hurricanes, tsunamis, and earthquakes (Dauvergne, 2012; Hernandez-Truyol and Johns, 1997; Molnar and Gill, 2018; Zúñiga and Hernández-León, 2005). In planning for these events, it is important to remember that they may lead to migration (Miller, 2015, 2016; Molnar and Gill, 2018; Money, 1998; Morris, 2002, 2016; Motomura, 1999; Nethery and Holman, 2016). Those that decide to move away may only do so on a temporary basis and will return if the danger subsides to an acceptable level (Acer and Goodman, 2009; Ackerman and Furman, 2014; Adelman, 2002; Aynsley-Green et al., 2012; Bacon, 1996). Others are happy to be resettled in a new region as long as they have a comparative lifestyle (Guild, 2001; Miller, 2016; Ryan and Mitsilegas, 2010; Wexler, 2007; Wilcox, 2009). However, the reality is that these environmental immigrants end up leading new lives of abject poverty and social discrimination (Peberdy, 2001; Ramji-Nogales, 2007; Rubio-Marín, 2014; Ruhs, 2010; Ryan and Mitsilegas, 2010; Saadi et al., 2020; Samers, 2004). They are now forced to rely on aid since their means of a livelihood are often destroyed by the triggering event (Heisler, 2000; Hernandez-Truyol and Johns, 1997; Hollifield, Martin, and Orrenius, 2014; Jacobson, 1996; Johnson, 1996).

The second category is that of environmental forced migrants (Hernandez-Truyol and Johns, 1997; Hollifield, Martin, and Orrenius, 2014; Jacobson, 1996; Johnson, 1996; Joppke, 1998). This group comprises people who have to leave due to deteriorating environmental conditions (Nethery and Holman, 2016; Newman, Proctor, and Dudley, 2013; Oberman, 2016; Orfanos, 2019; Ozdowski, 1985). A case in point are communities that are forced to change location due to a slow deterioration of their environment, such as deforestation and coastal deterioration (Hollifield, Martin, and

Orrenius, 2014; Jacobson, 1996; Johnson, 1996; Joppke, 1998, 1999, 2010). In recent times, there has been an example in the village of Satabhaya which is located in the Kendrapara district of Odisha within India (Fiske, 2016; Flynn, 2013; Frederking, 2012; Gilman, 2013; Guia, Koulish, and Mitsilegas, 2016; Guild, 2001; Guild and Niessen, 1996). Another example emerged in Nepal where many villages in mass migration has been reported from Shivalik Hills or Chure regions (Joppke, 1998, 1999, 2010; Kasimis, 2012; Kelson and DeLaet, 1999; King, 2009; Lopez, 2005; Lorentzen, 2014). These movements are due to water scarcity which remains a common theme in environmental migration (Dudley et al., 2012; Dunn, 2001, 2010; Exdell, 2009; Fiske, 2016; Flynn, 2013; Frederking, 2012; Gilman, 2013).

The third category comprises environmental motivated migrants also known as environmentally induced economic migrants (Mehan, 1997; Melis, 2001; Miller, 2015, 2016; Molnar and Gill, 2018; Money, 1998; Morris, 2002, 2016). These are people who choose to leave to avoid possible future problems (Brané and Lundholm, 2007; Flynn, 2013; Joppke, 2010; Newman, Proctor, and Dudley, 2013; Sassen, 1997). Some issues that might inspire them to plan a move include declining crop productivity caused by desertification (Brochmann and Hammar, 2020; Chavez, 2001; Chin, 1999; Cook, 2003; Cornelisse, 2004, 2010; Costello, 2012). In these cases, the environment has a proximate effect on migration (Becerra, 2016; Fiske, 2016; Joppke, 1999; Nethery and Holman, 2016; Sassen, 1996). It is not a direct cause of migration and that is why it is always recognized as falling within the criterion for asylum (Becerra, 2016; Brané and Lundholm, 2007; Brochmann and Hammar, 2020; Chavez, 2001; Chin, 1999; Cook, 2003). The next section explores some existential migration patterns.

4.4. EXISTENTIAL MIGRATION PATTERNS

Existential migration is a term coined by Greg Madison (2006) in "*Existential Analysis*," an article published in the Journal of the Society for Existential Analysis (Kasimis, 2012; Kelson and DeLaet, 1999; King, 2009; Lopez, 2005; Lorentzen, 2014; Mehan, 1997; Melis, 2001). That article describes expatriates or voluntary emigrants who supposedly have an "existential" motivation (Bangarth, 2003; Barak-Erez, 2008; Becerra, 2016; Brané and Lundholm, 2007; Brochmann and Hammar, 2020; Chavez, 2001). This motivation is unlike economic migration which seeks to find job opportunities and business avenues (Kasimis, 2012; Kelson and DeLaet, 1999; King, 2009; Lopez, 2005; Lorentzen, 2014; Mehan, 1997; Melis,

2013; Frederking, 2012; Gilman, 2013; Guia, Koulish, and Mitsilegas, 2016). The funding that is required for such adventures can be significant (Molnar and Gill, 2018; Money, 1998; Morris, 2002, 2016; Motomura, 1999; Nethery and Holman, 2016). Additionally, global nomads tend to be privileged with the kinds of passports that allow them to travel widely and freely (Acer and Goodman, 2009; Ackerman and Furman, 2014; Adelman, 2002; Aynsley-Green et al., 2012; Bacon, 1996). That criterion effectively rules out people from the developing world whose travel is severely restricted, unless they are immensely privileged (Morris, 2002, 2016; Motomura, 1999; Nethery and Holman, 2016; Newman, Proctor, and Dudley, 2013; Oberman, 2016).

The global nomad lifestyle challenges many of the dominant norms and ideals in Western societies (Webber, 2012; Welch, 2002; Wexler, 2007; Wilcox, 2009; Zúñiga and Hernández-León, 2005; Zwi and Mares, 2015). Some of these ideals are focused on the capitalist lifestyle including accumulation of wealth, nationalism, homeownership, and strong roots (Saadi et al., 2020; Samers, 2004; Sampson, Mitchell, and Bowring, 2011; Sanggaran, Haire, and Zion, 2016). However, a successful global nomad will require a powerful passport that opens, rather than closes, immigration doors (Wexler, 2007; Wilcox, 2009; Zúñiga and Hernández-León, 2005; Zwi and Mares, 2015). Even as they become more mobile and global, these nomads are still citizens of rich and powerful countries. This apparent contradiction or paradox suggests that global nomadism is yet another privilege to be enjoyed by those born in the right countries at the right time (Acer and Goodman, 2009; Ackerman and Furman, 2014; Adelman, 2002; Aynsley-Green et al., 2012; Bacon, 1996). That is why some critics argue that global nomads are privileged people who are indulging in their pastimes (Spijkerboer and Van Walsum, 2007; Taylor, 2000; Thym, 2008; Webber, 2012; Welch, 2002; Wexler, 2007; Wilcox, 2009).

The fact that global nomads are citizens of a powerful or influential country affords them the ability to indulge their lifestyle choices (Barak-Erez, 2008; Becerra, 2016; Brané and Lundholm, 2007; Brochmann and Hammar, 2020; Chavez, 2001; Chin, 1999). Those who deny the racism and xenophobia inherent in the current immigration framework in developed countries argue that the controls are born out of economic realities (Orfanos, 2019; Ozdowski, 1985; Paz, 2016; Peberdy, 2001; Ramji-Nogales, 2007; Rubio-Marín, 2014; Ruhs, 2010). It follows that people from the developing world will have an incentive to remain in developed countries and that is why their entry is controlled (Hollifield, Martin, and Orrenius, 2014; Jacobson, 1996; Johnson, 1996; Joppke, 1998, 1999, 2010). By contrast, those that are citizens of developed nations have no visible reason to move to developing nations (Hollifield, Martin, and Orrenius, 2014; Jacobson, 1996; Johnson, 1996; Joppke, 1998, 1999, 2010; Kasimis, 2012). However, such an assertion fails to understand the individuality of motivations (Dauvergne, 2012; Hernandez-Truyol and Johns, 1997; Molnar and Gill, 2018; Zúñiga and Hernández-León, 2005). There are many people in the developed world who are looking for opportunities (including jobs) from the developing world (Taylor, 2000; Thym, 2008; Webber, 2012; Welch, 2002; Wexler, 2007; Wilcox, 2009; Zúñiga and Hernández-León, 2005). What remains clear is that being a global nomad is a privilege that is still restricted to people from the developed world (Baldwin-Edwards, 2006; Bangarth, 2003; Barak-Erez, 2008; Becerra, 2016; Brané and Lundholm, 2007).

TCK or third culture individuals (TCI) are people who were raised in a culture other than their parents' or the culture of their country of nationality (Acer and Goodman, 2009; Chavez, 2001; Guild and Niessen, 1996; King, 2009; Ozdowski, 1985; Shohamy and McNamara, 2009). Such people live in a different environment during a significant part of their child development years (Money, 1998; Morris, 2002, 2016; Motomura, 1999; Nethery and Holman, 2016; Newman, Proctor, and Dudley, 2013). They typically have a complex cultural exposure and are markedly different from children that have never left their home countries (Dunn, 2010; Exdell, 2009; Fiske, 2016; Flynn, 2013; Frederking, 2012; Gilman, 2013; Guia, Koulish, and Mitsilegas, 2016). The term applies to both adults and children. This is because the term "kid" refers to the individual's formative or developmental years, rather than their current adult state (Saadi et al., 2020; Samers, 2004; Sampson, Mitchell, and Bowring, 2011; Sanggaran, Haire, and Zion, 2016). A more precise terms is that of an adult third culture kid or ATCK (Hailbronner, 2000; Hayter, 2000; Heisler, 2000; Hernandez-Truyol and Johns, 1997; Hollifield, Martin, and Orrenius, 2014). Generally speaking, TCK come from relatively privileged backgrounds and will have led an international lifestyle, for all its worth.

That is not to say that being a third culture kid is all fun and games. For example, these children may face the problem of confused cultural loyalties between their home and countries they visit (Adelman, 2002; Cook, 2003; Hayter, 2000; Lorentzen, 2014; Peberdy, 2001; Soysal, 2012). This can translate into confusion about their politics and values (Costello, 2012; Dauvergne, 2012; Den Heijer, 2010; Dudley et al., 2012; Dunn, 2001, 2010; Exdell, 2009; Fiske, 2016). A case in point is the reconciliation of values when traveling back and forth between collectivist to individualist cultures

(Acer and Goodman, 2009; Ackerman and Furman, 2014; Adelman, 2002; Aynsley-Green et al., 2012; Bacon, 1996). Perhaps one explanation for this is that the values within each culture are different from the other and yet these children are expected to rationalize or harmonize them (Baldwin-Edwards, 2006; Bangarth, 2003; Barak-Erez, 2008; Becerra, 2016; Brané and Lundholm, 2007; Brochmann and Hammar, 2020).

CHAPTER 4 SUMMARY

This chapter has explored a number of communities that are experiencing migration in one form or another. These include diasporas, environmental immigrants, existential migrants, global nomads, and TCK. One of the emerging themes that is emphasized throughout the chapter is the fact that migration and its experience can be qualitative in nature. That means that the reductivist notions of migrants do not always capture this level of complexity. It is also clear that experiences of migration can have long lasting effects beyond the immediate event within which they occur. In the next chapter, we try to redefine immigration categories.

CHAPTER 5

REDEFINING MIGRATION CATEGORIES

CONTENTS

This chapter explores the possibilities and limitations of migration categories. In so doing, the chapter highlights some new definitions and conceptualizations that are changing the way in which we understand migration categories. The first section in this chapter examines the notion of digital nomads. In the second section, we will look at perpetual travelers and backpackers. The third section highlights the possibilities and limitations of global citizenship. In the fourth section, we look at tax exiles and their impact. The chapter will close with an overview of how expatriates are privileged over and above other immigrants who are labeled in negative (and ultimately harmful) ways. Let us begin the chapter by examining the notion of digital nomads.

5.1. THE NATURE AND IMPACT OF DIGITAL NOMADS

Digital nomads use telecommunications technology to earn a living. However, these people conduct their lives in a nomadic pattern that does not fit into the traditional conceptualization of a migrant (Hollifield, Martin, and Orrenius, 2014; Jacobson, 1996; Johnson, 1996; Joppke, 1998, 1999, 2010). Such workers often work remotely from foreign countries. Anthropological studies have extensively examined their preferred operational spaces, including coffee shops, co-working spaces, public libraries, and recreational vehicles (Acer and Goodman, 2009; Ackerman and Furman, 2014; Adelman, 2002; Aynsley-Green et al., 2012; Bacon, 1996). This type of mobile and remote working is often accomplished through the use of devices that have wireless Internet capabilities (Brochmann and Hammar, 2020; Chavez, 2001; Chin, 1999; Cook, 2003; Cornelisse, 2004, 2010; Costello, 2012). Successful digital nomads typically have a financial cushion to fall back on in case things do not work out (Ryan and Mitsilegas, 2010; Saadi et al., 2020; Samers, 2004; Sampson, Mitchell, and Bowring, 2011; Sanggaran, Haire, and Zion, 2016). Alternatively, they need to develop high levels of self-reliance and self-discipline to maintain a certain level of income and expenditure that is sustainable in both the short and long run (Morris, 2002; Motomura, 1999; Nethery and Holman, 2016; Newman, Proctor, and Dudley, 2013; Oberman, 2016). Digital nomads have a very utilitarian view of spaces (see Figure 5.1), and this allows them to make use of cosmopolitan areas.

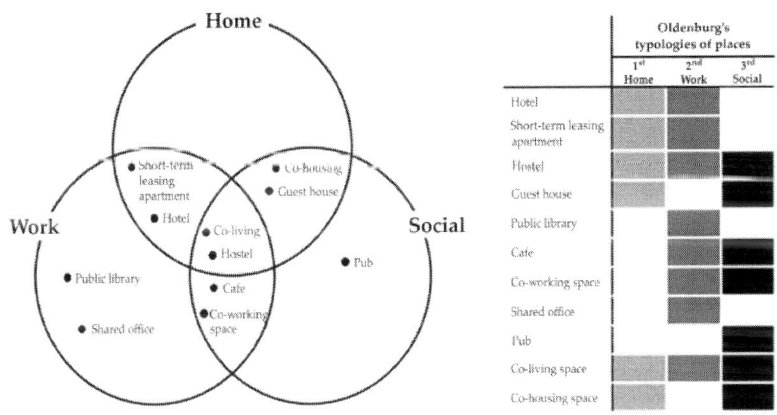

Figure 5.1: Utilitarian perception of spaces among digital nomads.

Source: Ahreum Lee via ResearchGate.

There is a host of technologies that have come into fashion so as to support digital nomads (Becerra, 2016; Fiske, 2016; Joppke, 1999; Nethery and Holman, 2016; Sassen, 1996). For example, services such as TransferWise and PayPal are popular among digital nomads. Skype, Zoom, and Slack are common tools for people to use to communicate through voice, text, and video chat across long distances. YouTube and Instagram have been used by digital nomads as a means by which to earn revenue through content directly or indirectly through sponsorship and merchandising without having to have a central workplace or living space. An important step in being a digital nomad is ensuring that all relevant documentation (such as visas and passports) is kept up to date (Cook, 2003; Cornelisse, 2004, 2010; Costello, 2012; Dauvergne, 2012; Den Heijer, 2010; Dudley et al., 2012). Failure to do so can lead to legal difficulties when traveling abroad (Hayter, 2000; Heisler, 2000; Hernandez-Truyol and Johns, 1997; Hollifield, Martin, and Orrenius, 2014; Jacobson, 1996). A solid grasp of any official languages of the countries visited is also important because failure to do so can prevent a person from engaging with the locals (Ruhs, 2010; Ryan and Mitsilegas, 2010; Saadi et al., 2020; Samers, 2004; Sampson, Mitchell, and Bowring, 2011). It also creates the risk of complication when accessing medical services (Hayter, 2000; Heisler, 2000; Hernandez-Truyol and Johns, 1997; Hollifield, Martin, and Orrenius, 2014; Jacobson, 1996).

There are psychosocial costs that are associated with digital nomadism. For example, feelings of loneliness are an inevitable consequence of living and working alone (Cornelisse, 2010; Gilman, 2013; Kelson and DeLaet, 1999; Orfanos, 2019; Thym, 2008). Indeed, nomadism often requires freedom from personal attachments, a key example being marriage (Kasimis, 2012; Kelson and DeLaet, 1999; King, 2009; Lopez, 2005; Lorentzen, 2014; Mehan, 1997; Melis, 2001). The need for intimacy and family life may be a motive to undertake digital nomadism as an intermittent or temporary activity (Exdell, 2009; Fiske, 2016; Flynn, 2013; Frederking, 2012; Gilman, 2013; Guia, Koulish, and Mitsilegas, 2016; Guild, 2001). Another option involves traveling as a digital nomad couple as long as both partners are interested in lifestyle (Soysal, 2012; Spijkerboer and Van Walsum, 2007; Taylor, 2000; Thym, 2008; Webber, 2012; Welch, 2002; Wexler, 2007). The next section considers the nature of perpetual travelers and backpackers.

5.2. BACKPACKERS AND PERPETUAL TRAVELERS

Backpacking is a form of low-cost, independent travel. This modality of migration often includes staying in inexpensive lodgings. Typically, the backpacker will carry all necessary possessions in a backpack, hence the name for them (Wexler, 2007; Wilcox, 2009; Zúñiga and Hernández-León, 2005; Zwi and Mares, 2015). At one point, backpacking was seen as a marginal form of travel undertaken only through necessity (Joppke, 1999, 2010; Kasimis, 2012; Kelson and DeLaet, 1999; King, 2009; Lopez, 2005; Lorentzen, 2014; Mehan, 1997). More recently, it has become a mainstream form of tourism and therefore has attracted significant research interest (Nethery and Holman, 2016; Newman, Proctor, and Dudley, 2013; Oberman, 2016; Orfanos, 2019; Ozdowski, 1985). For the most part, backpacker tourism is generally a form of youth travel (Motomura, 1999; Nethery and Holman, 2016; Newman, Proctor, and Dudley, 2013; Oberman, 2016; Orfanos, 2019). Others utilize it as an inexpensive way to spend gap years between high school and university admission (Morris, 2002, 2016; Motomura, 1999; Nethery and Holman, 2016; Newman, Proctor, and Dudley, 2013; Oberman, 2016). However, older people can become backpackers during a career break or retirement (Ramji-Nogales, 2007; Rubio-Marín, 2014; Ruhs, 2010; Ryan and Mitsilegas, 2010; Saadi et al., 2020; Samers, 2004). Backpackers tend to be from Western Europe, North America, and Asia (Shohamy and McNamara, 2009; Smith, 2014; Soysal, 2012; Spijkerboer and Van Walsum, 2007; Taylor, 2000; Thym, 2008). Related activities such as hiking are increasing in popularity, as exemplified by the trend in the USA (see Figure 5.2).

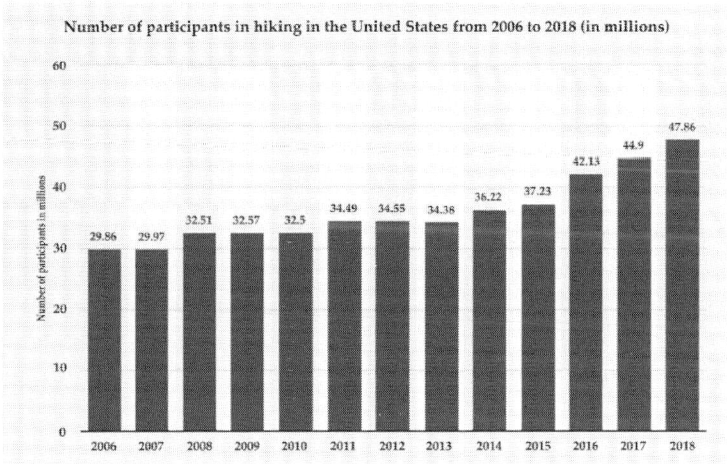

Figure 5.2: Number of hikers in the USA 2006 through 2018.

Source: Outdoor Freedom via Statista.

There are certain characteristics that differential backpacking from other forms of travel or tourism (Cornelisse, 2004, 2010; Costello, 2012; Dauvergne, 2012; Den Heijer, 2010; Dudley et al., 2012; Dunn, 2001). For example, backpackers tend to travel mostly via public transport. This is done in order to save costs. Such travelers also do not want to be tied down by the process of obtaining a private car or driving license (Ozdowski, 1985; Paz, 2016; Peberdy, 2001; Ramji-Nogales, 2007; Rubio-Marín, 2014; Ruhs, 2010; Ryan and Mitsilegas, 2010). In order to budget effectively for an extended period of time, backpackers are typically found of using inexpensive lodging such as hostels or homestays (Becerra, 2016; Fiske, 2016; Joppke, 1999; Nethery and Holman, 2016; Sassen, 1996). However, on average backpacking involves a longer duration trip when compared with conventional vacations (Wexler, 2007; Wilcox, 2009; Zúñiga and Hernández-León, 2005; Zwi and Mares, 2015). Typical backpackers express and pursue an interest in meeting locals as well as seeing sights (Taylor, 2000; Thym, 2008; Webber, 2012; Welch, 2002; Wexler, 2007; Wilcox, 2009; Zúñiga and Hernández-León, 2005; Zwi and Mares, 2015). Moreover, they have an interest in meeting other travelers (Cornelisse, 2010; Gilman, 2013; Kelson and DeLaet, 1999; Orfanos, 2019; Thym, 2008).

Recent research has showed that for Westerners, backpacking leads to acquired capabilities like effective communication and decision-making

(Webber, 2012; Welch, 2002; Wexler, 2007; Wilcox, 2009; Zúñiga and Hernández-León, 2005; Zwi and Mares, 2015). Others have reported improving their adaptability and problem solving following an experience of backpacking (Webber, 2012; Welch, 2002; Wexler, 2007; Wilcox, 2009; Zúñiga and Hernández-León, 2005; Zwi and Mares, 2015). All these skills contribute to an increase in self-efficacy among certain nationalities of backpackers, including for example, Chinese backpackers (Miller, 2016; Molnar and Gill, 2018; Money, 1998; Morris, 2002, 2016; Motomura, 1999; Nethery and Holman, 2016). Others have reported acquiring skills like time and money management (Taylor, 2000; Thym, 2008; Webber, 2012; Welch, 2002; Wexler, 2007; Wilcox, 2009; Zúñiga and Hernández-León, 2005; Zwi and Mares, 2015). Then there are those that benefit from language development and stress management following their experiences of backpacking (Cornelisse, 2004, 2010; Costello, 2012; Dauvergne, 2012; Den Heijer, 2010; Dudley et al., 2012; Dunn, 2001). Generally, this type of activity calls for a high level of self-motivation and has therefore been shown to provide a significant increase in self-efficacy (Johnson, 1996; Joppke, 1998, 1999, 2010; Kasimis, 2012; Kelson and DeLaet, 1999; King, 2009; Lopez, 2005). In that sense, backpacking can turn into a learning experience (Paz, 2016; Peberdy, 2001; Ramji-Nogales, 2007; Rubio-Marín, 2014; Ruhs, 2010; Ryan and Mitsilegas, 2010).

For many low-income communities in the developing world, the economic benefits of hosting backpackers outweigh their negative impacts (Costello, 2012; Guia, Koulish, and Mitsilegas, 2016; Melis, 2001; Rubio-Marín, 2014; Webber, 2012). That is why backpackers are welcomed despite the fact that they may not necessarily fit the profile of a typical tourist or expatriate (Exdell, 2009; Fiske, 2016; Flynn, 2013; Frederking, 2012; Gilman, 2013; Guia, Koulish, and Mitsilegas, 2016; Guild, 2001). Since backpackers tend to consume local products, they are in effect supporting local industry in ways which are not traditionally associated with tourism (Kelson and DeLaet, 1999; King, 2009; Lopez, 2005; Lorentzen, 2014; Mehan, 1997; Melis, 2001; Miller, 2015, 2016). Backpackers tend to stay in small guest houses, a source of income for small businesses and entrepreneurs (Paz, 2016; Peberdy, 2001; Ramji-Nogales, 2007; Rubio-Marín, 2014; Ruhs, 2010; Ryan and Mitsilegas, 2010; Saadi et al., 2020). They also tend to use locally owned ground transport which feeds back into the economy in terms of creating the necessary demand to support this infrastructure (Sassen, 1996, 1997; Shohamy and McNamara, 2009; Smith, 2014; Soysal, 2012; Spijkerboer and Van Walsum, 2007).

Research has shown that more of backpacker expenditure is retained in-country than in conventional mass tourism (Guild and Niessen, 1996; Hailbronner, 2000; Hayter, 2000; Heisler, 2000; Hernandez-Truyol and Johns, 1997). One of the prevailing complaints about conventional tourism is the fact that it is often owned and controlled by large conglomerates which have very limited attachment to the countries from which they extract sales revenue (Guild, 2001; Miller, 2016; Ryan and Mitsilegas, 2010; Wexler, 2007; Wilcox, 2009). Indeed, there has been instances in which these foreign-owned and controlled tourist companies have evaded taxes using any loopholes that they can exploit (Money, 1998; Morris, 2002, 2016; Motomura, 1999; Nethery and Holman, 2016; Newman, Proctor, and Dudley, 2013). Moreover, businesses that cater to backpackers are usually locally owned and profits tend to be retained within the country rather than flowing overseas to international hotel groups (Guia, Koulish, and Mitsilegas, 2016; Guild, 2001; Guild and Niessen, 1996; Hailbronner, 2000; Hayter, 2000; Heisler, 2000). That means that there is a net gain for the local economy from backpacking (Dauvergne, 2012; Den Heijer, 2010; Dudley et al., 2012; Dunn, 2001, 2010; Exdell, 2009; Fiske, 2016; Flynn, 2013). This even more so than in conventional tourism that is often promoted by the national authorities (Aynsley-Green et al., 2012; Bacon, 1996; Baldwin-Edwards, 2006; Bangarth, 2003; Barak-Erez, 2008; Becerra, 2016).

Nevertheless, there have been some criticism of backpacking as a model of travel and also as a tourism modality (Ackerman and Furman, 2014; Adelman, 2002; Aynsley-Green et al., 2012; Bacon, 1996; Baldwin-Edwards, 2006). Backpacker tourism of the hippie trail has been criticized for possibly encouraging urban liberal minorities while insulting Islamic traditionalist theology (Sassen, 1996, 1997; Shohamy and McNamara, 2009; Smith, 2014; Soysal, 2012; Spijkerboer and Van Walsum, 2007). Others see it as a continuation of harmful Western hegemony in which citizenry from Europe and North Africa engage in a rescue fantasy of solving the world's problems and "civilizing" communities that exist in the developing world (Brané and Lundholm, 2007; Flynn, 2013; Joppke, 2010; Newman, Proctor, and Dudley, 2013; Sassen, 1997). Some have argued that the backlash against this hegemony could possibly have led the Islamic reawakening in the late 1970s (Guild and Niessen, 1996; Hailbronner, 2000; Hayter, 2000; Heisler, 2000; Hernandez-Truyol and Johns, 1997). Even though one of the primary aims of backpacking is to seek the "authentic," the majority of backpackers spend most of their time interacting with other backpackers (Chin, 1999; Cook, 2003; Cornelisse, 2004, 2010; Costello, 2012; Dauvergne, 2012; Den

Heijer, 2010; Dudley et al., 2012). Backpacker tourism has been criticized for the transformation of some sleepy towns into hotbeds of antisocial behavior and foreign practices (Lorentzen, 2014; Mehan, 1997; Melis, 2001; Miller, 2015, 2016; Molnar and Gill, 2018; Money, 1998; Morris, 2016).

The perpetual travel is a variant on backpacking which so far has remained the privilege of those with passports that open (rather than close) doors for them (Miller, 2015, 2016; Molnar and Gill, 2018; Money, 1998; Morris, 2002, 2016; Motomura, 1999). The term "perpetual traveler" also approximates other terms such as "PT," "permanent tourist," or "prior taxpayer" (Ryan and Mitsilegas, 2010; Saadi et al., 2020; Samers, 2004; Sampson, Mitchell, and Bowring, 2011; Sanggaran, Haire, and Zion, 2016). It refers to the idea that by basing different aspects of one's life in different countries and not spending too long in any one place (Heisler, 2000; Hernandez-Truyol and Johns, 1997; Hollifield, Martin, and Orrenius, 2014; Jacobson, 1996; Johnson, 1996). The main objective in such instances is to simultaneously reduce civic duties whilst increasing personal freedom (Baldwin-Edwards, 2006; Dunn, 2001; Jacobson, 1996; Morris, 2016; Samers, 2004).

The perpetual traveler idea has been presented in terms of flag theory (Motomura, 1999; Nethery and Holman, 2016; Newman, Proctor, and Dudley, 2013; Oberman, 2016; Orfanos, 2019). The theory proposes a number of bases of living that should be in a separate country (Fiske, 2016; Flynn, 2013; Frederking, 2012; Gilman, 2013; Guia, Koulish, and Mitsilegas, 2016; Guild, 2001; Guild and Niessen, 1996). First is the passport and citizenship in a country that does not tax money earned outside the country or control actions (Welch, 2002; Wexler, 2007; Wilcox, 2009; Zúñiga and Hernández-León, 2005; Zwi and Mares, 2015). The legal residence is then located in a tax haven (Thym, 2008; Webber, 2012; Welch, 2002; Wexler, 2007; Wilcox, 2009; Zúñiga and Hernández-León, 2005; Zwi and Mares, 2015). The business base is where one earns one's money and the country should ideally have low corporate tax rates (Den Heijer, 2010; Miller, 2015; Ruhs, 2010; Welch, 2002; Zwi and Mares, 2015). The asset haven is where one keeps one's money (Sassen, 1996, 1997; Shohamy and McNamara, 2009; Smith, 2014; Soysal, 2012; Spijkerboer and Van Walsum, 2007). This is ideally somewhere with low taxation of passive income and capital gains (Spijkerboer and Van Walsum, 2007; Taylor, 2000; Thym, 2008; Webber, 2012; Welch, 2002; Wexler, 2007; Wilcox, 2009). Finally, there are the so-called playgrounds where one spends one's money (Acer and Goodman, 2009; Ackerman and Furman, 2014; Adelman, 2002; Aynsley-Green et al.,

2012; Bacon, 1996). This is ideally somewhere with low consumption taxes (Adelman, 2002; Cook, 2003; Hayter, 2000; Lorentzen, 2014; Peberdy, 2001; Soysal, 2012). In order for such flexibility to be widely available, the notion of global citizenship has to take root. This is the topic of the next section.

5.3. INTRODUCTION OF GLOBAL CITIZENSHIP

Global citizenship suggests that identity transcends geography and even traditional political borders (Cook, 2003; Cornelisse, 2004, 2010; Costello, 2012; Dauvergne, 2012; Den Heijer, 2010; Dudley et al., 2012). In that case, there is an assumption that all the rights derived from membership in a broader class of citizenship accrue to everyone or "humanity" (Guia, Koulish, and Mitsilegas, 2016; Guild, 2001; Guild and Niessen, 1996; Hailbronner, 2000; Hayter, 2000; Heisler, 2000). This does not mean that global citizens always have to denounce or waive their nationality and local identities (Sampson, Mitchell, and Bowring, 2011; Sanggaran, Haire, and Zion, 2016; Sassen, 1996, 1997; Shohamy and McNamara, 2009).

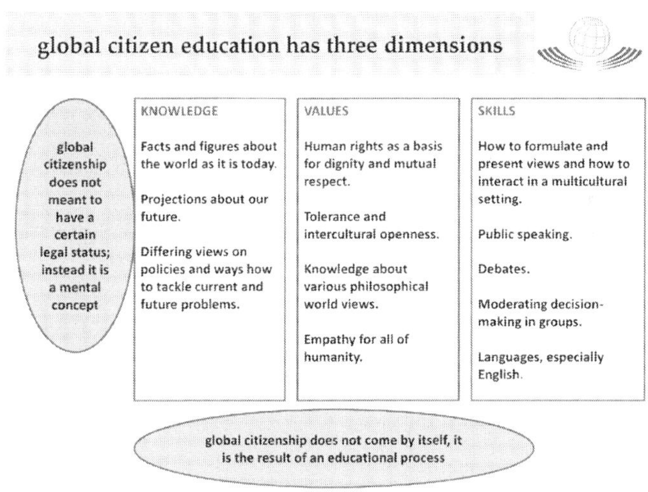

Figure 5.3: Dimensions of global citizenship.

Source: ISSUU.

Rather it means that such identities are given "second place" to their membership in a global community (Joppke, 1999, 2010; Kasimis, 2012; Kelson and DeLaet, 1999; King, 2009; Lopez, 2005; Lorentzen, 2014; Mehan, 1997). Critics have argued that global citizenship is just a few steps away from one-world governments that are determined to diminish the role, responsibility, and dynamic of sovereign nation-states. Figure 5.3 highlights the dimensions of global citizenship.

We already know that globalization is reducing the importance of nation-states (Aynsley-Green et al., 2012; Bacon, 1996; Baldwin-Edwards, 2006; Bangarth, 2003; Barak-Erez, 2008; Becerra, 2016). Hence, the idea of global citizenship may require a redefinition of ties between civic engagement and geographical location (King, 2009; Lopez, 2005; Lorentzen, 2014; Mehan, 1997; Melis, 2001; Miller, 2015, 2016; Molnar and Gill, 2018). For example, absentee ballots opened the way for expatriates to vote while living in another country. This allows global citizens to exercise national citizenship rights even as they enjoy a rather less parochial lifestyle (Peberdy, 2001; Ramji-Nogales, 2007; Rubio-Marín, 2014; Ruhs, 2010; Ryan and Mitsilegas, 2010; Saadi et al., 2020; Samers, 2004). Another interpretation of global citizenship that is given by several scholars is the possibility that citizenship becomes a changed institution (Adelman, 2002; Aynsley-Green et al., 2012; Bacon, 1996; Baldwin-Edwards, 2006; Bangarth, 2003; Barak-Erez, 2008). This is true even if citizenship is situated within territorial boundaries that are national (Paz, 2016; Peberdy, 2001; Ramji-Nogales, 2007; Rubio-Marín, 2014; Ruhs, 2010; Ryan and Mitsilegas, 2010; Saadi et al., 2020). The main requirement for such a radical interpretation of citizenship is the possibility that the meaning of the national itself has changed (Fiske, 2016; Flynn, 2013; Frederking, 2012; Gilman, 2013; Guia, Koulish, and Mitsilegas, 2016; Guild, 2001; Guild and Niessen, 1996). It then follows that the meaning of being a citizen of any nation changes accordingly (Melis, 2001; Miller, 2015, 2016; Molnar and Gill, 2018; Money, 1998; Morris, 2002, 2016; Motomura, 1999). In the next section, we consider tax exiles as a unique form of immigration status.

5.4. IMPACT OF TAX EXILES

A tax exile is a person who deliberately leaves a country (typically the home country) to avoid the payment of income tax or other taxes (Sampson, Mitchell, and Bowring, 2011; Sanggaran, Haire, and Zion, 2016; Sassen, 1996, 1997; Shohamy and McNamara, 2009). This definition includes people who already owe money to the tax authorities and are trying to escape liability (Frederking, 2012; Gilman, 2013; Guia, Koulish, and Mitsilegas, 2016; Guild, 2001; Guild and Niessen, 1996; Hailbronner, 2000). It also includes those that wish to avoid being liable in the future to taxation at what they consider to be high tax rates (Bangarth, 2003; Barak-Erez, 2008; Becerra, 2016; Brané and Lundholm, 2007; Brochmann and Hammar, 2020; Chavez, 2001). These people opt to reside in a foreign country or jurisdiction which has no taxes or lower tax rates (Chavez, 2001; Chin, 1999; Cook, 2003; Cornelisse, 2004, 2010; Costello, 2012; Dauvergne, 2012; Den Heijer, 2010). In return, tax exiles may have to give up all their voting privileges and are often looked at with scorn by the home community for failing to contribute to national development. As Figure 5.4 shows, the ability to collect revenue is key to the government fulfilling its responsibilities and controlling deficits. That means that tax exiles are in one way or another harming their home government, even if they do not expressly intend to do so (Baldwin-Edwards, 2006; Dunn, 2001; Jacobson, 1996; Morris, 2016; Samers, 2004).

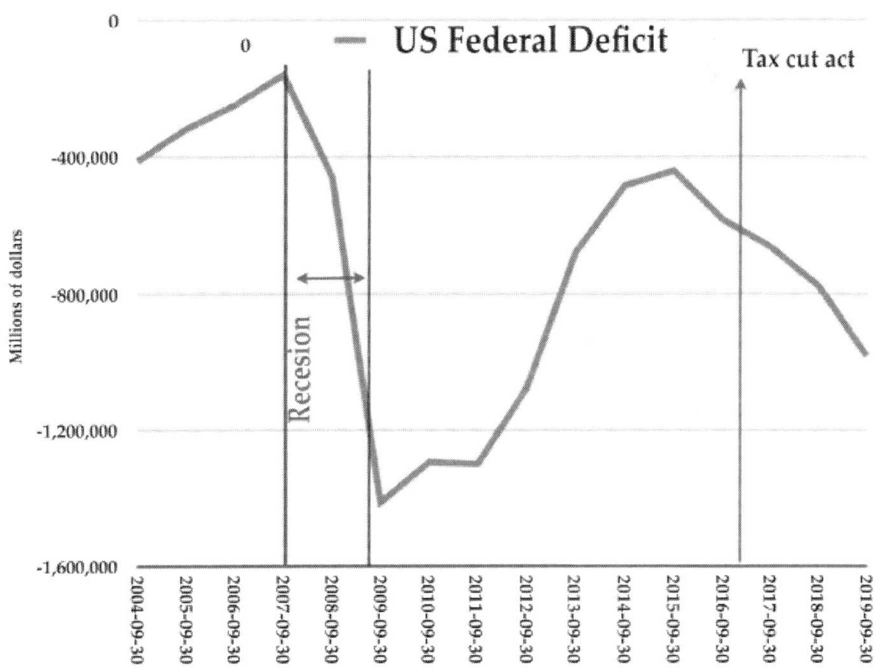

Figure 5.4: Lower taxes lead to increased government deficits in the USA.

Source: Economics Help.

There are certain conditions that will attract tax exiles and some countries deliberately set out their immigration policies in such a way as to attract tax exiles (Rubio-Marín, 2014; Ruhs, 2010; Ryan and Mitsilegas, 2010; Saadi et al., 2020; Samers, 2004; Sampson, Mitchell, and Bowring, 2011). Without an extradition agreement between countries which covers extradition for outstanding tax liabilities, there is a loophole that can be exploited (Acer and Goodman, 2009; Chavez, 2001; Guild and Niessen, 1996; King, 2009; Ozdowski, 1985; Shohamy and McNamara, 2009). Going into tax exile is a form of tax mitigation or avoidance and is frowned upon in many nations as an unpatriotic sign of personal greed (Sassen, 1997; Shohamy and McNamara, 2009; Smith, 2014; Soysal, 2012; Spijkerboer and Van Walsum, 2007). A tax exile normally cannot return to their home country without being subject to outstanding tax liabilities (Aynsley-Green et al., 2012; Cornelisse, 2004; Heisler, 2000; Mehan, 1997; Ramji-Nogales, 2007; Spijkerboer and Van Walsum, 2007). Any attempts to let them in may prove to be too politically controversial, especially if the public becomes aware of the decision in advance. Any outstanding liabilities may prevent them from leaving the country until they have been paid (Bacon, 1996; Dudley et al., 2012; Hollifield, Martin, and Orrenius, 2014; Money, 1998; Saadi et al., 2020). This chapter will close by reviewing the privileges of expatriates over other categories of migrants such as asylum seekers and refugees.

5.5. PRIVILEGING OF EXPATRIATES

An expatriate (often shortened to expat) is a person residing in a country other than their native country (Aynsley-Green et al., 2012; Bacon, 1996; Baldwin-Edwards, 2006; Bangarth, 2003; Barak-Erez, 2008; Becerra, 2016). In common usage, the term often refers to professionals, skilled workers, or artists taking positions outside their home country. These may have traveled independently, or they could have been sent abroad by their employers (Brané and Lundholm, 2007; Brochmann and Hammar, 2020; Chavez, 2001; Chin, 1999; Cook, 2003; Cornelisse, 2004). However, the term 'expatriate' is also used for retirees and others who have chosen to live outside their native country (Hernandez-Truyol and Johns, 1997; Hollifield, Martin, and Orrenius, 2014; Jacobson, 1996; Johnson, 1996; Joppke, 1998). Historically, it has also referred to exiles (Dunn, 2001, 2010; Exdell, 2009; Fiske, 2016; Flynn, 2013; Frederking, 2012; Gilman, 2013; Guia, Koulish, and Mitsilegas, 2016). More recently, some popular media outlets have used the time to de-stigmatize emigres from wealthier nations whilst simultaneously stigmatizing immigrants who are referred to using demeaning and dehumanizing terms such as "illegals" or "aliens" (Dudley et al., 2012; Dunn, 2001, 2010; Exdell, 2009; Fiske, 2016; Flynn, 2013; Frederking, 2012; Gilman, 2013). In some cases, expatriates are escaping unfair treatment and harassment at home; a recent example being of Black Americans leaving the USA to escape racism (see Figure 5.5).

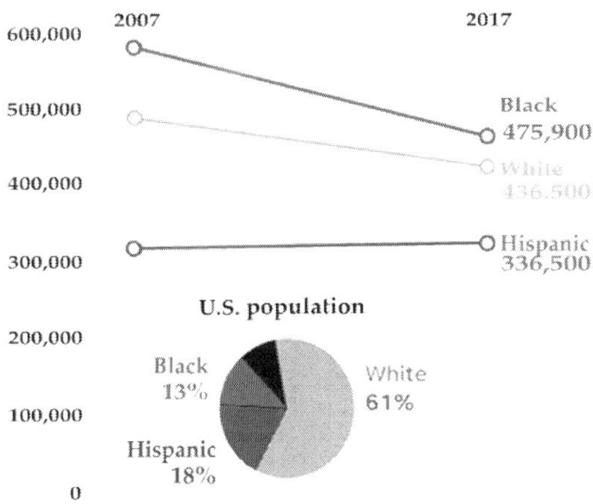

Figure 5.5: Black Americans leaving the USA to escape racism.

Source: USA Today.

The varying use of these terms for different groups of foreigners can thus be seen as implying nuances about wealth, intended length of stay, perceived motives for moving, nationality, and even race (Hailbronner, 2000; Hayter, 2000; Heisler, 2000; Hernandez-Truyol and Johns, 1997; Hollifield, Martin, and Orrenius, 2014). This has caused controversy, with many asserting that the traditional use of the word has had racist connotations (Den Heijer, 2010; Dudley et al., 2012; Dunn, 2001, 2010; Exdell, 2009; Fiske, 2016; Flynn, 2013; Frederking, 2012). For example, Anglo centrism is evident in British media when referring to British emigres as expatriates while others remain immigrants if they are outside their country of birth (Mehan, 1997; Melis, 2001; Miller, 2015, 2016; Molnar and Gill, 2018; Money, 1998; Morris, 2002, 2016).

Some neologisms have emerged to specify the exact nature of expatriates (Baldwin-Edwards, 2006; Bangarth, 2003; Barak-Erez, 2008; Becerra, 2016; Brané and Lundholm, 2007; Brochmann and Hammar, 2020). For example, a flexpatriate is an employee who often travels internationally for business (Bangarth, 2003; Dunn, 2010; Johnson, 1996; Morris, 2002; Sampson, Mitchell, and Bowring, 2011). By contrast, an inpatriate is an employee sent from a foreign subsidiary to work in the country where the employer has its headquarters (Joppke, 2010; Kasimis, 2012; Kelson and DeLaet, 1999; King, 2009; Lopez, 2005; Lorentzen, 2014; Mehan, 1997). A rex-pat is a repeat expatriate who is often someone who has chosen to return to a foreign country after completing a work assignment (Brané and Lundholm, 2007; Brochmann and Hammar, 2020; Chavez, 2001; Chin, 1999; Cook, 2003; Cornelisse, 2004). During colonial times, expatriates were often sent abroad to administer newly acquired territories (Acer and Goodman, 2009; Ackerman and Furman, 2014; Adelman, 2002; Aynsley-Green et al., 2012; Bacon, 1996). Some remained there at the end of the colonization while others returned (Ackerman and Furman, 2014; Adelman, 2002; Aynsley-Green et al., 2012; Bacon, 1996; Baldwin-Edwards, 2006). Then there are those that remained for some time and became settlers (Lorentzen, 2014; Mehan, 1997; Melis, 2001; Miller, 2015, 2016; Molnar and Gill, 2018; Money, 1998; Morris, 2016). The status of these people and their descendants has caused tensions in the developing world, Zimbabwe, and the appropriation of white farmers' land being a case in point (Dunn, 2001, 2010; Exdell, 2009; Fiske, 2016; Flynn, 2013; Frederking, 2012; Gilman, 2013; Guia, Koulish, and Mitsilegas, 2016).

CHAPTER 5 SUMMARY

This chapter has examined additional categories of immigrants, including digital nomads, perpetual travelers, backpackers, and expatriates. One of the emerging themes and facts of immigration policy is the reality that the freedom to travel is directly linked to the relative power and economic clout of one's home country. In effect, most of immigration controls are designed to prevent people from developing countries from traveling across the globe whilst simultaneously opening up boundaries and horizons for those that are privileged to be either "white" or a citizen of a highly industrialized nation. In that sense, the management of immigration emphasizes the inequalities across the globe. In the next chapter, we look that issues surrounding the plight of vulnerable migrants.

CHAPTER 6

VULNERABLE MIGRANT GROUPS

CONTENTS

This chapter examines the plight of vulnerable migrants in context. The first section considers the plight of women who happen to be migrants from developing countries. In the second section of this chapter, we will explore the various controls on geographic mobility and how they have impacted the lives of vulnerable migrant groups. The third section examines the plight of people and communities that are facing a range of human crises. In the fourth section, we will explore the ongoing stigmatization of illegal immigrants and how that impacts on their responses to the communities in which they live. The chapter will close with a section on the diversity of enforcement actions that are taken against illegal immigrants.

6.1. WOMEN MIGRANTS FROM DEVELOPING COUNTRIES

Women migrant workers from developing countries engage in paid employment in countries where they are not citizens (Acer and Goodman, 2009; Ackerman and Furman, 2014; Adelman, 2002; Aynsley-Green et al., 2012; Bacon, 1996). Here they face double discrimination due to issues of intersectionality (Baldwin-Edwards, 2006; Bangarth, 2003; Barak-Erez, 2008; Becerra, 2016; Brané and Lundholm, 2007). Women have traditionally been considered companions to their husbands in the migratory process and that has meant that not enough attention is paid to their needs and perspectives (Brochmann and Hammar, 2020; Chavez, 2001; Chin, 1999; Cook, 2003; Cornelisse, 2004, 2010). However, currently most adult migrant women are employed in their own right and deserving of specific attention (Costello, 2012; Dauvergne, 2012; Den Heijer, 2010; Dudley et al., 2012; Dunn, 2001, 2010; Exdell, 2009). For example, by 2017, statistics indicated that of the 168 million migrant workers, over 68 million were women. The increase in proportion of women migrant workers since the early 20th century is often referred to as the "feminization of migration" (Fiske, 2016; Flynn, 2013; Frederking, 2012; Gilman, 2013; Guia, Koulish, and Mitsilegas, 2016; Guild, 2001). Some have argued that this feminization of the entire migration process has led to a deterioration of conditions for migrants generally since women have traditionally only been allowed to engage in low paying jobs (Guild and Niessen, 1996; Hailbronner, 2000; Hayter, 2000; Heisler, 2000; Hernandez-Truyol and Johns, 1997). In Figure 6.1, we can see some of the gender variation across various geographical patterns of migration. Yet, the issue of gender disparities is not given sufficient attention when dealing with vulnerable migrants in general (Hollifield, Martin, and Orrenius, 2014; Jacobson, 1996; Johnson, 1996; Joppke, 1998, 1999, 2010).

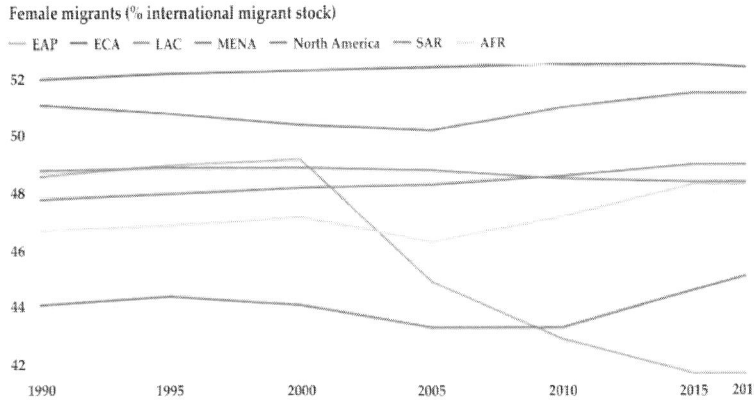

Figure 6.1: Variances in gender composition of international migration.

Source: World Bank Blogs.

The majority of migration involves people moving from developing countries to developed countries (Kasimis, 2012; Kelson and DeLaet, 1999; King, 2009; Lopez, 2005; Lorentzen, 2014; Mehan, 1997; Melis, 2001). Most women workers immigrate from developing countries to high-income countries (Miller, 2015, 2016; Molnar and Gill, 2018; Money, 1998; Morris, 2002, 2016; Motomura, 1999). These gendered patterns of migration lead to significant impacts on both countries of origin and destination countries (Nethery and Holman, 2016; Newman, Proctor, and Dudley, 2013; Oberman, 2016; Orfanos, 2019; Ozdowski, 1985). Women migrant workers send upwards of $300 billion in remittances to their countries of origin each year (Taylor, 2000; Thym, 2008; Webber, 2012; Welch, 2002; Wexler, 2007; Wilcox, 2009; Zúñiga and Hernández-León, 2005; Zwi and Mares, 2015). Women migrants often use this money to pay for their families' basic health, housing, and education needs (Sassen, 1996, 1997; Shohamy and McNamara, 2009; Smith, 2014; Soysal, 2012; Spijkerboer and Van Walsum, 2007). On a macroeconomic level, remittances from emigrant workers can account for up to 25% of national gross domestic product (Saadi et al., 2020; Samers, 2004; Sampson, Mitchell, and Bowring, 2011; Sanggaran, Haire, and Zion, 2016). Women migrants are therefore helping many developing countries to cope with trade deficits and external debts (Paz, 2016; Peberdy, 2001; Ramji-Nogales, 2007; Rubio-Marín, 2014; Ruhs, 2010; Ryan and Mitsilegas, 2010).

Despite all these contributions and benefits, there is a high price that women must pay if they are to become successful migrants (Nethery and Holman, 2016; Newman, Proctor, and Dudley, 2013; Oberman, 2016; Orfanos, 2019; Ozdowski, 1985). For example, women migrant workers have to leave their countries of origin to provide financial assistance to their families back at home (Kasimis, 2012; Kelson and DeLaet, 1999; King, 2009; Lopez, 2005; Lorentzen, 2014; Mehan, 1997; Melis, 2001). They are often separated from their own families, which can lead to psychosocial challenges (Miller, 2015, 2016; Molnar and Gill, 2018; Money, 1998; Morris, 2002, 2016; Motomura, 1999). At the same time, women are important contributors to the economic development of the countries where they settle, even if their contribution is habitually ignored as being secondary or conditional (Saadi et al., 2020; Samers, 2004; Sampson, Mitchell, and Bowring, 2011; Sanggaran, Haire, and Zion, 2016). For example, immigrant women help address the care worker shortage in the health industry (Saadi et al., 2020; Samers, 2004; Sampson, Mitchell, and Bowring, 2011; Sanggaran, Haire, and Zion, 2016; Sassen, 1996). This has the positive effect of enabling more local women to enter the workforce because of the support that is being provided at home (Dunn, 2010; Exdell, 2009; Fiske, 2016; Flynn, 2013; Frederking, 2012; Gilman, 2013; Guia, Koulish, and Mitsilegas, 2016). In countries of origin, the emigration of large numbers of women forces other members of the community to shoulder greater domestic work burdens (Acer and Goodman, 2009; Chavez, 2001; Guild and Niessen, 1996; King, 2009; Ozdowski, 1985; Shohamy and McNamara, 2009). Besides, the contributions of women migrants are often ignored during the generalized marginalization and stigmatization of migrants (Flynn, 2013; Frederking, 2012; Gilman, 2013; Guia, Koulish, and Mitsilegas, 2016; Guild, 2001; Guild and Niessen, 1996).

Women migrant workers typically pursue gendered professions such as domestic work and disproportionately work in private homes (Hollifield, Martin, and Orrenius, 2014; Jacobson, 1996; Johnson, 1996; Joppke, 1998, 1999, 2010; Kasimis, 2012). As a result, they are comparatively "hidden" from society and are more vulnerable to exploitation and abuse (Lopez, 2005; Lorentzen, 2014; Mehan, 1997; Melis, 2001; Miller, 2015, 2016; Molnar and Gill, 2018; Money, 1998). A variety of governmental policies have also increased the vulnerability of these women migrant workers to abuse (Miller, 2015, 2016; Molnar and Gill, 2018; Money, 1998; Morris, 2002, 2016; Motomura, 1999). For example, in the Arab states, migrant domestic workers depend on their employers for legal status (Miller, 2015,

2016; Molnar and Gill, 2018; Money, 1998; Morris, 2002, 2016; Motomura, 1999). This has the effect of causing the migrant women workers to tolerate a significant amount of abuse for fear of deportation (Mehan, 1997; Melis, 2001; Miller, 2015, 2016; Molnar and Gill, 2018; Money, 1998; Morris, 2002, 2016). Several countries also prohibit women migrant workers from having sex or becoming pregnant (Sassen, 1997; Shohamy and McNamara, 2009; Smith, 2014; Soysal, 2012; Spijkerboer and Van Walsum, 2007). Not only is this an abuse of their human rights, but such a rule is also self-contradictory rule given the fact that many of these women face sexual harassment at work (Exdell, 2009; Fiske, 2016; Flynn, 2013; Frederking, 2012; Gilman, 2013; Guia, Koulish, and Mitsilegas, 2016; Guild, 2001). In the next section, we consider the various controls that are placed on geographic mobility in the world today.

6.2. CONTROLS ON GEOGRAPHIC MOBILITY

The reality is that only the wealthy and well-connected are truly free to travel in the current global immigration system (Orfanos, 2019; Ozdowski, 1985; Paz, 2016; Peberdy, 2001; Ramji-Nogales, 2007; Rubio-Marín, 2014; Ruhs, 2010). There are a host of controls that are placed on people who are poor in order to prevent them from traveling from one place to another (Oberman, 2016; Orfanos, 2019; Ozdowski, 1985; Paz, 2016; Peberdy, 2001; Ramji-Nogales, 2007; Rubio-Marín, 2014). All these measures are defined as border control, although the term may also refer to non-human traffic (Newman, Proctor, and Dudley, 2013; Oberman, 2016; Orfanos, 2019; Ozdowski, 1985; Paz, 2016; Peberdy, 2001). Border control comprises all the measures taken by a state or a bloc of states to monitor its borders (Nethery and Holman, 2016; Newman, Proctor, and Dudley, 2013; Oberman, 2016; Orfanos, 2019; Ozdowski, 1985). The ultimate aim is to regulate the movement of people, animals, and goods across the border (Motomura, 1999; Nethery and Holman, 2016; Newman, Proctor, and Dudley, 2013; Oberman, 2016; Orfanos, 2019). Although there is a significant focus on human traffic in the form of immigrants, the reality is that border control is a much more holistic term that describes measures that allow countries to maintain strict control of who and what enters their borders (Morris, 2002, 2016; Motomura, 1999; Nethery and Holman, 2016; Newman, Proctor, and Dudley, 2013; Oberman, 2016). Border controls can be in response to humanitarian crisis, a case in point is Germany reducing unauthorized border entries following the Syrian Crisis (see Figure 6.2).

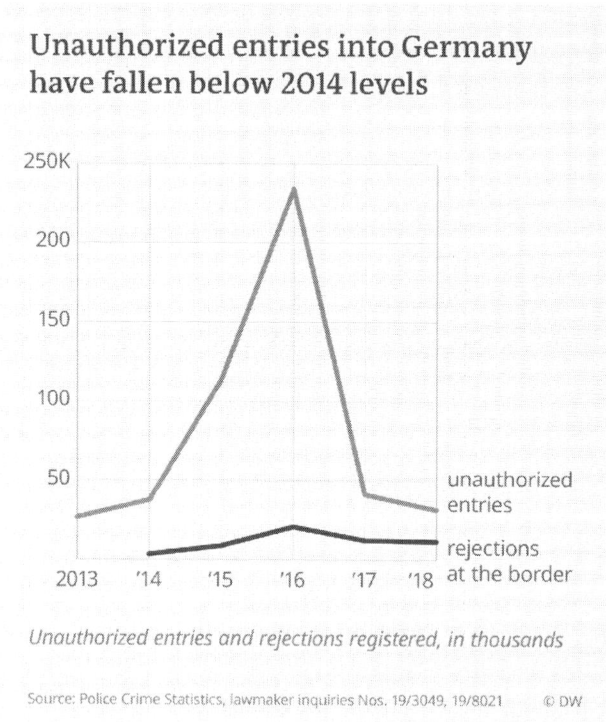

Figure 6.2: Effective German border control following Syrian immigrant crisis.

Source: DW.

There are various aspects of border control which makes it a complex and integrated system of checks (Morris, 2002; Motomura, 1999; Nethery and Holman, 2016; Newman, Proctor, and Dudley, 2013; Oberman, 2016). For example, quarantine policies exist to control the spread of disease through the control of the entry of unknown animal species (Money, 1998; Morris, 2002, 2016; Motomura, 1999; Nethery and Holman, 2016; Newman, Proctor, and Dudley, 2013). When applied as a component of border control, such policies focus primarily on mitigating the entry of infected individuals, plants, or animals into a country (Molnar and Gill, 2018; Money, 1998; Morris, 2002, 2016; Motomura, 1999; Nethery and Holman, 2016). By contrast, customs are about ensuring that controlling imports and exports for purposes of maximizing tax revenue or protecting local markets (Miller, 2016; Molnar and Gill, 2018; Money, 1998; Morris, 2002, 2016; Motomura, 1999; Nethery and Holman, 2016).

Each country has its own laws and regulations for the import and export of goods into and out of a country, depending on the policy objectives that are set out by the political class (Miller, 2015, 2016; Molnar and Gill, 2018; Money, 1998; Morris, 2002, 2016; Motomura, 1999; Nethery and Holman, 2016). The import or export of some goods may be restricted or forbidden for health and safety reasons, or even to protect local (Melis, 2001; Miller, 2015, 2016; Molnar and Gill, 2018; Money, 1998; Morris, 2002, 2016; Motomura, 1999). Customs enforcement at borders can also entail collecting excise tax and preventing the smuggling of dangerous or illegal goods (Mehan, 1997; Melis, 2001; Miller, 2015, 2016; Molnar and Gill, 2018; Money, 1998; Morris, 2002, 2016).

Border security measures are border control policies adopted by a country or group of countries. These measures and resources are organized in such a way as to prevent unauthorized travel or trade across its borders. They have also been used to limit illegal immigration of certain people from certain countries. Additionally, border checks can be used to combat transnational crime. A case in point is where wanted criminals are intercepted and prevented from traveling (Joppke, 1998, 1999, 2010; Kasimis, 2012; Kelson and DeLaet, 1999; King, 2009; Lopez, 2005; Lorentzen, 2014). A worried and skeptical publicly routinely demands for stringent border checks and controls. Meanwhile, human rights activists call for a more human approach to vulnerable people such as refugees or people that are running away from humanitarian crises. The next section considers the immigration experiences of those that have been impacted by humanitarian crises.

6.3. VICTIMS OF HUMANITARIAN CRISES

A humanitarian crisis is also known as a humanitarian disaster in some literature. It is defined as a singular event or a series of events that are threatening in terms of health, safety or well-being of a community or large group of people (Kasimis, 2012; Kelson and DeLaet, 1999; King, 2009; Lopez, 2005; Lorentzen, 2014; Mehan, 1997; Melis, 2001; Miller, 2015). Such an event may be an internal or external conflict that impacts on the lives of people (Joppke, 2010; Kasimis, 2012; Kelson and DeLaet, 1999; King, 2009; Lopez, 2005; Lorentzen, 2014; Mehan, 1997). A humanitarian crisis usually occurs throughout a large land area and may even cross borders in the process (Joppke, 1999, 2010; Kasimis, 2012; Kelson and DeLaet, 1999; King, 2009; Lopez, 2005; Lorentzen, 2014; Mehan, 1997). Local, national, and international responses are necessary in such events and there are specific rules concerning responses once a crisis has been declared (Joppke, 1998, 1999, 2010; Kasimis, 2012; Kelson and DeLaet, 1999; King, 2009; Lopez, 2005; Lorentzen, 2014). Figure 6.3 highlights the relationships between immigration and humanitarian crises in Latin America. This is a region that is often ignored in the immigration debate that is taking place in Europe despite the fact that a significant portion of immigrants are from South America (Johnson, 1996; Joppke, 1998, 1999, 2010; Kasimis, 2012; Kelson and DeLaet, 1999; King, 2009; Lopez, 2005).

PEOPLE OF CONCERN - 2017 [PROJECTED]

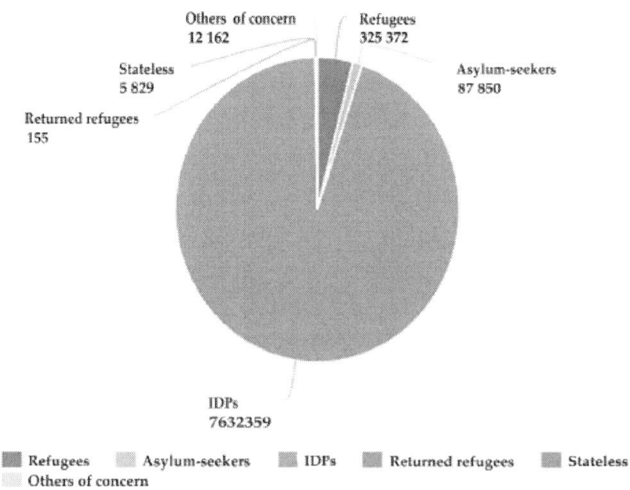

Figure 6.3: Humanitarian crises and immigration in Latin America.

Source: World Economic Forum.

Each humanitarian crisis is caused by different factors, which can be quite diverse and complex (Soysal, 2012; Spijkerboer and Van Walsum, 2007; Taylor, 2000; Thym, 2008; Webber, 2012; Welch, 2002; Wexler, 2007). The implication is that each different humanitarian crisis requires a unique response targeted towards the specific sectors affected (Smith, 2014; Soysal, 2012; Spijkerboer and Van Walsum, 2007; Taylor, 2000; Thym, 2008; Webber, 2012; Welch, 2002). Unfortunately, that requires a lot of resources and planning in order to get the right response for the right crisis (Shohamy and McNamara, 2009; Smith, 2014; Soysal, 2012; Spijkerboer and Van Walsum, 2007; Taylor, 2000; Thym, 2008). Many governments prefer to use a one-size-fits all approach which is based on generalities and a quantitative approach (Sassen, 1997; Shohamy and McNamara, 2009; Smith, 2014; Soysal, 2012; Spijkerboer and Van Walsum, 2007). This can result in either short-term or long-term damage which is hidden in the wider statistics (Shohamy and McNamara, 2009; Smith, 2014; Soysal, 2012; Spijkerboer and Van Walsum, 2007; Taylor, 2000; Thym, 2008). Humanitarian crises can either be natural disasters, manmade disasters, or complex emergencies; each requiring unique responses that can be significantly expensive (Sassen, 1996, 1997; Shohamy and McNamara, 2009; Smith, 2014; Soysal, 2012; Spijkerboer and Van Walsum, 2007). In such cases, complex emergencies occur as a result of several factors or events that prevent a large group of people from accessing their fundamental needs. Hence, there is concern about access to food, clean water, or safe shelter (Sanggaran, Haire, and Zion, 2016; Sassen, 1996, 1997; Shohamy and McNamara, 2009; Smith, 2014).

Examples of humanitarian crises include armed conflicts, epidemics, famine, natural disasters, and other major emergencies (Sampson, Mitchell, and Bowring, 2011; Sanggaran, Haire, and Zion, 2016; Sassen, 1996, 1997; Shohamy and McNamara, 2009). If such a crisis causes large movements of people, it could also become a refugee crisis (Samers, 2004; Sampson, Mitchell, and Bowring, 2011; Sanggaran, Haire, and Zion, 2016; Sassen, 1996, 1997). For these reasons, humanitarian crises are often interconnected and complex (Saadi et al., 2020; Samers, 2004; Sampson, Mitchell, and Bowring, 2011; Sanggaran, Haire, and Zion, 2016; Sassen, 1996). It is within that spirit that several national and international agencies play roles in the repercussions of the incidences (Ryan and Mitsilegas, 2010; Saadi et al., 2020; Samers, 2004; Sampson, Mitchell, and Bowring, 2011; Sanggaran, Haire, and Zion, 2016). There is no simple categorization of humanitarian crises however (Ruhs, 2010; Ryan and Mitsilegas, 2010; Saadi et al., 2020; Samers, 2004; Sampson, Mitchell, and Bowring, 2011).

Different communities and agencies tend to have definitions related to the concrete situations they face (Rubio-Marín, 2014; Ruhs, 2010; Ryan and Mitsilegas, 2010; Saadi et al., 2020; Samers, 2004; Sampson, Mitchell, and Bowring, 2011). Internationally, the humanitarian response sector has tended to distinguish between natural disasters and complex emergencies which are related to armed conflict and wars (Gilman, 2013; Guia, Koulish, and Mitsilegas, 2016; Guild, 2001; Guild and Niessen, 1996; Hailbronner, 2000; Hayter, 2000). One of the key concerns will be in ensuring that people who are fleeing from a humanitarian crisis have the possibility of settling in a new place with a lifestyle that is dignified and productive. Whereas they may not be able to replicate their exact initial status; the new location and opportunities should be broadly consistent with basic human rights. The next section focuses on the stigmatization of undocumented or illegal immigrants.

6.4. STIGMATIZING ILLEGAL IMMIGRANTS

Illegal immigration refers to the migration of people into a country in violation of the immigration laws of that country (Frederking, 2012; Gilman, 2013; Guia, Koulish, and Mitsilegas, 2016; Guild, 2001; Guild and Niessen, 1996; Hailbronner, 2000). It also refers to the continued residence without the legal right to live in that country (Flynn, 2013; Frederking, 2012; Gilman, 2013; Guia, Koulish, and Mitsilegas, 2016; Guild, 2001; Guild and Niessen, 1996). Illegal immigration tends to move from poorer countries to richer countries and is hence considered to be financially upward (Fiske, 2016; Flynn, 2013; Frederking, 2012; Gilman, 2013; Guia, Koulish, and Mitsilegas, 2016; Guild, 2001; Guild and Niessen, 1996). Illegal residence in another country creates the risk of detention, deportation, and other sanctions if apprehended by the authorities (Exdell, 2009; Fiske, 2016; Flynn, 2013; Frederking, 2012; Gilman, 2013; Guia, Koulish, and Mitsilegas, 2016; Guild, 2001). As Figure 6.4 illustrates, migrants are at the center of different complex crisis points.

Figure 6.4: Multiplicity of crises afflicting immigrants.

Source: International Journal for Equity in Health.

One of the most vulnerable groups of immigrants is that of asylum of seekers whose application has unlikely chances of being accepted (Dunn,

2010; Exdell, 2009; Fiske, 2016; Flynn, 2013; Frederking, 2012; Gilman, 2013; Guia, Koulish, and Mitsilegas, 2016). Asylum seekers who are denied asylum may face impediment to expulsion if the home country refuses to receive the person or if new asylum evidence emerges after the decision (Dunn, 2001, 2010; Exdell, 2009; Fiske, 2016; Flynn, 2013; Frederking, 2012; Gilman, 2013; Guia, Koulish, and Mitsilegas, 2016). In some cases, these people are considered illegal aliens, and in others, they may receive a temporary residence permit (Dudley et al., 2012; Dunn, 2001, 2010; Exdell, 2009; Fiske, 2016; Flynn, 2013; Frederking, 2012; Gilman, 2013). A case in point is the reference to the principle of non-refoulement in the international Refugee Convention (Den Heijer, 2010; Dudley et al., 2012; Dunn, 2001, 2010; Exdell, 2009; Fiske, 2016; Flynn, 2013; Frederking, 2012). The European Court of Human Rights, referring to the European Convention on Human Rights, has shown in a number of indicative judgments that there are enforcement barriers to expulsion to certain countries due to the risks that are associated with returning to those countries. A case in point is the risk of torture or inhuman treatment for political dissidents (Dauvergne, 2012; Den Heijer, 2010; Dudley et al., 2012; Dunn, 2001, 2010; Exdell, 2009; Fiske, 2016; Flynn, 2013).

6.5. DIVERSITY OF ENFORCEMENT ACTION AGAINST ILLEGAL IMMIGRATION

Many governments consider it their sacred duty to control immigration (Barak-Erez, 2008; Becerra, 2016; Brané and Lundholm, 2007; Brochmann and Hammar, 2020; Chavez, 2001; Chin, 1999). Those who do not follow the rules are often deported and prevented from returning to the country in question (Bangarth, 2003; Barak-Erez, 2008; Becerra, 2016; Brané and Lundholm, 2007; Brochmann and Hammar, 2020; Chavez, 2001). This acts as a punishment and also as a deterrent to the would-be immigrant in the future (Baldwin-Edwards, 2006; Bangarth, 2003; Barak-Erez, 2008; Becerra, 2016; Brané and Lundholm, 2007; Brochmann and Hammar, 2020). At the same time, strong enforcement action might be used to calm down the local communities who may be worried about the short term and long-term effects of uncontrolled immigration. The way in which enforcement is carried out may sway the public towards even harsher enforcement; while at other times public outcry calls for a more humanitarian approach (Adelman, 2002; Aynsley-Green et al., 2012; Bacon, 1996; Baldwin-Edwards, 2006; Bangarth, 2003; Barak-Erez, 2008). As Figure 6.5 shows, enforcement action is less effective than temporary visas in stemming illegal immigration (Ackerman and Furman, 2014; Adelman, 2002; Aynsley-Green et al., 2012; Bacon, 1996; Baldwin-Edwards, 2006).

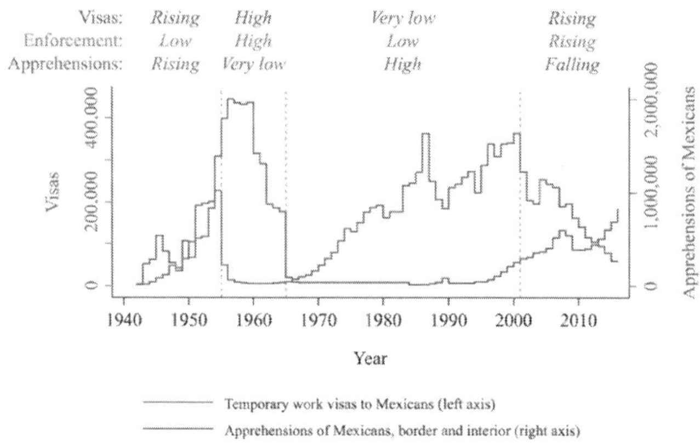

Figure 6.5: Inverse relationship between temporary work visas and illegal immigration apprehensions.

Source: Center for Global Development.

One of the countries that is facing a problem with illegal immigration in South Africa, not least because it is by far the most developed nation in the entire Sub-Saharan Africa (Acer and Goodman, 2009; Ackerman and Furman, 2014; Adelman, 2002; Aynsley-Green et al., 2012; Bacon, 1996). No accurate estimates of the number of illegal migrants living in South Africa exist. Estimates that have been published vary widely (Dauvergne, 2012; Den Heijer, 2010; Dudley et al., 2012; Dunn, 2001, 2010; Exdell, 2009; Fiske, 2016; Flynn, 2013). The lack of clarity about the true number of illegal immigrants can lead to civil unrest as vigilante groups attempt to mete out mob justice to suspected immigrants (Dunn, 2001, 2010; Exdell, 2009; Fiske, 2016; Flynn, 2013; Frederking, 2012; Gilman, 2013; Guia, Koulish, and Mitsilegas, 2016). In South Africa, there are disturbing xenophobic and racist overtones to the vigilante groups that attack suspected migrants (Dunn, 2010; Exdell, 2009; Fiske, 2016; Flynn, 2013; Frederking, 2012; Gilman, 2013; Guia, Koulish, and Mitsilegas, 2016). They tend to focus on poor African migrants rather than their wealthier white counterparts (Fiske, 2016; Flynn, 2013; Frederking, 2012; Gilman, 2013; Guia, Koulish, and Mitsilegas, 2016; Guild, 2001; Guild and Niessen, 1996).

Regardless of wealth or status, each country will have its own illegal immigration challenges to contend with. Even relatively poor countries may have to contend with an immigration problem (Guia, Koulish, and Mitsilegas, 2016; Guild, 2001; Guild and Niessen, 1996; Hailbronner, 2000; Hayter, 2000; Heisler, 2000). For example, there are about 1.2 million Indians living in Bangladesh illegally as of 2014 (Guild, 2001; Guild and Niessen, 1996; Hailbronner, 2000; Hayter, 2000; Heisler, 2000; Hernandez-Truyol and Johns, 1997). Other countries have such longstanding immigration problems that they end up legalizing the migrants (Hernandez-Truyol and Johns, 1997; Hollifield, Martin, and Orrenius, 2014; Jacobson, 1996; Johnson, 1996; Joppke, 1998). For example, Brazil has long been part of international migration routes (Hollifield, Martin, and Orrenius, 2014; Jacobson, 1996; Johnson, 1996; Joppke, 1998, 1999, 2010; Kasimis, 2012). Through bilateral agreements with the countries of origin, Brazil has occasionally regularized migrants as opposed to pursuing them over a long period of time. Besides, Brazil provides certain freedoms for illegal immigrants which are not found elsewhere. For example, illegal immigrants residing in Brazil enjoy the same legal privileges as native Brazilians regarding access to social services such as public education and the Brazilian public healthcare system (Kasimis, 2012; Kelson and DeLaet, 1999; King, 2009; Lopez, 2005; Lorentzen, 2014; Mehan, 1997; Melis, 2001; Miller, 2015).

CHAPTER 6 SUMMARY

This chapter has explored the plight and experiences of migrants that are considered to be particularly vulnerable. For example, we have seen that women migrants make a significant contribution to the home and destination countries. Yet, their efforts and issues are under-recognized in the policy formulation process. We have also seen the systematic and systemic stigmatization of economic and illegal immigrants. The chapter has demonstrated the limitations of harsh enforcement in preventing immigration. The penultimate chapter in this book will explore certain immigration hotspots across the globe.

CHAPTER 7

KEY MIGRATION HOTSPOTS IN THE WORLD TODAY

CONTENTS

The penultimate chapter in this book considers some of the migration hotspots in the world today, if only to illustrate the extent of the problem and its possible solutions. The first section will consider how Europe has become a magnet for economic, social, and political migrants due to its perceived prosperity and liberalism. The second section turns to chapter as an upcoming economic power that has specific immigration and emigration patterns. In the third section, we will consider offshoring as a round-about-way of using foreign labor and its impact on domestic job markets. The fourth section is concerned with political demography as a critical aspect of the immigration debate by politicians. The chapter will close with a review of the vulnerabilities of LGBT migrants.

7.1. DESIRABILITY OF LEGAL STATUS IN EUROPE

To many migrants, particularly those from the poorest parts of the world, Europe is an attractive destination (Motomura, 1999; Nethery and Holman, 2016; Newman, Proctor, and Dudley, 2013; Oberman, 2016; Orfanos, 2019). For a start, many European countries engaged in extensive colonial campaigns, which means that they share official languages with many of their impoverished former colonies (Bacon, 1996; Baldwin-Edwards, 2006; Bangarth, 2003; Barak-Erez, 2008; Becerra, 2016; Brané and Lundholm, 2007). That removes the language barrier that can be problematic for many less-educated immigrants (Lopez, 2005; Lorentzen, 2014; Mehan, 1997; Melis, 2001; Miller, 2015, 2016; Molnar and Gill, 2018; Money, 1998). Immigration to Europe has a long history. However, such immigration increased substantially in the later 20th century (Baldwin-Edwards, 2006; Bangarth, 2003; Barak-Erez, 2008; Becerra, 2016; Brané and Lundholm, 2007). Europe is dealing with a migrant problem that is similar to other wealthy nations such as China which attract migrant labor (see Figure 7.1).

In contemporary globalization, migrations to Europe have accelerated in speed and scale since World War II and some of the countries claim that they are struggling to cope with the influx (Fiske, 2016; Flynn, 2013; Frederking, 2012; Gilman, 2013; Guia, Koulish, and Mitsilegas, 2016; Guild, 2001; Guild and Niessen, 1996). Over the last decades, there has been an increase in negative attitudes towards immigration, partly as a response to the gradual naturalization of those migrants that have met the citizenship requirements of European countries (Welch, 2002; Wexler, 2007; Wilcox, 2009; Zúñiga and Hernández-León, 2005; Zwi and Mares, 2015).

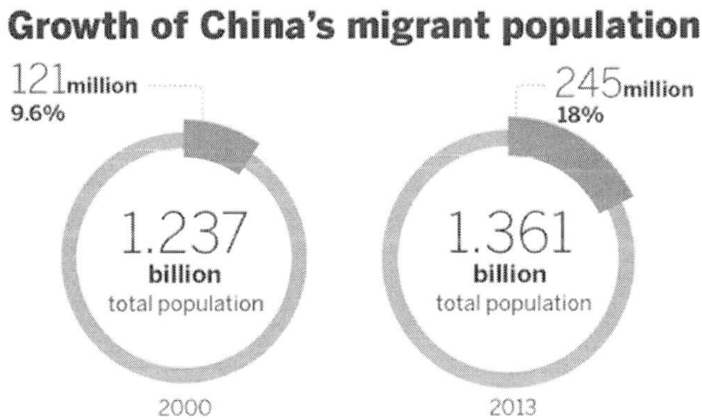

Figure 7.1: Growth in China's migrant population 2000 through 2013.

Source: State Council of TPRoC via China Daily.

For example, many studies have emphasized marked differences in the strength of anti-immigrant attitudes among European countries, not least because of the differing attitudes towards the notion of "free movement" (Thym, 2008; Webber, 2012; Welch, 2002; Wexler, 2007; Wilcox, 2009; Zúñiga and Hernández-León, 2005; Zwi and Mares, 2015). Beginning in 2004, the European Union has granted EU citizens a freedom of movement and residence within the EU and that has meant that it is almost impossible to restrict movement of Europeans within the union (Den Heijer, 2010; Miller, 2015; Ruhs, 2010; Welch, 2002; Zwi and Mares, 2015). Hence, the term "immigrant" has since been used to refer to non-EU citizens, although many of the complaints about "immigrants" include Europeans. Another term that is emerging is that of the "foreign national" which allows for discussion of immigration issues including Europeans (Sassen, 1996, 1997; Shohamy and McNamara, 2009; Smith, 2014; Soysal, 2012; Spijkerboer and Van Walsum, 2007). Nevertheless, the meaning that EU citizens are not to be defined as immigrants within the EU territory has taken root (Spijkerboer and Van Walsum, 2007; Taylor, 2000; Thym, 2008; Webber, 2012; Welch, 2002; Wexler, 2007; Wilcox, 2009).

The European Commission defines "immigration" as the action by which a person from a non-EU country establishes his or her usual residence in the territory of an EU country for a period that is or is expected to be at least 12 months (Acer and Goodman, 2009; Ackerman and Furman, 2014; Adelman, 2002; Aynsley-Green et al., 2012; Bacon, 1996). A large proportion of immigrants in western European states have come from former eastern bloc states in the 1990s. These states did not have the same standards of living as Western and Northern European states. Hence, there was a natural gravitation towards those states with good job opportunities. Other migrants were accused of targeting countries like the UK because of their perceived lax welfare systems that did not put many restrictions on European applicants. The countries that experienced a high level of middle-income European immigrants included Spain, Greece, Germany, Italy, Portugal, and the United Kingdom (Becerra, 2016; Brané and Lundholm, 2007; Brochmann and Hammar, 2020; Chavez, 2001; Chin, 1999; Cook, 2003).

Many of these Polish immigrants to the UK have since returned to Poland, after the serious economic crisis in the UK (Ackerman and Furman, 2014; Adelman, 2002; Aynsley-Green et al., 2012; Bacon, 1996; Baldwin-Edwards, 2006). Nevertheless, free movement of EU nationals is now an important aspect of migration within the EU, since there are now 27 member states, and has resulted in serious political tensions between Italy and Romania, since Italy has expressed the intention of restricting free movement of EU nationals (Acer and Goodman, 2009; Ackerman and Furman, 2014; Adelman, 2002; Aynsley-Green et al., 2012; Bacon, 1996). Such an action is contrary to Treaty obligations and the clear jurisprudence of the European Court of Justice (Brané and Lundholm, 2007; Brochmann and Hammar, 2020; Chavez, 2001; Chin, 1999; Cook, 2003; Cornelisse, 2004). Another migration trend has been that of Northern Europeans moving toward Southern Europe (Joppke, 2010; Kasimis, 2012; Kelson and DeLaet, 1999; King, 2009; Lopez, 2005; Lorentzen, 2014; Mehan, 1997). Because these are relatively wealthy migrants, they hardly register in the debates concerning the impact of immigration. Spain is the most favored destination for Western Europeans considering to move from their own country and seek jobs elsewhere in the EU (Dunn, 2010; Exdell, 2009; Fiske, 2016; Flynn, 2013; Frederking, 2012; Gilman, 2013; Guia, Koulish, and Mitsilegas, 2016).

Some scholars claim that the increase in immigration flows from the 1980s is due to global inequalities between poor and rich countries (Brané and Lundholm, 2007; Brochmann and Hammar, 2020; Chavez, 2001; Chin, 1999; Cook, 2003; Cornelisse, 2004). These inequalities have worsened over time and inspired even more people to seek sanctuary and opportunities in a few premier countries. That is why by 2017, over 800,000 persons acquired citizenship of a member state of the European Union. This was down by nearly 100,000 successful applications when compared to the previous year.

The largest groups acquiring European citizenship were nationals of Albania, India, Morocco, Turkey, and Pakistan. It is estimated that nearly 2.5 million non-EU migrants entered the EU in 2017. In addition, cheaper transportation and more advanced technology have further aided migration (Aynsley-Green et al., 2012; Bacon, 1996; Baldwin-Edwards, 2006; Bangarth, 2003; Barak-Erez, 2008; Becerra, 2016). The Nordic countries have differed in their approach to immigration (King, 2009; Lopez, 2005; Lorentzen, 2014; Mehan, 1997; Melis, 2001; Miller, 2015, 2016; Molnar and Gill, 2018). While Norway and Sweden used to have generous immigration policies, Denmark, and Finland had more restricted immigration (Brochmann and Hammar, 2020; Frederking, 2012; Kasimis, 2012; Oberman, 2016; Taylor, 2000). Recently Denmark has been demanding that migrants return to their country of origin if conditions that led them to flee have improved in a significant way. In the next section, we consider the migration patterns in China.

7.2. MIGRATION PATTERNS INTO CHINA

Internal migration in the People's Republic of China is one of the most extensive in the world according to the International Labor Organization (ILO) (Bacon, 1996; Dudley et al., 2012; Hollifield, Martin, and Orrenius, 2014; Money, 1998; Saadi et al., 2020). This is because migrants in China are commonly members of a floating population, a situation unlike any other developed country (Peberdy, 2001; Ramji-Nogales, 2007; Rubio-Marín, 2014; Ruhs, 2010; Ryan and Mitsilegas, 2010; Saadi et al., 2020; Samers, 2004). This term refers primarily to migrants in China without local household registration status through the Chinese Hukou system (Adelman, 2002; Aynsley-Green et al., 2012; Bacon, 1996; Baldwin-Edwards, 2006; Bangarth, 2003; Barak-Erez, 2008).

There is a lot of discrimination against internal migrants in China, with restrictions on movement that sometimes mirror those that are placed on international visitors. In general, rural-urban migrant workers are most excluded from support services such as local educational resources, citywide social welfare programs and many jobs. This exclusion is because of their lack of Hukou status, an internal control for movements among populations (Paz, 2016; Peberdy, 2001; Ramji-Nogales, 2007; Rubio-Marín, 2014; Ruhs, 2010; Ryan and Mitsilegas, 2010; Saadi et al., 2020). Migrant workers are not necessarily rural workers. Indeed, research has shown that the category includes people living in urban areas with rural household registration (Fiske,

2016; Flynn, 2013; Frederking, 2012; Gilman, 2013; Guia, Koulish, and Mitsilegas, 2016; Guild, 2001; Guild and Niessen, 1996). These migrants (the foreign ones at least) significantly contribute to the growing volume of remittances that are sent to low-income and middle-income countries (see Figure 7.2).

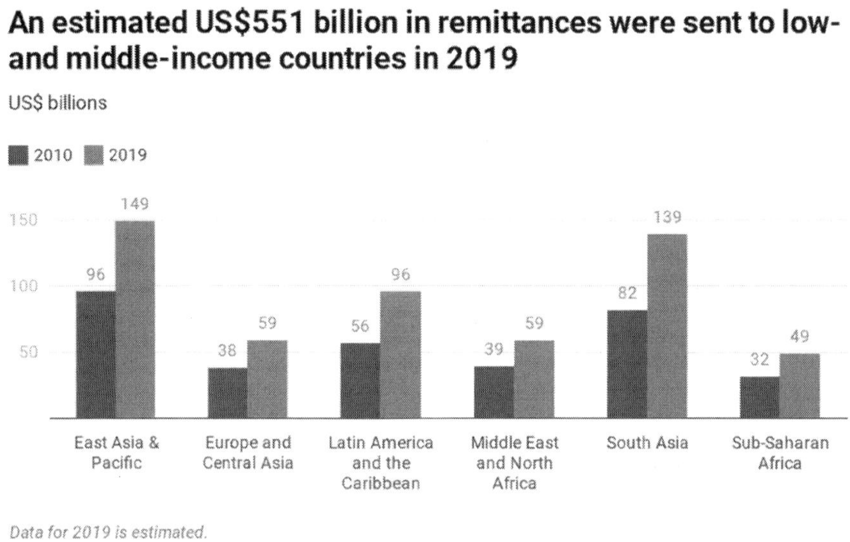

Figure 7.2: Migrant remittances to middle income countries.

Source: World Bank-KNOMAD via The Conversation.

Millions of Chinese migrant workers are reported by the authorities and in some cases, they can go as high as 270 million per year (Melis, 2001; Miller, 2015, 2016; Molnar and Gill, 2018; Money, 1998; Morris, 2002, 2016; Motomura, 1999). Of these, just over half are internal migrants who move from province to province within China in search of work (Brochmann and Hammar, 2020; Frederking, 2012; Kasimis, 2012; Oberman, 2016; Taylor, 2000). The gender split is 3:1 (male to female), meaning that the vast majority of these workers are men. It is anticipated that by 2025, China will be dealing with an annual influx of migrants that easily exceed 200 million every year population (Hollifield, Martin, and Orrenius, 2014; Jacobson, 1996; Johnson, 1996; Joppke, 1998, 1999, 2010; Kasimis, 2012). The implication is that the most populous nation on earth will have the most immigrants on earth. The crucial difference with China is that it counts internal movements in its figures. Yet, other comparable nations such as the USA, China, and Brazil allow for free movement of citizens within its borders.

Because of the system of floating migrants, statistics are hard to come by; let alone verifying their accuracy (Brochmann and Hammar, 2020; Chavez, 2001; Chin, 1999; Cook, 2003; Cornelisse, 2004, 2010). There are reports that 20% of all workers in the major cities of China is an immigrant (Hollifield, Martin, and Orrenius, 2014; Jacobson, 1996; Johnson, 1996; Joppke, 1998, 1999, 2010; Kasimis, 2012). Clearly, this is a country that is well on the way to accumulating a significant number of people that have changed location in order to find work (Chavez, 2001; Chin, 1999; Cook, 2003; Cornelisse, 2004, 2010; Costello, 2012; Dauvergne, 2012; Den Heijer, 2010). In response, the Chinese government has attempted to control the patterns of settlement using the Hukou permanent residence registration system (Johnson, 1996; Joppke, 1998, 1999, 2010; Kasimis, 2012; Kelson and DeLaet, 1999; King, 2009; Lopez, 2005). Under this modality, being a citizen is not enough to secure work legally. You have to also have permission and registration in the locality that you are searching for work. The system extends to issues such as purchasing land, rents, incentives, and access to infrastructure. In doing so, the Chinese government hopes to provide incentives and disincentives that ensure minimal movement of internal workers. Ideally, this should lead to balanced development where there are no pockets of high levels of deprivation. Such a system may not be workable in other countries with constitutions that explicitly allow for the movement of labor within the border. In the next section, we will consider offshoring as a business response to restrictions on the importation of foreign labor.

7.3. OFFSHORING TO OVERCOME MIGRATION RESTRICTIONS

Offshoring is the relocation of a business process from one country to another (Sampson, Mitchell, and Bowring, 2011; Sanggaran, Haire, and Zion, 2016; Sassen, 1996, 1997; Shohamy and McNamara, 2009). This is typically an operational process that is meant to rationalize costs and leverage any competitive advantages in particular locations. Offshoring occurs in major industries such as manufacturing, administration support, finance, and accountancy (Frederking, 2012; Gilman, 2013; Guia, Koulish, and Mitsilegas, 2016; Guild, 2001; Guild and Niessen, 1996; Hailbronner, 2000). Typically, offshoring refers to a company business whose efforts to control costs mean that it has to search for alternative labor pools elsewhere.

However, there are also instances where state governments employ offshoring in order to access value for money (Bangarth, 2003; Barak-Erez, 2008; Becerra, 2016; Brané and Lundholm, 2007; Brochmann and Hammar, 2020; Chavez, 2001).

More recently, new industries such as technical and administrative services have experimented with offshoring in order to test their viability in this modality (Chavez, 2001; Chin, 1999; Cook, 2003; Cornelisse, 2004, 2010; Costello, 2012; Dauvergne, 2012; Den Heijer, 2010). Offshoring and outsourcing are not mutually inclusive. Hence, there are some institutions that will offshore without outsourcing or outsource without offshoring (Acer and Goodman, 2009; Chavez, 2001; Guild and Niessen, 1996; King, 2009; Ozdowski, 1985; Shohamy and McNamara, 2009). One of the formats for offshoring is what is known as intertwined (offshore outsourcing). Other institutions engage in offshoring individually or jointly. Moreover, there is a distinction between partially and completely reversed offshoring. Other related terms have emerged in existing literature including reshoring, in-shoring, and insourcing (Sassen, 1997; Shohamy and McNamara, 2009; Smith, 2014; Soysal, 2012; Spijkerboer and Van Walsum, 2007).

Offshoring is when the offshored work is done by means of an internal and captive delivery model in order to minimize the risks of operational failure (Aynsley-Green et al., 2012; Cornelisse, 2004; Heisler, 2000; Mehan, 1997; Ramji-Nogales, 2007; Spijkerboer and Van Walsum, 2007). This is sometimes referred to as in-house offshore and gives the organization much more control over the activities that are being undertaken (Bacon, 1996; Dudley et al., 2012; Hollifield, Martin, and Orrenius, 2014; Money, 1998; Saadi et al., 2020). Countries like India which are facing immigration hotspots (see Figure 7.3), may benefit from offshoring which picks up the excess labor supply on their shores (Rubio-Marín, 2014; Ruhs, 2010; Ryan and Mitsilegas, 2010; Saadi et al., 2020; Samers, 2004; Sampson, Mitchell, and Bowring, 2011). It is a great way for countries to access the job market of other countries without having to go through the challenges of obtaining a long-term work visa.

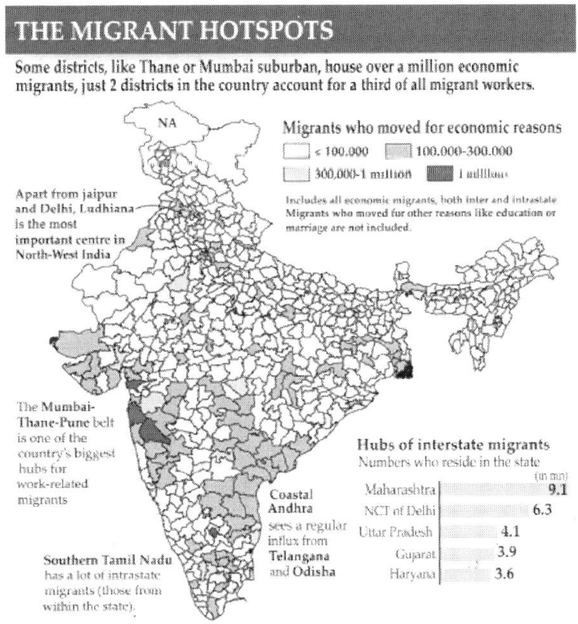

Figure 7.3: Migrant hotspots in India.

Source: Census 2011 vi Mint.

Imported services from subsidiaries or other closely related suppliers are included in offshoring (Baldwin-Edwards, 2006; Dunn, 2001; Jacobson, 1996; Morris, 2016; Samers, 2004). However, the decision to include them can raise question about the quality of service that is being delivered and whether it inconveniences clients in the long run. The classic definition of offshoring excludes intermediate goods such as cars or computers that are still in the manufacturing process and waiting to be finished in the home location (Soysal, 2012; Spijkerboer and Van Walsum, 2007; Taylor, 2000; Thym, 2008; Webber, 2012; Welch, 2002; Wexler, 2007). Lower cost and increased corporate profitability are often the motivation for offshoring, although some companies have no choice but to follow existing patterns of offshoring anyway. This is what economists refer to as labor arbitrage, a key concept for organizations that are operation as multinational corporations (Barak-Erez, 2008; Exdell, 2009; Joppke, 1998; Motomura, 1999; Sanggaran, Haire, and Zion, 2016).

More recently, offshoring drivers also include access to qualified personnel abroad who are used to complete tasks that are critical to the production process. The home country may be experiencing shortages in particular specializations yet another location has them in plenty. This type of offshoring occurs within technical professions and is associated with an increasing operational process (Joppke, 1998, 1999, 2010; Kasimis, 2012; Kelson and DeLaet, 1999; King, 2009; Lopez, 2005; Lorentzen, 2014).

Jobs are added in the destination country providing the goods or services and are subtracted from the higher-cost labor country when estimating the impact of the offshoring process (Thym, 2008; Webber, 2012; Welch, 2002; Wexler, 2007; Wilcox, 2009; Zúñiga and Hernández-León, 2005; Zwi and Mares, 2015). Because of the different levels of accuracy across industry, sometimes the true impact of offshoring in this way is underestimated or overestimated, a major problem for policy formulation. The increased safety net costs of the unemployed may be absorbed by the government through contributions by taxpayers in the high-cost country. They can also be absorbed by the company doing the offshoring itself (Den Heijer, 2010; Dudley et al., 2012; Dunn, 2001, 2010; Exdell, 2009; Fiske, 2016; Flynn, 2013; Frederking, 2012). This highlights the close cooperation between the government and individual companies in order to make offshoring an effective business modality. A comparative analysis of Europe and the USA demonstrates some of the implications of policy and cultural barriers during the offshoring process. For example, Europe experienced less offshoring than the United States due to policies that applied more costs to corporations. There were also cultural barriers that impacted on the perceptions of and responses to offshoring (Welch, 2002; Wexler, 2007; Wilcox, 2009; Zúñiga and Hernández-León, 2005; Zwi and Mares, 2015).

After its accession to the World Trade Organization (WTO) in 2001, the People's Republic of China opened up to the world. One of its achievements since then is becoming a prominent destination for production offshoring (Molnar and Gill, 2018; Money, 1998; Morris, 2002, 2016; Motomura, 1999; Nethery and Holman, 2016). This is because China has very cheap labor and highly controlled workplace practices which reduce liabilities for employers and hence increase business efficiency. Another focus area has been the software industry as part of global software development and developing global information systems (Morris, 2002, 2016; Motomura, 1999; Nethery and Holman, 2016; Newman, Proctor, and Dudley, 2013; Oberman, 2016). China has been accused of pilfering business ideas and technology, then producing them at a fraction of the cost that they would be produced in Europe and North America. Indeed, this was one of the key anchors of the Donald Trump policy of trade sanctions against China.

Specific industries lend themselves to the process of offshoring and are therefore more likely to have an element of foreign-located labor. Countries like India have specifically targeted these industries as a source of income and also as a mean of reducing the local unemployment rates. After technical progress in telecommunications improved the possibilities of trade in services, India became one prominent destination for such offshoring. For example, India was providing call center services to UK banks with some success (Ozdowski, 1985; Paz, 2016; Peberdy, 2001; Ramji-Nogales, 2007; Rubio-Marín, 2014; Ruhs, 2010; Ryan and Mitsilegas, 2010). Occasionally, there were operational problems such as language barriers when running the offshoring outfit. However, the vast majority of business transactions were effectively completed at a fraction of the cost that they would have been conducted locally. Nevertheless, there was some resentment about entire departments being sent abroad and therefore increasing the local unemployment rate.

Over time, many parts of the world are now emerging as offshore destinations (Aynsley-Green et al., 2012; Bacon, 1996; Baldwin-Edwards, 2006; Bangarth, 2003; Barak-Erez, 2008; Becerra, 2016). Indeed, there was a time when Africa expressed some ambitions for becoming an offshoring center but was then let down by the poor infrastructure and political instability of many African countries. One of the complaints about offshoring is that it depresses quality and working conditions in the country that is losing the jobs (Brané and Lundholm, 2007; Brochmann and Hammar, 2020; Chavez, 2001; Chin, 1999; Cook, 2003; Cornelisse, 2004). Nevertheless, it is one of the ways in which an organization can escape unfavorable labor markets in industrialized nations (Dunn, 2010; Exdell, 2009; Fiske, 2016; Flynn, 2013; Frederking, 2012; Gilman, 2013; Guia, Koulish, and Mitsilegas, 2016). The next section focuses on political demography as an important aspect of the immigration debate.

7.4. IMPLICATIONS OF POLITICAL DEMOGRAPHY

Political demography is the study of the relationship between politics and population change (Dunn, 2010; Exdell, 2009; Fiske, 2016; Flynn, 2013; Frederking, 2012; Gilman, 2013; Guia, Koulish, and Mitsilegas, 2016). In undertaking such studies, it is possible to reconcile political aspirations and priorities with the realities of a population structure that is changing over time. Population change is driven by classic demographic mechanisms. Some of the known ones include births, deaths, and changes in age structure.

For purposes of this book, it is also worth considering the role of migration in changing populations and communities (Hernandez-Truyol and Johns, 1997; Hollifield, Martin, and Orrenius, 2014; Jacobson, 1996; Johnson, 1996; Joppke, 1998).

That is not to say that changes in populations are always undesirable. For example, there is always scope for assimilation as well as boundary and identity change (Dunn, 2001, 2010; Exdell, 2009; Fiske, 2016; Flynn, 2013; Frederking, 2012; Gilman, 2013; Guia, Koulish, and Mitsilegas, 2016). When new people come in, they change the way in which we see ourselves and the world around us. Such events and issues can redraw the boundaries of populations in a way that is not possible with biological populations (Dudley et al., 2012; Dunn, 2001, 2010; Exdell, 2009; Fiske, 2016; Flynn, 2013; Frederking, 2012; Gilman, 2013). Typically, political-demographic projections can account for both demographic factors. They can also arise out of transitions which are caused by social change (Hailbronner, 2000; Hayter, 2000; Heisler, 2000; Hernandez-Truyol and Johns, 1997; Hollifield, Martin, and Orrenius, 2014). For example, migrants intermarry with the local population and produce children that do not entirely belong to either community. Instead, these children form a new community that challenges and enriches the existing communities. As Figure 7.4 demonstrates, even in a free movement region such as the European Union; there are economic impacts when people from place to place in search of work and other opportunities (Den Heijer, 2010; Dudley et al., 2012; Dunn, 2001, 2010; Exdell, 2009; Fiske, 2016; Flynn, 2013; Frederking, 2012).

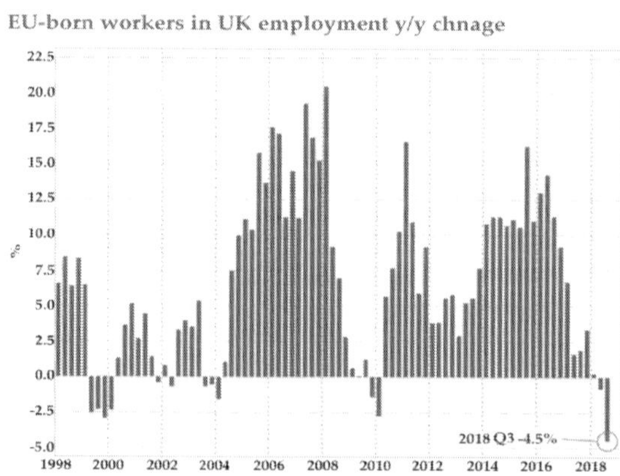

Figure 7.4: EU workers in the UK 1998 to 2018.

Source: The Independent.

Some of the issues which are studied in the context of political demography include surges of young people in the developing world (Mehan, 1997; Melis, 2001; Miller, 2015, 2016; Molnar and Gill, 2018; Money, 1998; Morris, 2002, 2016). Whereas young people are a key resource, they are less so if they are undereducated and have no realistic prospect of finding a good job. That is why all the talk of Africa's vibrant young population has as yet to deliver its ambitions of becoming a developed region. Political demography is also interested in the significantly increasing aging in the developed world (Costello, 2012; Dauvergne, 2012; Den Heijer, 2010; Dudley et al., 2012; Dunn, 2001, 2010; Exdell, 2009; Fiske, 2016). Indeed, there is such a crisis in countries such as Germany that the countries have resorted to importing young people from other parts of the world in order to replenish its aging population.

Another area of increasing interest is the impact of increasing urbanization (Dunn, 2010; Exdell, 2009; Fiske, 2016; Flynn, 2013; Frederking, 2012; Gilman, 2013; Guia, Koulish, and Mitsilegas, 2016). As more and more people move to urban centers, rural areas may be turning into backwaters. The situation is made even more serious by the tendency of key demographics such as migrant labor and young people to move towards urban centers and away from rural areas. Political demographers study issues like population growth in a political context and how those issues play out in a modern urban context (Baldwin-Edwards, 2006; Bangarth, 2003; Barak-Erez, 2008; Becerra, 2016; Brané and Lundholm, 2007; Brochmann and Hammar, 2020). A population's growth is impacted by the relative balance of variables like mortality, fertility, and immigration (Bangarth, 2003; Dunn, 2010; Johnson, 1996; Morris, 2002; Sampson, Mitchell, and Bowring, 2011). These are key variables which policymakers target in order to control population changes.

Many of the present world's most powerful nations are aging quickly, and that is happening in mainly the most industrialized nations. Hence, the demographic dividend appears to be creating problems for developed nations in the long run. Developed nations are also grappling with major decreases in fertility rates. At the same time, there are major increases in life expectancies meaning that many more people are living for much longer than before (Joppke, 2010; Kasimis, 2012; Kelson and DeLaet, 1999; King, 2009; Lopez, 2005; Lorentzen, 2014; Mehan, 1997). As the labor pools in these nations shrink, and spending on the elderly increases, their economies are likely to slow down (Brané and Lundholm, 2007; Brochmann and Hammar, 2020; Chavez, 2001; Chin, 1999; Cook, 2003; Cornelisse, 2004).

This is a ticking timebomb unless those populations can rebalance their structures to include more and more young healthy people.

Political demography has some overlaps with theories of evolution (Becerra, 2016; Brané and Lundholm, 2007; Brochmann and Hammar, 2020; Chavez, 2001; Chin, 1999; Cook, 2003). For example, differential reproductive success is the mechanism through which evolution takes place (Joppke, 1999, 2010; Kasimis, 2012; Kelson and DeLaet, 1999; King, 2009; Lopez, 2005; Lorentzen, 2014; Mehan, 1997). That means that highly populated communities have a high level of reproductive success. However, if that reproductive success is not matched by productive success; these communities will slide into dependency and economic decline.

Countries are already well-versed in the processes and effects of population changes. For much of human history, this occurred through migrations and wars of conquest. Other major events that changed populations included disease outbreaks. Certain countries like Ireland experienced high mortality through famine. The effects of war, particularly World War I meant that old empires were collapsing, partly due to changes in population structures. Population levels and characteristics have the power to impact on empires, tribes, and city-states (Sampson, Mitchell, and Bowring, 2011; Sanggaran, Haire, and Zion, 2016; Sassen, 1996, 1997; Shohamy and McNamara, 2009). Differential fertility means that various countries in the world are dealing with entirely different population issues. For example, Europe is dealing with an aging population, whereas Africa is dealing with a young population that is underemployed. This chapter will close by exploring the vulnerabilities of LGBT migrants.

7.5. LGBT MIGRANTS AND THEIR VULNERABILITIES

LGBT migration is the movement of lesbian, gay, bisexual, transgender, and queer (LGBT) people around the world and domestically (Frederking, 2012; Gilman, 2013; Guia, Koulish, and Mitsilegas, 2016; Guild, 2001; Guild and Niessen, 1996; Hailbronner, 2000). This is often done in order to escape discrimination or ill-treatment due to their sexuality (Baldwin-Edwards, 2006; Dunn, 2001; Jacobson, 1996; Morris, 2016; Samers, 2004). Globally, many LGBT people attempt to leave discriminatory regions in search of more tolerant ones (Heisler, 2000; Hernandez-Truyol and Johns, 1997; Hollifield, Martin, and Orrenius, 2014; Jacobson, 1996; Johnson, 1996). Historically, LGBT people have suffered discrimination and the threat of imprisonment or deportation due to their identification or sexuality (Heisler, 2000; Hernandez-Truyol and Johns, 1997; Hollifield, Martin, and Orrenius, 2014; Jacobson, 1996; Johnson, 1996). In countries like China which generally exclude migrants (Figure 7.5), LGBT migrants will find it even harder to secure a safe space to live (Lorentzen, 2014, Mehan, 1997; Melis, 2001; Miller, 2015, 2016; Molnar and Gill, 2018; Money, 1998; Morris, 2016). As a consequence, these countries are not preferred destinations even if they may have other job opportunities (Chin, 1999; Cook, 2003; Cornelisse, 2004, 2010; Costello, 2012; Dauvergne, 2012; Den Heijer, 2010; Dudley et al., 2012).

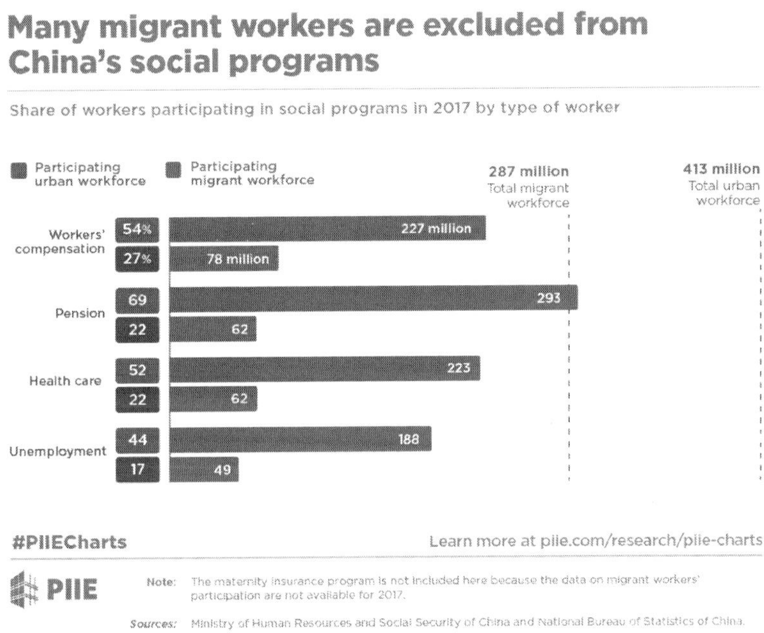

Figure 7.5: Exclusion of migrants from social programs in China.

Source: Peterson Institute for International Economics.

Other countries have had similarly challenging environments for LGBT people. For example, in the beginning of the 20th century, homosexuality was considered a mental illness and used to bar homosexuals from settling in North America (Guild and Niessen, 1996; Hailbronner, 2000; Hayter, 2000; Heisler, 2000; Hernandez-Truyol and Johns, 1997). LGBT people were referenced as "sexual deviates" and banned from entering the country. Immigration authorities were required by law to deport LGBT people for no other reason than the fact that they were non-heterosexual and non-cis-gender (Sassen, 1996, 1997; Shohamy and McNamara, 2009; Smith, 2014; Soysal, 2012; Spijkerboer and Van Walsum, 2007).

The Lavender Scare of the anti-communist 1950's America is an example of the kind of mass hysteria that surrounds the migration of LGBT people. This particular scare created additional persecution of homosexuals. There was a generalized fear among people with same-sex attraction, and many had to go underground in order to avoid the wrath of the moral majority (Ackerman and Furman, 2014; Adelman, 2002; Aynsley-Green et al., 2012; Bacon, 1996; Baldwin-Edwards, 2006). After the war, a "Pervert Elimination Campaign" was initiated in Washington D.C. by the U.S. Park Police. Consequently, there were a number of highly publicized sex charge arrests of gay men, many of whom subsequently lost their jobs (Aynsley-Green et al., 2012; Bacon, 1996; Baldwin-Edwards, 2006; Bangarth, 2003; Barak-Erez, 2008; Becerra, 2016). For a long time, LGBT people were not allowed to openly serve in the military.

LGBT people face challenges in gaining asylum or sanctuary based on persecution based on their identification or sexuality (Money, 1998; Morris, 2002, 2016; Motomura, 1999; Nethery and Holman, 2016; Newman, Proctor, and Dudley, 2013). For example, under US immigration laws, homosexuality must be socially visible in order for sexual persecution to be a viable complaint (Guild, 2001; Miller, 2016; Ryan and Mitsilegas, 2010; Wexler, 2007; Wilcox, 2009). Additionally, homosexuality must be a permanent and inherent characteristic to be considered a justified reason for migrating under the asylum provisions (Guild and Niessen, 1996; Hailbronner, 2000; Hayter, 2000; Heisler, 2000; Hernandez-Truyol and Johns, 1997). LGBT individuals who are applying for asylum often have a difficult time representing themselves properly in court and many are embarrassed by the intrusive evaluation interviews (Paz, 2016; Peberdy, 2001; Ramji-Nogales, 2007; Rubio-Marín, 2014; Ruhs, 2010; Ryan and Mitsilegas, 2010; Saadi et al., 2020).

Other seemingly liberal communities have also engaged in acts of violence against LGBT citizenry. This has the effect of forcing LGBT people to flee their homelands (Kelson and DeLaet, 1999; King, 2009; Lopez, 2005; Lorentzen, 2014; Mehan, 1997; Melis, 2001; Miller, 2015, 2016). Indeed, some anti-LGBT campaigners express this as their ultimate goal to clear entire countries of "homosexuals and perverts." Mexico has reported the second-highest rate of homophobic crimes in the world after Brazil, despite its apparent embrace of equality (Exdell, 2009; Fiske, 2016; Flynn, 2013; Frederking, 2012; Gilman, 2013; Guia, Koulish, and Mitsilegas, 2016; Guild, 2001). Researchers have found that the most frequent types of discrimination include prevention from employment, extortion, and arbitrary detention (Costello, 2012; Guia, Koulish, and Mitsilegas, 2016; Melis, 2001; Rubio-Marín, 2014; Webber, 2012).

Developing countries have adopted increasingly harsh measures against LGBT people that have forced them to flee (Webber, 2012; Welch, 2002; Wexler, 2007; Wilcox, 2009; Zúñiga and Hernández-León, 2005; Zwi and Mares, 2015). For example, some African countries punish homosexuality with the death sentence or a life sentence (Paz, 2016; Peberdy, 2001; Ramji-Nogales, 2007; Rubio-Marín, 2014; Ruhs, 2010; Ryan and Mitsilegas, 2010). Mauritania, Sudan, and northern Nigeria have been reported as places where lesbians and gays are sometimes stoned to death (Johnson, 1996; Joppke, 1998, 1999, 2010; Kasimis, 2012; Kelson and DeLaet, 1999; King, 2009; Lopez, 2005). Institutional sexual persecution is also rampant in Cameroon, Burundi, Uganda, and Gambia (Cornelisse, 2004, 2010; Costello, 2012; Dauvergne, 2012; Den Heijer, 2010; Dudley et al., 2012; Dunn, 2001). As a consequence, there have been reports of LGBT applicants for asylum from these countries.

There are many other examples of LGBT people simply denied the possibility of living peacefully in their home countries (Smith, 2014; Soysal, 2012; Spijkerboer and Van Walsum, 2007; Taylor, 2000; Thym, 2008; Webber, 2012; Welch, 2002). For example, corrective rape is a major problem in South Africa (Miller, 2015, 2016; Molnar and Gill, 2018; Money, 1998; Morris, 2002, 2016; Motomura, 1999; Nethery and Holman, 2016). This is despite South Africa's record of legislative prohibitions against LGBT discrimination (Webber, 2012; Welch, 2002; Wexler, 2007; Wilcox, 2009; Zúñiga and Hernández-León, 2005; Zwi and Mares, 2015). This amounts to the rape of LGBT people in order to "correct" their "pathologies" (Jacobson, 1996; Johnson, 1996; Joppke, 1998, 1999, 2010; Kasimis, 2012; Kelson and DeLaet, 1999). It is a particularly frightening practice given the high instance of HIV/AIDS in South Africa (Taylor, 2000; Thym, 2008; Webber, 2012; Welch, 2002; Wexler, 2007; Wilcox, 2009; Zúñiga and Hernández-León, 2005). Given these incidents of harassment and discrimination, it seems highly likely that LGBT people will continue to migrate away from socially conservative nations into the more liberal industrialized nations

(Acer and Goodman, 2009; Chavez, 2001; Guild and Niessen, 1996; King, 2009; Ozdowski, 1985; Shohamy and McNamara, 2009).

CHAPTER 7 SUMMARY

This chapter has explored some of the immigration hotspots that have been reported in the world today. One of the emerging patterns is the emphasis on preventing people from poorer countries coming to developed nations. However, there are also specific groups such as LGBT migrants that need specific protections based on their unique needs, which may not necessarily fall within the remit of the mainstream service provision. Through the study of political demography, we are able to predict some of the short term and long-term effects of migration as well as other factors such as birth control. The final chapter in this book accepts the inevitability of migrations, but then posits some solutions for managing its effects in the future.

CHAPTER 8

PLANNING FOR INEVITABLE MIGRATIONS

CONTENTS

Given the virtual inevitability of migrations, the most practical response to this phenomenon is to plan and manage the process. This chapter specifically highlights some general policy responses to immigration that bear in mind the law and human rights. The first section of this final chapter will explore the implications of the refugee roulette and religious migration. The second section tackles replacement immigration and separation barriers. The third section deals with the thorny issue of settler colonialism. The fourth section will focus on migrant worker rights and the possibilities of allowing free movement of labor. The chapter will close with an overview of the reformation prospects for migration management generally.

8.1. ARBITRARINESS IN MIGRATION DECISIONS

There have been reports of arbitrariness and inconsistencies in asylum decisions. This has been referred to as refugee roulette (Webber, 2012; Welch, 2002; Wexler, 2007; Wilcox, 2009; Zúñiga and Hernández-León, 2005; Zwi and Mares, 2015). Recent research suggests that the outcome of asylum determinations largely depends upon the identity of the particular adjudicator (and by extension their perspectives or prejudices) rather than the merits of the case (Costello, 2012; Guia, Koulish, and Mitsilegas, 2016; Melis, 2001; Rubio-Marín, 2014; Webber, 2012). Ideally, different adjudicators should come to the same conclusion about the same facts of the case, but this is not always the case. The implications are that the resulting disparities in rates of granting asylum are problematic (Exdell, 2009; Fiske, 2016; Flynn, 2013; Frederking, 2012; Gilman, 2013; Guia, Koulish, and Mitsilegas, 2016; Guild, 2001). On the other hand, some commentators state that a good deal of disparity is inevitable given the human judgment which is subjective by definition (Kelson and DeLaet, 1999; King, 2009; Lopez, 2005; Lorentzen, 2014; Mehan, 1997; Melis, 2001; Miller, 2015, 2016). Figure 8.1 highlights the various levels at which these disparities occur during asylum determination process in the USA.

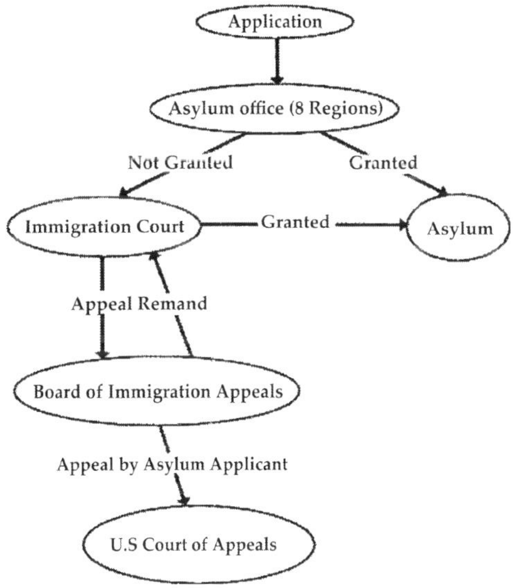

Figure 8.1: Various levels of adjudication disparities in refugee roulette.

Source: Semantic Scholar.

Researchers used the term "refugee roulette" following an empirical analysis of decision-making at all four levels of the asylum process (Sassen, 1996, 1997; Shohamy and McNamara, 2009; Smith, 2014; Soysal, 2012; Spijkerboer and Van Walsum, 2007). Results indicated an unacceptable level of disparities in grant rates, meaning that the case was not being tried on its own merits but rather the beliefs and perceptions of the decision-maker (Guild, 2001; Miller, 2016; Ryan and Mitsilegas, 2010; Wexler, 2007; Wilcox, 2009). Given the seriousness of asylum decisions, the notion that it is based on biases and prejudices of the adjudicator is unacceptable to some human rights advocates (Money, 1998; Morris, 2002, 2016; Motomura, 1999; Nethery and Holman, 2016; Newman, Proctor, and Dudley, 2013). This is contrary to all the rules and recommendations that are made under international law regarding the management of asylum claims (Guia, Koulish, and Mitsilegas, 2016; Guild, 2001; Guild and Niessen, 1996; Hailbronner, 2000; Hayter, 2000; Heisler, 2000).

As a case in point, we might consider how asylum cases based on religious persecution are handled. Whereas this is not as high profile as political persecution, it affects the lives of people. Indeed, many Christians in the USA are worried that not enough attention is given to people who are fleeing religious intolerance (Dauvergne, 2012; Den Heijer, 2010; Dudley et al., 2012; Dunn, 2001, 2010; Exdell, 2009; Fiske, 2016; Flynn, 2013). This can be a tough task if the country where the applicant proposes to move is not particularly religious or is actually anti-religious in its public administration (Aynsley-Green et al., 2012; Bacon, 1996; Baldwin-Edwards, 2006; Bangarth, 2003; Barak-Erez, 2008; Becerra, 2016). Changes in religious demography are often consequences, and often goals, of human mass migration to other territories (Ackerman and Furman, 2014; Adelman, 2002; Aynsley-Green et al., 2012; Bacon, 1996; Baldwin-Edwards, 2006).

Often, the goals of a political migration involve establishing a territory and governments biased towards and welcoming of members of the same sect (Sassen, 1996, 1997; Shohamy and McNamara, 2009; Smith, 2014; Soysal, 2012; Spijkerboer and Van Walsum, 2007). Recently the USA has been at the forefront of protecting Christians across the globe (particularly in Muslim-majority countries like Iran). However, the same government also instituted bans and restrictions on migrants from Muslim-majority governments. This demonstrates that often disjointed and contradictory policies that underpin controversial immigration processes (Brané and Lundholm, 2007; Flynn, 2013; Joppke, 2010; Newman, Proctor, and Dudley, 2013; Sassen, 1997). In the next section, we consider similar problems in replacement migration and the construction of separation barriers.

8.2. REPLACEMENT IMMIGRATION AND SEPARATION BARRIERS

Replacement migration has been one of the key debates and topics in political demography in recent years. In demography, replacement migration is a theory of migration needed for a region to achieve a particular objective which could be demographic, economic, or social (Guild and Niessen, 1996; Hailbronner, 2000; Hayter, 2000; Heisler, 2000; Hernandez-Truyol and Johns, 1997). Generally, studies using this concept have as an objective to avoid the decline of the total population. There is even more concern about the potential decline of the working-age population (Chin, 1999; Cook, 2003; Cornelisse, 2004, 2010; Costello, 2012; Dauvergne, 2012; Den Heijer, 2010; Dudley et al., 2012). Often, these overall declines in the population are influenced by low fertility rates and are particularly problematic among the most developed nations which are the premium destinations for economic migrants (Lorentzen, 2014; Mehan, 1997; Melis, 2001; Miller, 2015, 2016; Molnar and Gill, 2018; Money, 1998; Morris, 2016). In these cases, fertility is lower than the replacement level of 2.1 children per woman. Additionally, there is a longer life expectancy. The combination of these factors changes the age structure over time (Miller, 2015, 2016; Molnar and Gill, 2018; Money, 1998; Morris, 2002, 2016; Motomura, 1999). Countries in Western Europe and North America are facing this particular problem (Ryan and Mitsilegas, 2010; Saadi et al., 2020; Samers, 2004; Sampson, Mitchell, and Bowring, 2011; Sanggaran, Haire, and Zion, 2016). In Figure 8.2, we see how replacement immigration has impacted on the Canadian population.

	Total fertility rate			Immigration			Life expectancy M/F		
Projection	L	M	H	L	M	H	H	M	L
1971 census	1.8	2.2	2.6	120,000	...	160,000		70.2/ 78.3	
1976 census	1.7	...	2.1	125,000	150,000	175,000		70.2/ 78.3	
1981 census	1.4	1.66	2.2	100,000	...	150,000		74.9/ 81.6	
1986 census	1.2	1.67	2.1	140,000	...	200,000		77.2/ 84.0	
1991 census	1.5	1.7	1.9	150,000	250,000	330,000	81.0/ 86.0	78.5/ 84.0	77.0/ 83.0
1996 census	1.3	1.48	1.8	180,000	225,000	270,000	81.5/ 85.0	80.0/ 84.0	78.5/ 83.0

Figure 8.2: Impact of replacement immigration on the Canadian population.

Source: 1. Statistics Canada, 1974: 26, 59; 1979: 21, 29; 1985: 27, 41; 1990: 12, 26; 1994: 59; 2001: 57
2. Statistics Canada, demography division, special tabulations.

Overall, the population will start to decline as there will not be enough children born to replace the population of people lost and the proportion of older individuals composing the population will continue to increase (Heisler, 2000; Hernandez-Truyol and Johns, 1997; Hollifield, Martin, and Orrenius, 2014; Jacobson, 1996; Johnson, 1996). One concern from this is that the age-dependency ratio will be affected. In effect, the working-age population will have more dependents in older age to support (Baldwin-Edwards, 2006; Dunn, 2001; Jacobson, 1996; Morris, 2016; Samers, 2004). Therefore, replacement migration has been a proposed mechanism to try and combat declining population size and rebalance the population structure (Frederking, 2012; Gilman, 2013; Guia, Koulish, and Mitsilegas, 2016; Guild, 2001; Guild and Niessen, 1996; Hailbronner, 2000).

Projections calculating migration replacement are primarily demographics and theoretical exercises. They are not forecasts or recommendations for specific policy interventions (Kelson and DeLaet, 1999; King, 2009; Lopez, 2005; Lorentzen, 2014; Mehan, 1997; Melis, 2001; Miller, 2015, 2016). However, this demographic information can help prompt governments to facilitate replacement migration by making policy changes (Cornelisse, 2010; Costello, 2012; Dauvergne, 2012; Den Heijer, 2010; Dudley et al., 2012; Dunn, 2001, 2010). The concept of replacement migration may vary according to the study and depending on the context in which it applies (Taylor, 2000; Thym, 2008; Webber, 2012; Welch, 2002; Wexler, 2007; Wilcox, 2009; Zúñiga and Hernández-León, 2005). It may be a number of annual immigrants. Others consider a net migration compared to an ideal scenario (Motomura, 1999; Nethery and Holman, 2016; Newman, Proctor, and Dudley, 2013; Oberman, 2016; Orfanos, 2019). Government policies to encourage younger immigrants in countries like Germany and UK have proved to be highly controversial (Bacon, 1996; Baldwin-Edwards, 2006; Bangarth, 2003; Barak-Erez, 2008; Becerra, 2016; Brané and Lundholm, 2007). That is why there is always a concern that replacement migration is all about changing the character of the native population. This can lead to a backlash that ushers in rightwing governments with a decidedly anti-immigrant stance, as happened in the USA, Italy, and Australia.

One of the consequences of such disquiet about replacement immigration has been advocacy for separation barriers to prevent even more migrants from arriving (Lopez, 2005; Lorentzen, 2014; Mehan, 1997; Melis, 2001; Miller, 2015, 2016; Molnar and Gill, 2018; Money, 1998). A separation barrier or separation wall is a barrier, wall, or fence, constructed to limit the movement of people across a certain line or border, or to separate peoples or cultures (Baldwin-Edwards, 2006; Bangarth, 2003; Barak-Erez, 2008; Becerra, 2016; Brané and Lundholm, 2007). A separation barrier that runs along an internationally recognized border is known as a border barrier (Saadi et al., 2020; Samers, 2004; Sampson, Mitchell, and Bowring, 2011; Sanggaran, Haire, and Zion, 2016). Some experts have posited that separation barriers are being built at a record rate around the world along borders. These barriers do not only surround dictatorships or pariah states, but are found on borders between two democracies such as the USA and Mexico (Fiske, 2016; Flynn, 2013; Frederking, 2012; Gilman, 2013; Guia, Koulish, and Mitsilegas, 2016; Guild, 2001; Guild and Niessen, 1996). The next section considers the ongoing problem of settler colonialism.

8.3. THE PROBLEM OF SETTLER COLONIALISM

Settler colonialism is a form of colonialism that seeks to replace the original population of the colonized territory with a new society of settlers, often without the consent of the original population (Thym, 2008; Webber, 2012; Welch, 2002; Wexler, 2007; Wilcox, 2009; Zúñiga and Hernández-León, 2005; Zwi and Mares, 2015). Like other types of colonialism, it is based on exogenous domination and the subjugation of people that are considered to be inferior in some way (Den Heijer, 2010; Miller, 2015; Ruhs, 2010; Welch, 2002; Zwi and Mares, 2015). Such a program is typically organized or supported by an imperial authority and is by definition exploitative in nature (Sassen, 1996, 1997; Shohamy and McNamara, 2009; Smith, 2014; Soysal, 2012; Spijkerboer and Van Walsum, 2007).

Settler colonialism is enacted by a variety of means that are always destructive and humiliating. These can include depopulation through violent means. Due to a fear of a political backlash on the international stage, the aggressor nation may use subtle means such as the enactment of laws that implicitly or explicitly support settler colonialism. The legal means are then embedded in the constitution whilst simultaneously avoiding the assimilation or recognition of indigenous identity within a colonial framework (Spijkerboer and Van Walsum, 2007; Taylor, 2000; Thym, 2008; Webber, 2012; Welch, 2002; Wexler, 2007; Wilcox, 2009). Settler colonialism contrasts with exploitation colonialism, which entails a national economic policy of conquering a country to exploit its population as cheap or free labor. In the case of the great colonial powers such as Britain, France, and recently the USA, this type of colonialism aims to exploit natural resources as a raw material for industrialization (Acer and Goodman, 2009; Ackerman and Furman, 2014; Adelman, 2002; Aynsley-Green et al., 2012; Bacon, 1996). As Figure 8.3 shows, settler colonialism is not merely a relic of the past but a phenomenon that still has reverberations today (Adelman, 2002; Cook, 2003; Hayter, 2000; Lorentzen, 2014; Peberdy, 2001; Soysal, 2012).

Figure 8.3: Modern examples of settler colonialism.

Source: Visualizing Palestine 101.

Unlike other forms of colonialism, the imperial power does not always represent the same nationality as the settlers (Cook, 2003; Cornelisse, 2004, 2010; Costello, 2012; Dauvergne, 2012; Den Heijer, 2010; Dudley et al., 2012). However, the colonizing authority generally views the settlers as racially superior to the previous inhabitants (Guia, Koulish, and Mitsilegas, 2016; Guild, 2001; Guild and Niessen, 1996; Hailbronner, 2000; Hayter, 2000; Heisler, 2000). This may give settlers' social movements and political demands greater legitimacy than those of colonized peoples in the eyes of the home colonies (Sampson, Mitchell, and Bowring, 2011; Sanggaran, Haire, and Zion, 2016; Sassen, 1996, 1997; Shohamy and McNamara, 2009). Despite the end of the European colonial empires, settler populations typically remain and are still privileged in some parts of the world (Becerra, 2016; Brané and Lundholm, 2007; Brochmann and Hammar, 2020; Chavez, 2001; Chin, 1999; Cook, 2003). In this way, settler colonialism lasts indefinitely, except in the rare event of complete evacuation or settler decolonization (Oberman, 2016; Orfanos, 2019; Ozdowski, 1985; Paz, 2016; Peberdy, 2001; Ramji-Nogales, 2007; Rubio-Marín, 2014).

Settler colonialism is generally discussed in terms of the one-way flow of the values of the imperial master. These are deliberately designed to overtake and repudiate the culture and history of the indigenous community

(Bacon, 1996; Baldwin-Edwards, 2006; Bangarth, 2003; Barak-Erez, 2008; Becerra, 2016; Brané and Lundholm, 2007). Transnational and global studies of settler colonialism often give more importance to the histories of imperial emigrants rather than of the displaced indigenous peoples (Dunn, 2001, 2010; Exdell, 2009; Fiske, 2016, Flynn, 2013; Frederking, 2012; Gilman, 2013; Guia, Koulish, and Mitsilegas, 2016). Indeed, the subjugated people may even be forced to learn the history of the conqueror. Legal proceedings in some settler colonies have challenged settler rights in order to address historical wrongs. Robert Mugabe of Zimbabwe famously complained about settlers who had acquired large swathes of land to the detriment of the indigenous population. That then led to a land reform agenda which was opposed by the great powers who imposed crippling sanctions on the Zimbabwe economy in an attempt to oust Mugabe.

These histories of settler colonies highlight the hypocrisies of the great powers who imposed their own migrants on indigenous people but are now completely unwilling to accept economic migrants from their former colonies. There are lasting effects of colonial takeovers and the continued displacement of Indigenous peoples at the start of the 21st century which underpin some of the modern inequalities in the world (Lorentzen, 2014; Mehan, 1997; Melis, 2001; Miller, 2015, 2016; Molnar and Gill, 2018; Money, 1998; Morris, 2016). In the United States, Western Australia and South Africa, governments used land allotment as a legal way to take possession of indigenous peoples' land (Ackerman and Furman, 2014; Adelman, 2002; Aynsley-Green et al., 2012; Bacon, 1996; Baldwin-Edwards, 2006). Any requests for compensation and public apologies have often met with resistance from the descendants of settler colonialists who feel that they should not be held responsible for the actions of their ancestors. The next section briefly discusses migrant worker rights and the possibility of free movement.

8.4. MIGRANT WORKER RIGHTS AND FREE MOVEMENT

One of the key reform areas for modern migration policy is the protection of workers who happen to be migrants (Acer and Goodman, 2009; Ackerman and Furman, 2014; Adelman, 2002; Aynsley-Green et al., 2012; Bacon, 1996). The International Convention on the Protection of the Rights of All Migrant Workers and Members of Their Families is a United Nations multilateral treaty governing the protection of migrant workers and families

(Brané and Lundholm, 2007; Brochmann and Hammar, 2020; Chavez, 2001; Chin, 1999; Cook, 2003; Cornelisse, 2004). The agreement was signed on the 18th of December 1990. Subsequently, it entered into force on the 1st of July 2003 after the threshold of 20 ratifying States was reached in March 2003. The Committee on Migrant Workers (CMW) monitors implementation of the convention and is one of the seven UN-linked human rights treaty bodies (Joppke, 2010; Kasimis, 2012; Kelson and DeLaet, 1999; King, 2009; Lopez, 2005; Lorentzen, 2014; Mehan, 1997). In Figure 8.4, we see the kind of segmented labor market that encourages migrant labor and therefore calls for protections for those workers that cross borders (Bangarth, 2003; Dunn, 2010; Johnson, 1996; Morris, 2002; Sampson, Mitchell, and Bowring, 2011). Because of the international nature of migrant worker movements, the reference to international law is increasingly becoming important when developing strategies to deal with immigration issues.

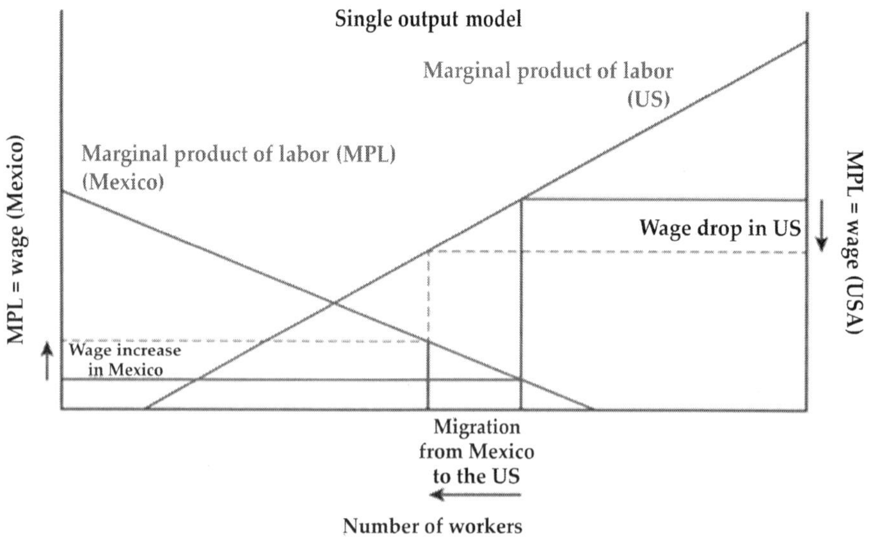

Figure 8.4: Model of segmented labor market in the USA and Mexican immigration.

Source: IZA World of Labor.

The United Nations Convention constitutes a comprehensive international treaty regarding the protection of migrant workers' rights (Baldwin-Edwards, 2006; Bangarth, 2003; Barak-Erez, 2008; Becerra, 2016; Brané and Lundholm, 2007; Brochmann and Hammar, 2020). It emphasizes the connection between migration and human rights, which is increasingly becoming a crucial policy topic worldwide (Dunn, 2010; Exdell, 2009; Fiske, 2016; Flynn, 2013; Frederking, 2012; Gilman, 2013; Guia, Koulish, and Mitsilegas, 2016). The convention aims at protecting migrant workers and members of their families, despite the fact that they lack the full citizenship rights available in their countries of destination (Costello, 2012; Dauvergne, 2012; Den Heijer, 2010; Dudley et al., 2012; Dunn, 2001, 2010; Exdell, 2009; Fiske, 2016). Hence, its existence sets a moral standard, and serves as a guide and stimulus for the promotion of migrant rights in each country (Mehan, 1997; Melis, 2001; Miller, 2015, 2016; Molnar and Gill, 2018; Money, 1998; Morris, 2002, 2016).

The primary objective of the convention is to foster respect for migrants' human rights and calls for a human approach to handling issues of immigration (Den Heijer, 2010; Dudley et al., 2012; Dunn, 2001, 2010; Exdell, 2009; Fiske, 2016; Flynn, 2013; Frederking, 2012). Migrants are not only workers, they are also human beings (Hailbronner, 2000; Hayter, 2000; Heisler, 2000; Hernandez-Truyol and Johns, 1997; Hollifield, Martin, and Orrenius, 2014). The convention does not create new rights for migrants but aims at guaranteeing equality of treatment. For example, it references the need to harmonize working conditions. The protocol has been used to make a case for protecting temporary workers, vulnerable migrants, and nationals who are working low-status jobs (Dudley et al., 2012; Dunn, 2001, 2010; Exdell, 2009; Fiske, 2016; Flynn, 2013; Frederking, 2012; Gilman, 2013). The convention innovates because it relies on the fundamental notion that all migrants should have access to a minimum degree of protection (Dunn, 2001, 2010; Exdell, 2009; Fiske, 2016; Flynn, 2013; Frederking, 2012; Gilman, 2013; Guia, Koulish, and Mitsilegas, 2016).

The convention recognizes that regular migrants have the legitimacy to claim more rights than irregular immigrants and therefore addresses one of the concerns for hosting countries (Hernandez-Truyol and Johns, 1997; Hollifield, Martin, and Orrenius, 2014; Jacobson, 1996; Johnson, 1996; Joppke, 1998). It is important to note that the convention does not encourage criminal activity and expressly discourages people trafficking or exploitation of migrant workers. However, the agreement stresses that irregular migrants must see their fundamental human rights respected, like all human beings (Dunn, 2010; Exdell, 2009; Fiske, 2016; Flynn, 2013; Frederking, 2012; Gilman, 2013; Guia, Koulish, and Mitsilegas, 2016). This can be a problem in countries that have a starting point of viewing undocumented workers as criminals who must first be punished for breaking the law. Moreover, the convention proposes that actions be taken to eradicate clandestine movements. One of the modalities that is of concern is the wide dissemination of misleading information inciting people to migrate irregularly with promises of a better life abroad. Governments can reference the convention as they develop a number of policy options such as sanctions against traffickers and employers of undocumented migrants (Brané and Lundholm, 2007; Brochmann and Hammar, 2020; Chavez, 2001; Chin, 1999; Cook, 2003; Cornelisse, 2004). This chapter will close with a suggestion for reforming immigration laws to reflect modern realities and complexities.

8.5. REFORMING IMMIGRATION LAWS

It is inevitable that there will be calls for reforming immigration laws, not least because of the changing context within which they are supposed to be operating (Aynsley-Green et al., 2012; Bacon, 1996; Baldwin-Edwards, 2006; Bangarth, 2003; Barak-Erez, 2008; Becerra, 2016). Immigration laws vary around the world and throughout history, according to the social and political climate of the place and time (King, 2009; Lopez, 2005; Lorentzen, 2014; Mehan, 1997; Melis, 2001; Miller, 2015, 2016; Molnar and Gill, 2018). This is because the acceptance of immigrant (or not, as the case may be) sways from the widely inclusive to the deeply nationalist and isolationist (Brochmann and Hammar, 2020; Frederking, 2012; Kasimis, 2012; Oberman, 2016; Taylor, 2000). National laws regarding the immigration of citizens of that country are regulated by international law (Bacon, 1996; Dudley et al., 2012; Hollifield, Martin, and Orrenius, 2014; Money, 1998; Saadi et al., 2020). The United Nations' International Covenant on Civil and Political Rights mandates that all countries allow entry to their own citizens, but not to non-citizens (Peberdy, 2001; Ramji-Nogales, 2007; Rubio-Marín, 2014; Ruhs, 2010; Ryan and Mitsilegas, 2010; Saadi et al., 2020; Samers, 2004). However, there are countries that still deny the right of re-entry to citizens, sometimes on the pretext that they have not obtained an exit visa. As Figure 8.5 shows, traditional solutions such as mass deportations have potentially very significant costs that render them undesirable in the modern age (Adelman, 2002; Aynsley-Green et al., 2012; Bacon, 1996; Baldwin-Edwards, 2006; Bangarth, 2003; Barak-Erez, 2008).

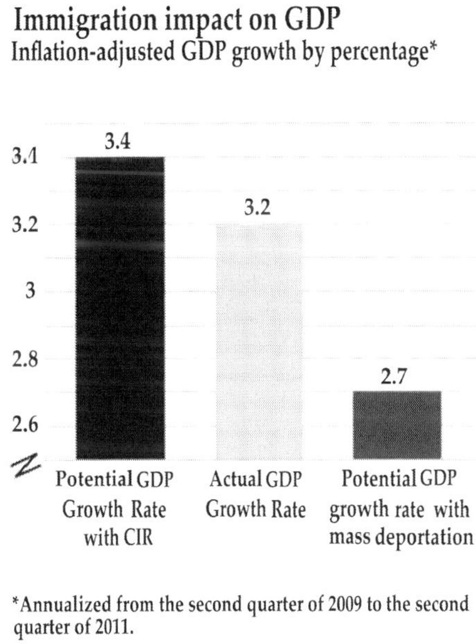

Figure 8.5: Costs of mass deportations on GDP.

Source: Center for American Progress.

Reform should ideally focus on letting in the right people and excluding the wrong people (Paz, 2016; Peberdy, 2001; Ramji-Nogales, 2007; Rubio-Marín, 2014; Ruhs, 2010; Ryan and Mitsilegas, 2010; Saadi et al., 2020). However, those are subjective terms that can even become emotive when they are politicized (Fiske, 2016; Flynn, 2013; Frederking, 2012; Gilman, 2013; Guia, Koulish, and Mitsilegas, 2016; Guild, 2001; Guild and Niessen, 1996). For example, it is generally recognized that the restrictions put on other forms of immigration has put place on the asylum system (Melis, 2001; Miller, 2015, 2016; Molnar and Gill, 2018; Money, 1998; Morris, 2002, 2016; Motomura, 1999). That means that many economic migrants have no option by to apply for asylum if they are to be let in (Brochmann and Hammar, 2020; Frederking, 2012; Kasimis, 2012; Oberman, 2016; Taylor, 2000). If countries wish to effectively control immigration, they must consider both the push and pull factors (Hollifield, Martin, and Orrenius, 2014; Jacobson, 1996; Johnson, 1996; Joppke, 1998, 1999, 2010; Kasimis, 2012). Currently, too much emphasis is put on the pull factors without consider why people are forced out of their countries (Orfanos, 2019; Ozdowski, 1985; Paz, 2016; Peberdy, 2001; Ramji-Nogales, 2007; Rubio-Marín, 2014; Ruhs, 2010). If the international community can work in unison, it is possible to reduce the impact of factors such as political instability, climate change, discrimination, and economic instability (Brochmann and Hammar, 2020; Chavez, 2001; Chin, 1999; Cook, 2003; Cornelisse, 2004, 2010).

CHAPTER 8 SUMMARY

This final chapter in the book has highlighted some potential areas of reform in the immigration systems across the globe. First, asylum claims should be made based on the veracity and admissibility of the allegations rather than the arbitrary inclinations of the assessor. The chapter has shown that replacement immigration must be handled with sensitivity to reduce the risk of a public backlash. We have seen settler-colonialism is still impacting on the modern world, despite the apparent end of imperialism. There should be efforts to improve workers' rights because they contribute to the global economy.

CONCLUDING REMARKS

Immigration remains one of the hot topics in global politics today. No politician wants to come out on the side of the besieged immigrants. All sorts of stories and myths have emerged concerning migrants. This book attempts to bring a human rights perspective to the debates surrounding immigration. Ultimately, the book concludes that immigration is an inevitable part of human existence. Therefore, the authorities should try to reform it so that it is fair and equipped to deal with the modern challenges of immigration. I hope you have enjoyed reading the book and will explore the other items in the series.

BIBLIOGRAPHY

1. Acer, E., & Goodman, J., (2009). Reaffirming rights: Human rights protections of migrants, asylum seekers, and refugees in immigration detention. *Geo. Immigr. LJ., 24*, 507.
2. Ackerman, A. R., & Furman, R., (2014). *The Criminalization of Immigration*. Contexts and consequences.
3. Adelman, H., (2002). Canadian borders and immigration post 9/11. *International Migration Review, 36*(1), 15–28.
4. Aynsley-Green, A., Cole, T. J., Crawley, H., Lessof, N., Boag, L. R., & Wallace, R. M. M., (2012). Medical, statistical, ethical, and human rights considerations in the assessment of age in children and young people subject to immigration control. *British Medical Bulletin, 102*(1), 17–42.
5. Bacon, D., (1996). For an immigration policy based on human rights. *Social Justice, 23*(3(65), 137–153.
6. Baldwin-Edwards, M., (2006). 'Between a rock and a hard place': North Africa as a region of emigration, immigration and transit migration. *Review of African Political Economy, 33*(108), 311–324.
7. Bangarth, S., (2003). 'We are not asking you to open wide the gates for Chinese immigration': The committee for the repeal of the Chinese immigration act and early human rights activism in Canada. *Canadian Historical Review, 84*(3), 395–422.

8. Barak-Erez, D., (2008). Israel: Citizenship and immigration law in the vise of security, nationality, and human rights. *Int'l J. Const. L., 6*, 184.
9. Becerra, D., (2016). Anti-immigration policies and fear of deportation: A human rights issue. *Journal of Human Rights and Social Work, 1*(3), 109–119.
10. Brané, M., & Lundholm, C., (2007). Human rights behind bars: Advancing the rights of immigration detainees in the United States through human rights frameworks. *Geo. Immigr. LJ., 22*, 147.
11. Brochmann, G., & Hammar, T., (2020). *Mechanisms of Immigration Control: A Comparative Analysis of European Regulation Policies*. Routledge.
12. Chavez, L. R., (2001). *Covering Immigration: Popular Images and the Politics of the Nation* (pp. 176–192). Berkeley: University of California Press.
13. Chin, K. L., (1999). *Smuggled Chinese: Clandestine Immigration to the United States* (Vol. 216). Temple University Press.
14. Cook, M., (2003). Banished for minor crimes: The aggravated felony provision of the immigration and nationality act as human rights violation. *BC Third World LJ., 23*, 293.
15. Cornelisse, G., (2004). Human rights for immigration detainees in Strasbourg: Limited sovereignty or a limited discourse? *European Journal of Migration and Law, 6*(2), 93–110.
16. Cornelisse, G., (2010). *Immigration Detention and Human Rights: Rethinking Territorial Sovereignty*. Brill.
17. Costello, C., (2012). Human rights and the elusive universal subject: Immigration detention under international human rights and EU law. *Indiana Journal of Global Legal Studies, 19*(1), 257–303.
18. Dauvergne, C., (2012). International human rights in Canadian immigration law-the case of the immigration and refugee board of Canada. *Indiana Journal of Global Legal Studies, 19*(1), 305–326.
19. Den, H. M., (2010). Europe beyond its borders: Refugee and human rights protection in extraterritorial immigration control. In: *Extraterritorial Immigration Control* (pp. 163–194). Brill Nijhoff.
20. Dudley, M., Steel, Z., Mares, S., & Newman, L., (2012). Children and young people in immigration detention. *Current Opinion in Psychiatry, 25*(4), 285–292.

21. Dunn, T. J., (2001). Border militarization via drug and immigration enforcement: Human rights implications. *Social Justice, 28*(2(84), 7–30.
22. Dunn, T. J., (2010). *Blockading the Border and Human Rights: The El Paso Operation that Remade Immigration Enforcement*. University of Texas Press.
23. Exdell, J., (2009). Immigration, nationalism, and human rights. *Metaphilosophy, 40*(1), 131–146.
24. Fiske, L., (2016). *Human Rights, Refugee Protest, and Immigration Detention*. London: Palgrave Macmillan.
25. Flynn, M., (2013). *The Hidden Costs of Human Rights: The Case of Immigration Detention*. Available at SSRN 2344193.
26. Frederking, L. C., (2012). A comparative study of framing immigration policy after 11 September 2001. *Policy Studies, 33*(4), 283–296.
27. Gilman, D., (2013). Realizing liberty: The use of international human rights law to realign immigration detention in the United States. *Fordham Int'l LJ., 36*, 243.
28. Guia, M. J., Koulish, R., & Mitsilegas, V., (2016). *Immigration Detention, Risk and Human Rights.* Cham: Springer.
29. Guild, E., & Niessen, J., (1996). *The Developing Immigration and Asylum Policies of the European Union: Adopted Conventions, Resolutions, Recommendations, Decisions and Conclusions*. Brill Nijhoff.
30. Guild, E., (2001). *Immigration Law in the European Community*. Brill Nijhoff.
31. Hailbronner, K., (2000). *Immigration and Asylum Law and Policy of the European Union*. Brill Nijhoff.
32. Hayter, T., (2000). *Open Borders: The Case Against Immigration Controls*. Sterling, London.
33. Heisler, B. S., (2000). The sociology of immigration. *Migration Theory: Talking Across Disciplines* (pp. 80–84). New York.
34. Hernandez-Truyol, B. E., & Johns, K. A., (1997). Global rights, local wrongs, and legal fixes: An international human rights critique of immigration and welfare reform. *S. Cal. L. Rev., 71,* 547.
35. Hollifield, J., Martin, P. L., & Orrenius, P., (2014). *Controlling Immigration: A Global Perspective*. Stanford University Press.

36. Jacobson, D., (1996). *Rights Across Borders: Immigration and the Decline of Citizenship*. Brill.
37. Johnson, K. R., (1996). "Aliens" and the US immigration laws: The social and legal construction of nonpersons. *The University of Miami Inter-American Law Review*, 263–292.
38. Joppke, C., (1998). *Challenge to the Nation-State: Immigration in Western Europe and the United States*. Oxford University Press on demand.
39. Joppke, C., (1999). *Immigration and the Nation-State: The United States, Germany, and Great Britain*. Clarendon Press.
40. Joppke, C., (2010). *Citizenship and Immigration* (Vol. 2). Polity.
41. Kasimis, C., (2012). Greece: Illegal immigration in the midst of crisis. *Migration Information Source Online Journal, 8*.
42. Kelson, G. A., & DeLaet, D. L., (1999). *Gender and Immigration* (p. 2). London: Macmillan.
43. King, S. M., (2009). US immigration law and the traditional nuclear conception of family: Toward a functional definition of family that protects children's fundamental human rights. *Colum. Hum. Rts. L. Rev., 41*, 509.
44. Lopez, M. P., (2005). The intersection of immigration law and civil rights law: Noncitizen workers and the international human rights paradigm. *Brandeis LJ., 44*, 611.
45. Lorentzen, L. A., (2014). *Hidden Lives and Human Rights in the United States: Understanding the Controversies and Tragedies of Undocumented Immigration* [3 Volumes]. ABC-CLIO.
46. Mehan, H., (1997). The discourse of the illegal immigration debate: A case study in the politics of representation. *Discourse and Society, 8*(2), 249–270.
47. Melis, B., (2001). *Negotiating Europe's Immigration Frontiers*. Brill Nijhoff.
48. Miller, D., (2015). Justice in immigration. *European Journal of Political Theory, 14*(4), 391–408.
49. Miller, D., (2016). *Strangers in Our Midst: The Political Philosophy of Immigration*. Harvard University Press.
50. Molnar, P., & Gill, L., (2018). *Bots at the Gate: A Human Rights Analysis of Automated Decision-Making in Canada's Immigration*

and Refugee System. Toronto: University of Toronto, Faculty of Law. International Human Rights Program.

51. Money, J., (1998). Human rights norms and immigration control. *UCLA J. Int'l L. and Foreign Aff., 3*, 497.
52. Morris, J., (2016). In the market of morality: International human rights standards and the immigration detention 'improvement' complex. In: *Intimate Economies of Immigration Detention* (pp. 51–69). Routledge.
53. Morris, L., (2002). Britain's asylum and immigration regime: The shifting contours of rights. *Journal of Ethnic and Migration Studies, 28*(3), 409–425.
54. Motomura, H., (1999). Federalism, international human rights, and immigration exceptionalism. *U. Colo. L. Rev., 70*, 1361.
55. Nethery, A., & Holman, R., (2016). Secrecy and human rights abuse in Australia's offshore immigration detention centers. *The International Journal of Human Rights, 20*(7), 1018–1038.
56. Newman, L., Proctor, N., & Dudley, M., (2013). Seeking asylum in Australia: Immigration detention, human rights, and mental health care. *Australasian Psychiatry, 21*(4), 315–320.
57. Oberman, K., (2016). Immigration as a human right. *Migration in Political Theory: The Ethics of Movement and Membership, 109,* 32.
58. Orfanos, S. D., (2019). Drops of light into the darkness: Migration, immigration, and human rights. *Psychoanalytic Dialogues, 29*(3), 269–283.
59. Ozdowski, S. A., (1985). The law, immigration, and human rights: Changing the Australian immigration control system. *International Migration Review, 19*(3), 535–554.
60. Paz, M., (2016). Between the kingdom and the desert sun: Human rights, immigration, and border walls. *Berkeley J. Int'l L., 34*, 1.
61. Peberdy, S., (2001). Imagining immigration: Inclusive identities and exclusive policies in post-1994 South Africa. *Africa Today*, 15–32.
62. Ramji-Nogales, J., (2007). Global approach to secret evidence: How human rights law can reform our immigration system. *Colum. Hum. Rts. L. Rev., 39*, 287.
63. Rubio-Marín, R., (2014). *Human Rights and Immigration*. Oxford University Press.

64. Ruhs, M., (2010). Migrant rights, immigration policy and human development. *Journal of Human Development and Capabilities, 11*(2), 259–279.
65. Ryan, B., & Mitsilegas, V., (2010). *Extraterritorial Immigration Control: Legal Challenges*. Brill.
66. Saadi, A., Young, M. E. D. T., Patler, C., Estrada, J. L., & Venters, H., (2020). Understanding US immigration detention: Reaffirming rights and addressing social-structural determinants of health. *Health and Human Rights, 22*(1), 187.
67. Samers, M., (2004). An emerging geopolitics of 'illegal' immigration in the European Union. *European Journal of Migration and Law, 6*(1), 27–45.
68. Sampson, R., Mitchell, G., & Bowring, L., (2011). *There are Alternatives: A Handbook for Preventing Unnecessary Immigration Detention.* International Detention Coalition.
69. Sanggaran, J. P., Haire, B., & Zion, D., (2016). The health care consequences of Australian immigration policies. *PLoS Medicine, 13*(2), e1001960.
70. Sassen, S., (1996). Beyond sovereignty: Immigration policy making today. *Social Justice, 23*(3(65), 9–20.
71. Sassen, S., (1997). Immigration policy in a global economy. *SAIS Review, 17*(2), 1–19.
72. Shohamy, E., & McNamara, T., (2009). Language Tests for Citizenship, Immigration, and Asylum. Language Assessment Quarterly, *6*, 1-5.
73. Smith, R. M., (2014). National Obligations and noncitizens: Special rights, human rights, and immigration. *Politics and Society, 42*(3), 381–398.
74. Soysal, Y. N., (2012). Citizenship, immigration, and the European social project: Rights and obligations of individuality. *The British Journal of Sociology, 63*(1), 1–21.
75. Spijkerboer, T., & Van, W. S., (2007). *Women and Immigration Law: New Variations on Classical Feminist Themes*. Routledge.
76. Taylor, S., (2000). Protecting the human rights of immigration detainees in Australia: An evaluation of current accountability mechanisms. *Sydney L. Rev., 22*, 50.

77. Thym, D., (2008). Respect for private and family life under Article 8 ECHR in immigration cases: A human right to regularize illegal stay? *International and Comparative Law Quarterly*, 87–112.

78. Webber, F., (2012). UK: The real 'immigration debate.' *Race and Class, 53*(3), 91–98.

79. Welch, M., (2002). *Detained: Immigration Laws and the Expanding INS Jail Complex*. Temple University Press.

80. Wexler, L., (2007). The non-legal role of international human rights law in addressing immigration. *U. Chi. Legal F.,* 359.

81. Wilcox, S., (2009). The open borders debate on immigration. *Philosophy Compass, 4*(5), 813–821.

82. Zúñiga, V., & Hernández-León, R., (2005). *New Destinations: Mexican Immigration in the United States*. Russell Sage Foundation.

83. Zwi, K., & Mares, S., (2015). Stories from unaccompanied children in immigration detention: A composite account. *Journal of Pediatrics and Child Health, 51*(7), 658–662.

INDEX